Investing with Confidence

Investing with Confidence

*Understanding Political Risk
Management in the 21st Century*

*Kevin W. Lu, Gero Verheyen,
and Srilal M. Perera
Editors*

THE WORLD BANK
Washington, D.C.

This volume is a product of the staff of the International Bank for Reconstruction and Development / The World Bank. The findings, interpretations, and conclusions expressed in this volume do not necessarily reflect the views of the Executive Directors of The World Bank or the governments they represent.

The World Bank does not guarantee the accuracy of the data included in this work. The boundaries, colors, denominations, and other information shown on any map in this work do not imply any judgement on the part of The World Bank concerning the legal status of any territory or the endorsement or acceptance of such boundaries.

Rights and Permissions
The material in this publication is copyrighted. Copying and/or transmitting portions or all of this work without permission may be a violation of applicable law. The International Bank for Reconstruction and Development / The World Bank encourages dissemination of its work and will normally grant permission to reproduce portions of the work promptly.

For permission to photocopy or reprint any part of this work, please send a request with complete information to the Copyright Clearance Center Inc., 222 Rosewood Drive, Danvers, MA 01923, USA; telephone: 978-750-8400; fax: 978-750-4470; Internet: www.copyright.com.

All other queries on rights and licenses, including subsidiary rights, should be addressed to the Office of the Publisher, The World Bank, 1818 H Street NW, Washington, DC 20433, USA; fax: 202-522-2422; e-mail: pubrights@worldbank.org.

ISBN-13: 978-0-8213-7893-9
eISBN: 978-0-8213-7981-3
DOI: 10.1596/978-0-8213-7893-9

Library of Congress Cataloging-in-Publication Data
Investing with confidence : understanding political risk management in the 21st century / Kevin W. Lu, Gero Verheyen, and Srilal M. Perera, editors.
    p. cm.
Includes bibliographical references and index.
ISBN 978-0-8213-7893-9 (alk. paper) -- ISBN 978-0-8213-7981-3 (ebk.)
1. Country risk. 2. Investments, Foreign. 3. Risk management. I. Lu, Kevin W.
II. Verheyen, Gero. III. Perera, Srilal Mohan.

HG4538.I65438 2009
332.67'3--dc22
                                                2009032582

Contents

**Part I.   Global Finance and Potential for
              Political Risk Insurance**

Part II. Advancements in Recurring Issues and New Dimensions for Political Risk Insurance

Appendixes

Preface

Investing with Confidence: Understanding Political Risk Management in the 21st Century is based on papers presented at a symposium held on December 4, 2008, under the joint auspices of the Multilateral Investment Guarantee Agency (MIGA) of the World Bank Group and the Karl F. Landegger Program in International Business Diplomacy at the School of Foreign Service, Georgetown University. This was the sixth such symposium, held biennially, and brought together almost 200 senior practitioners from the political risk insurance (PRI) industry, including investors, insurers, brokers, lenders, academics, and members of the legal community.

The 2008 symposium also celebrated the 20th anniversary of the founding of MIGA in April 1988, and covered a number of important topics, including calculating compensation arising from claims; an Argentine perspective on that country's ongoing arbitration proceedings; pricing methodology from private, public, and multilateral perspectives; Islamic finance transactions; and sovereign wealth funds.

In addition to papers presented at the symposium, the editors have chosen to include a number of papers that complement the general topics that defined the discussion, and that provide a historical context for MIGA's evolution as an important player in the political risk insurance arena. The inclusion of a paper published in 1986 by the late Dr. Ibrahim Shihata, the former Senior Vice President and General Counsel of MIGA, on the roles of MIGA and the International Center for the Settlement of Investment Disputes (ICSID) offers the reader a foundation for the types of issues often faced by investors when considering the risks involved with undertaking a significant investment in a foreign country.

In an effort to look at new areas in which PRI can play an important role, the symposium's agenda included presentations on Islamic finance and sovereign wealth funds. Project financing through the medium of Islamic finance has existed for some time now, and has been served by PRI providers; however, only recently has PRI been used as a risk mitigator for a large infrastructure project in Djibouti under an Islamic financing structure. The success in putting together this project opens the door for PRI to support future complex projects with Islamic financing. Sovereign wealth funds have gained prominence in recent years as a result of the rate at which they have grown, as well as from the challenge issued by the president of the World Bank for the funds to dedicate 1 percent of their assets to development causes. With the value of the funds estimated at $3 trillion at the time, almost $30 billion would have been available for development projects. Although the financial crisis has caused the funds to lose some of their value and in some cases curtail their investment activities, as the market recovers and the fund managers begin to look for new avenues of investment, PRI can provide much needed support for new development projects.

Given the unprecedented—by recent standards—financial crisis that has devastated the world financial system and extended its reach into a number of other sectors, political risk insurance has become even more relevant. At the same time, questions remain as to whether PRI really covers those risks that investors need covered the most. Put another way, will the coverage offered by PRI providers actually cover events, and will the insurers step up to the plate when the situation in a country deteriorates rapidly and begins to threaten investment projects? Difficulties in the financial markets have also resulted in the evaporation of available credit as lenders have refocused their lending to keeping themselves and their subsidiaries liquid and adequately capitalized. The result has been the delay or outright cancellation of many projects. From MIGA's perspective, this has the potential to significantly adversely effect developing countries, many of which rely on foreign direct investment (FDI) to tackle important projects, thereby freeing domestic funds and resources for other critical projects.

The financial crisis has also raised concerns about a new wave of nationalizations as governments step in to rescue failing banks and enterprises. Does government support of major banks constitute nationalization and expropriation, or is it, in fact, limited to financial underpinning, much in the way the U.S. government stepped in to support AIG? Although the initial impact of the crisis on financial institutions has subsided somewhat, it will take time for institutions to recover; casualties will occur as those financial institutions too weak to recover either shut their doors or are taken over by those strong enough to do so.

How PRI providers respond to the challenges brought about by the crisis and adapt to the ever-changing investment landscape was addressed at the symposium through discussions on pricing methodology and the formulation of coverages, most notably for expropriation. With verdicts in the offing for a number of expropriation cases before the ICSID tribunal, much discussion will revolve around how to interpret the awards on both the investor and the government sides, and this will help to shape future developments in the structure of PRI cover.

The discussions at the symposium and the ideas presented in the papers included in this volume represent, despite any divergent opinions, a dedication to strengthening the PRI market and promoting FDI in developing and emerging markets. The potential for developmental impact is substantial and recognized by purchasers and practitioners of PRI alike. This development goal is also shared by the two institutions that joined together to sponsor this and the five previous symposia.

MIGA's mission is to promote sustainable FDI in its developing member countries by providing political risk guarantees. As such, it is fully integrated into and critical to the broader health of the PRI industry. The Karl F. Landegger Program in International Business Diplomacy at the Georgetown University School of Foreign Service is a leader in teaching and research of international risk analysis and management, public policy, relations between business and governments, and the role of multinational corporations in development. The shared objectives of these institutions, and their collaboration in the organization of the symposia, are to further the discussion on risk mitigation techniques, improve economic growth, and reduce poverty in developing countries.

We hope that the papers presented in this volume contribute to those shared objectives and that they instill in the readers a renewed dedication to continued innovation in the PRI markets.

The editors wish to express their gratitude to Dr. Ted Moran and Gerry West for their tireless efforts in organizing the symposium; and to Lola Brown and Kathleen Klingenberg at Georgetown University and May Eidi at MIGA for the support they provided to both Georgetown University and MIGA during the organization of the symposium.

Gero Verheyen
Editor

Gero Verheyen is an Reinsurance Syndications Officer at MIGA.

Foreword

Izumi Kobayashi

It gives me great pleasure to introduce *Investing with Confidence: Understanding Political Risk Management in the 21st Century*, the fifth volume in the International Political Risk Management series. The chapters that follow represent the latest thinking on political risk management issues. A number of the chapters were presented as papers at the 2008 Symposium on International Political Risk Management, hosted by the Multilateral Investment Guarantee Agency (MIGA) and Georgetown University on December 4, 2008. The symposium was the sixth such event, and coincided with MIGA's 20th anniversary.

Both of these milestones attest to the importance of political risk insurance (PRI) and the extent to which the PRI market has developed and grown during this period. The last 20 years have seen tremendous growth in both the number and value of projects that have been insured, and a steady and healthy increase in the number of PRI providers in the marketplace. MIGA, for one, has written over $20 billion in guarantees since the agency was established, and has worked with and received support from a wide range of private, public, and multilateral insurers. Events like the MIGA–Georgetown Symposium demonstrate that there is much to be learned through the sharing of experiences and thinking together about the critical issues that confront our industry as well as new products and ideas.

Izumi Kobayashi is Executive Vice President of MIGA.

The theme of this volume, understanding political risk management in the 21st century, is appropriate given the tremendous changes we have witnessed since the financial crisis started in 2008 in the subprime markets. We are in the midst of a crisis unprecedented since the Great Depression, and the list of casualties continues to grow. In the United States, two of the big three automakers have requested large amounts of government assistance; Chrysler has filed for Chapter 11 bankruptcy and will undergo restructuring. Banks continue to need financial assistance. However, with the restrictions that the U.S. government has put on executive compensation and bonuses, a number of institutions have refused such assistance. The European Union also put together a €200 billion stimulus package. Despite these government interventions, we have yet to see a significant increase in credit extended between financial institutions or to consumers.

External Environment

After recovering from the decline in capital flows in 2001, the economy experienced a rapid recovery through the beginning of 2008. This recovery was cut short, however, by the subprime crisis and the collapse of (i) the credit default swap (CDS) and collateralized debt obligation (CDO) markets, and (ii) major players such as AIG, Bear Stearns, and Lehman Brothers. We saw a rapid contraction of credit, and despite the enormous volume of government assistance to banks both in the United States and in Europe, credit flows to consumers and investors showed no marked improvement.

The crisis has also had a major impact on the ability of traditionally solid investors to undertake new projects, especially in developing countries. Sovereign wealth funds, which had experienced rapid growth during a time of high commodity prices, have seen substantial losses in the value of their portfolios—overall the decline has been estimated at 25 percent. Some funds that had been investing heavily in Africa have either reduced the scope of their projects or withdrawn from projects altogether.

It is precisely in this environment that foreign direct investment (FDI) is going to be needed more than ever to assist developing countries with little or no capacity. All countries are moving into a new danger zone with heightened risks to exports and investments, industry, credit, banking systems, budgets, and balance of payments, and the least developed countries with the smallest economies are especially vulnerable.

Within this context, political risk insurers have an important role to support developing markets by helping to catalyze new investment and demonstrate that noncommercial risk, while heightened, is still manageable. Such signals are critical in maintaining stability in countries experiencing difficulty, particularly in the financial sector. Supporting liquidity injections by international banks into their foreign subsidiaries demonstrates our confidence in the banks' staying power as well as their importance to the financial sectors in those countries. We are still in the midst of resolving arbitration proceedings dating back to 2001; the outcome of these proceedings will send an important signal about the effectiveness of the arbitral panels and, in a worst-case scenario, about the effectiveness of insurers in covering the nonhonoring of arbitration awards.

Making sure that critical projects remain on track will help to prevent developing countries from being hit even harder by the current crisis. For example, as we all know, FDI is critical to the forward momentum of most infrastructure projects in the developing world, helping with such essential tasks as building the roads that provide farmers with access to markets. And FDI also brings global knowledge and best practices.

New Potential in Political Risk Management

Despite the current crisis, political risk insurance can play a pivotal role in moving the recovery process forward in several areas. As the portfolios of the sovereign wealth funds (SWFs) begin to recover, PRI can provide critical support to new investments into developing or high-risk countries. SWFs have not typically relied on PRI; it may now seem more attractive to them as they begin to rebuild their portfolios. The recovery from the crisis is not expected to begin before 2010 and will proceed at a much lower rate than the rate at which the SWFs initially built themselves up; thus, the funds will most likely be more cautious and selective in the investments they choose to undertake.

Islamic finance represents another yet untapped market for political risk management. *Shariah*-compliant projects, while still a small portion of the overall volume of investments, are growing in number. They present opportunities not only to underwrite new projects, but also to enter new markets and provide support for investments into developing countries. The Islamic Corporation for the Insurance of Investments and Export Credit (ICIEC) provides such insurance. However, PRI is a largely fallow market, accounting for only about 7 percent of ICIEC's insurance portfolio. This is not unique to ICIEC; PRI represents a small share of the portfolio of most multi-line insurance providers, with the bulk of the portfolio going to trade credit and finance. Furthermore, entering the Islamic finance market provides opportunities for traditionally western insurers to bridge a cultural gap and promote greater cooperation.

Developments in Political Risk Management

The financial crisis has shed new light on the importance of solid and appropriate risk management tools, not only for insurance providers, but also for investors. Very few had anticipated the collapse of the subprime market and its effect on other markets, especially because so many of the papers had been rated AAA by the rating agencies. In addition to exposing the complexity of these security instruments, the crisis also exposed the extent to which decisions relied on analytical models tuned to such high levels of confidence that failure seemed impossible.

Risk managers have had to reassess the validity of their assumptions as well as the impact that even minute changes in those assumptions can have on the output of their models. This is certainly true for PRI providers, who must structure their coverage and pricing on the basis of the project itself and, equally important, on their assessment of the current and future risk in the host country. Such assessments must be made within the context of the insurer's overall portfolio, and must include measurements of the impact that each project will have. Refining models allows insurers to assess risk and offer the investor a product that provides an appropriate level of protection, while at the same time making business sense from a cost perspective. PRI providers must have the flexibility to adapt to a changing marketplace while continuing to support new investments. Adaptation can manifest itself in the form of a higher appetite for risk, or in the development of new coverage types for investors. One such example is expanding breach-of-contract coverage to include nonhonoring of sovereign obligations by state-owned enterprises, extending such coverage to subsovereign governments, or granting longer tenures.

As one consequence of the crisis, many have lost faith in the validity of risk assessments, particularly those of the rating agencies. It is paramount that this faith be restored, and that investors have confidence that those who are advising them on political risk issues and mitigation can demonstrate that a sound analytical foundation underpins their recommendations. In addition to providing a challenge to PRI providers, this situation presents an exceptional opportunity for them to reaffirm their relevance in the current environment and their unique ability to support new investments.

The crisis has also provided an opportunity for members of the PRI community to work more closely with one another in supporting investments. MIGA continues to focus on its core areas—post-conflict countries, frontier markets, South-South investments, and infrastructure projects—and has also looked to assist the World Bank–led project to provide facilities to financial institutions in Eastern Europe and the Former Soviet Union to support their ongoing operations and help prevent a collapse of the financial markets in that region. In many of its projects, MIGA works with public, private, and multilateral insurers, and has found that good cooperation with its counterparts raises the effectiveness of all parties involved. Because available capacity in key countries is severely restricted and in some countries, virtually unavailable, it is even more important for PRI providers to cooperate to continue supporting new investments.

Conclusion

The chapters presented in this volume provide the reader with important and current insights into the evolving world of political risk insurance and foreign direct investment. The financial crisis presents us incredible challenges, and at the same time, incredible opportunities. Through cooperation and innovation, we can emerge from the crisis in a stronger position. Making the most of the lessons we have learned from the past and applying new tools puts us in a position to mitigate the impact of the current crisis on those countries with the least resilience and with the greatest need for continued foreign direct investment, as well as to benefit from new opportunities as the recovery begins and credit flows and investment levels regain momentum.

Abbreviations

ABV	adjusted book value
APV	adjusted present value
BIT	bilateral investment treaty
BOC	breach of contract
CCF	capitalized cash flow
CFIUS	Committee on Foreign Investment in the United States
DCF	discounted cash flow
DIC	Dubai Investment Company
EC	economic capital
ECA	export credit agency
EDC	Export Development Canada
EFIC	Export and Finance Insurance Corporation
EX	expropriation
FCFF	free cash flows to the firm
FDI	foreign direct investment
FMV	fair market value
GAAP	Generally Accepted Accounting Principles
GAPP	Generally Accepted Principles and Practices
IAP	International Accounting Principles
ICSID	International Center for Settlement of Investment Disputes
IFI	international financial institution
IWG	International Working Group of Sovereign Wealth Funds
KBC	Karaha Bodas Company
MFN	most favored nation
MIGA	Multilateral Investment Guarantee Agency
NAFTA	North American Free Trade Agreement
NBIM	Norwegian Government Pension Fund

NPV	net present value
OECD	Organisation for Economic Co-operation and Development
OPIC	U.S. Overseas Private Investment Corporation
P/B	price-to-book ratio
P/E	price-to-earnings ratio
PML	probable maximum loss
PRC	project review committee
PRI	political risk insurance
P/S	price-to-sales ratio
RAROC	risk-adjusted return on capital
SWF	sovereign wealth fund
TR	currency inconvertibility or transfer restriction
UNCITRAL	United Nations Commission on International Trade Law
WACC	weighted average cost of capital
WCD	war and civil disturbance

PART I

Global Finance and Potential for Political Risk Insurance

Toward a Greater Depoliticization of Investment Disputes: The Roles of ICSID and MIGA

Ibrahim F. I. Shihata

The means to settle disputes between states and foreign investors have changed considerably in the course of time. In the last century and in the early years of this one,* such disputes were highly politicized and led to the frequent exercise of diplomatic protection, sometimes followed by the use of force.

Latin American countries in particular were exposed to abuses of diplomatic protection and, at times, to armed intervention and occupation by foreign forces dispatched by the governments of foreign investors.[1] The reaction of these countries found its expression in the formulation of a legal framework that would subject foreign

Ibrihim Shihata (1937–2001) was Vice President and General Counsel of the World Bank and Secretary-General, ICSID. This article, reprinted with permission, is an updated version (up to January 31, 1992) of a paper delivered by the author on July 31, 1985, at the International Congress on Commercial Arbitration held in Rio de Janeiro, Brazil, later published as an article in I ICSID Rev.-FILJ 1 (1986). At the time of the article's original publication, only four Latin American countries had signed the ICSID Convention. The number of Latin American signatories has since more than doubled to 12. A full list of ICSID signatories can be found on the ICSID Web site, www.worldbank.org/icsid/.
*References to this and the last century refer to the 20th and 19th centuries, respectively (editor).

investments to the exclusive jurisdiction of the host country. This was the object of the Drago Doctrine, which aimed at forbidding the use of force for the collection of the public debt of Latin American States.[2] The most famous theory advanced by the Latin American countries against the institution of diplomatic protection, however, was the Calvo Doctrine. Taking the principle of equality of states as a premise, the Calvo Doctrine denied that foreign nationals were entitled to special rights and privileges and emphasized that controversies related to the claims of such nationals against host states were to be settled exclusively under domestic law and by domestic tribunals. The intervention of the states of such foreign nationals in these controversies was simply seen as a violation of the territorial jurisdiction of the host states.[3]

The implications of this Latin American approach were thus not limited to the principle that disputes with foreign investors should be settled in accordance with the law of the host state and by using local judicial remedies. They included a rejection of any right of the investor's state to exercise diplomatic protection by the espousal of the claims of its national against the host state, unless the latter state itself agreed to international adjudication or arbitration of the dispute between the states involved. The Calvo Doctrine attempted, in other words, to formulate international law rules applicable to the relations among sovereign states. In order to relate it to the relations between a host country and foreign investors, the so-called Calvo Clause was devised. Consistently provided in contractual arrangements between Latin American countries and foreign investors, the Calvo Clause binds foreign investors to waive appeal to diplomatic protection, and permits them to seek redress only in the local courts and under the law of the host state.[4]

Principles emanating from the Calvo Doctrine were embodied in the constitutions and statutes of Latin American countries and in treaties concluded among them.[5] Such principles were restated in such inter-American instruments as the famous Decision 24 issued by the Andean Pact Commission in 1970[6] and the 1976 Opinion on Transnational Enterprises of the Inter-American Juridical Committee.[7] They even appeared in the 1974 U.N. Charter of Economic Rights and Duties of States[8] in the drafting of which Mexico played a leading role.

It would be a mistake, however, to overstate the value of the Calvo Doctrine in contemporary international law. From the viewpoint of the state whose nationals may have claims against another country, diplomatic protection is an established right under customary international law which cannot be unilaterally denied by any host country. A Calvo Clause may well be binding on the investor who accepts it, as upheld in the North American Dredging Company case decided by the United States–Mexican General Claims Commission in 1926.[9] This does not, however, mean that it deprives the government of the investor of its own right to present an international claim for an injury to its own interests arising from the alleged violation of international law that resulted in an injury to its national. Such a claim may be based on denial of justice to the state's nationals or on other grounds.[10] Neither the Calvo Doctrine in its general application, nor any specific Calvo Clause, has inhibited states outside the Latin American region from the espousal of the claims of their nationals against other states, when they deemed such action necessary or appropriate. Diplomatic protection remains very much part of the realities of international life, the Calvo Doctrine notwithstanding.

ICSID as a Means of Depoliticization of Investment Disputes

The Objectives and Main Features of ICSID

Since the Calvo Doctrine was formulated,[11] new and significant developments have occurred. International organizations have proliferated and the classification of countries underlying Calvo's writings has lost some of its significance. Although foreign direct investments still originate mainly in the United States and Europe (Japan has also become a major source in recent years), investment flows now move in all directions and appropriate international forums provide ample opportunities for the settlement of investment disputes.

The International Centre for Settlement of Investment Disputes (ICSID or the Centre), was created by the Convention on the Settlement of Investment Disputes (the ICSID Convention)[12] to provide a forum for conflict resolution in a framework which carefully balances the interests and requirements of all the parties involved, and attempts in particular to "depoliticize" the settlement of investment disputes.[13]

The arrangements made for ICSID's governing body, the Administrative Council, reflect this balance of interests. The Council consists of one representative of each Contracting State, the total number of which is at present 97. Each representative casts one vote. The ICSID Convention therefore ensures equal representation for all Contracting States. The Administrative Council, it should be noted, approves the Regulations and Rules governing the proceedings relating to investment disputes and elects the Secretary-General of ICSID.

Moreover, ICSID should not be regarded solely as a mechanism for the settlement of investment disputes. Its paramount objective is to promote a climate of mutual confidence between investors and states favorable to increasing the flow of resources to developing countries under reasonable conditions. Like the World Bank, with which it is closely associated, or the Multilateral Investment Guarantee Agency (MIGA or the Agency), which I will describe later, ICSID must be regarded as an instrument of international policy for the promotion of investments and of economic development. The main features of the system ICSID's founders devised for this instrument include its voluntary character, its flexibility, and its effectiveness.

ICSID's voluntary character. ICSID's facilities are available on a voluntary basis. States eligible to join ICSID (members of the World Bank and states invited to sign the ICSID Convention under its Article 67) are obviously free to decline to do so. Their decision has no bearing on their relations with the World Bank itself. Moreover, ratification of the ICSID Convention does not constitute an obligation to use the ICSID machinery. That obligation can arise only after the Contracting State concerned has specifically agreed to submit to ICSID arbitration a particular dispute or class of disputes. In other words, the decision of a state to consent to ICSID arbitration is a matter within the sole discretion of each Contracting State. Under Article 25(4) of the ICSID Convention, any Contracting State may in addition notify ICSID, either at the time of ratification or at any time thereafter, of the class or classes of disputes that it would or would not consider arbitrable under ICSID's auspices. However, only a few Contracting States have made such a notification. Saudi Arabia has indicated that it intends to exclude investment disputes relating to "oil and pertaining to acts of sovereignty" and Jamaica has excluded disputes relating to "minerals or other natural resources." Papua New Guinea has specified that "it will only consider submitting those disputes to the Centre which are fundamental to the investment itself" and Turkey has indicated that it will only consider submitting to ICSID disputes arising out of investments that have been approved in Turkey and do not relate to rights in land.[14]

Within this framework, parties have considerably more freedom to determine whether their transaction is suitable for ICSID arbitration than might be assumed from the limitation of the Centre's jurisdiction to investment disputes of a legal character. The ICSID Convention does not define the term "investment," and this lack of definition, which was deliberate, has enabled the ICSID Convention to accommodate both traditional types of investment in the form of capital contributions and new types of investment, including service contracts and transfers of technology.

Disputes submitted to the Centre concerning traditional types of investment have included disputes relating to the exploitation of natural resources, such as bauxite,[15] timber,[16] and petroleum;[17] industrial investments, such as the manufacture of fibers[18] and of bottles,[19] natural gas liquefaction,[20] and aluminum production;[21] a shrimp-farming joint venture;[22] and the construction of hotels,[23] tourist centers,[24] and urban housing.[25] Disputes relating to new types of "investment" have included disputes arising out of agreements for the construction of a chemical plant on a turnkey basis, coupled with a management contract,[26] a management contract for a cotton mill,[27] a contract for the equipping of vessels for fishing and training of their crews,[28] technical and licensing agreements for the manufacture of weapons,[29] and a branch operation of a bank.[30] Most of these cases, it may be added, related to genuine contractual disputes concerning the interpretation of investment agreements or matters of performance. Only a few concerned unilateral termination of investment agreements, for example, in the form of outright nationalization or the revocation of investment licenses.

Notably missing from the above inventory of disputes submitted to the Centre are disputes arising out of loan agreements. Parties are, of course, also free to decide not to submit their investment disputes to ICSID, and although provision for ICSID arbitration is sometimes made in transnational loans to foreign governments, it is no secret that lenders often continue to require the judicial adjudication of loan disputes before the domestic courts of New York or London.[31]

Flexibility of the ICSID system. The rules applicable to ICSID proceedings are flexible in the sense that the parties may derogate from them in order to accommodate their particular needs. For example, most of the provisions regarding the number of arbitrators and the method for their appointment are permissive, and apply only in the absence of agreement between the parties.[32] The ICSID Arbitration Rules also provide for a preliminary procedural consultation, during which the parties may express their views on such matters as those concerning the language or languages to be used in the proceedings, the sequence of procedural events, apportionment of costs, and other matters of interest to them, including the place of the proceedings.[33]

While they are highly flexible, the ICSID rules are specific enough to ensure that a party cannot frustrate the proceedings. For example, if one of the parties refuses to cooperate in the appointment of arbitrators, the tribunal may still be constituted through the appointment of arbitrators by the Chairman of the Administrative Council. In fact, the Chairman has acted as appointing authority in the majority of ICSID proceedings either in connection with the initial appointment of arbitrators or with regard to their replacement in the event of death or resignation. In that capacity, the Chairman endeavors to consult with the parties prior to making the necessary appointment, and indeed is required to do so "as far as possible."[34] Even if a party fails to participate in the proceedings, the ICSID Convention ensures that the proceedings can continue[35] and lead to an award. In practice, there has been little occasion for these provisions to be used, in view of the high degree of state participation in the proceedings and of their frequent termination by means of amicable settlement.

Effectiveness of the ICSID System. While parties are free to decide whether to make use of the ICSID machinery, the ICSID Convention (Article 25(1)) assures both parties that once they have consented to submit disputes to ICSID conciliation or arbitration, neither party can unilaterally revoke its consent. This rule, which is indispensable to ICSID's effectiveness, has been upheld in three decisions of arbitral tribunals in connection with disputes between foreign investors and Jamaica.[36]

The exclusivity of the ICSID system also contributes to its effectiveness. Under the ICSID Convention (Article 26), consent of the parties to ICSID arbitration is deemed to be exclusive of any other remedy, unless the parties otherwise agree. This rule has several consequences, one of which is that ICSID proceedings are insulated in all Contracting States from any form of judicial intervention or control. In its application by national courts, this principle has on several occasions led to decisions denying the authority of such courts to issue provisional or conservatory measures in the context of ICSID cases unless the parties have agreed otherwise.[37]

The ICSID Convention furthermore assures the effectiveness of an ICSID award once it has been rendered. Article 53(1) of the ICSID Convention provides that such an award is binding on the parties, while Article 54(2) provides that a party may obtain recognition and enforcement of the award by furnishing a certified copy thereof to the competent court or other authority designated for the purpose by each Contracting State. This simple procedure eliminates the problems of the recognition and enforcement of foreign arbitral awards, which subsist in domestic laws and under other international conventions. Under the ICSID Convention, there is no exception to the binding character of ICSID awards and the role of the courts of Contracting States is purely to assist in the recognition of ICSID awards. This has been acknowledged by a French decision granting recognition to an ICSID award rendered against the People's Republic of Congo.[38]

On recognition, an ICSID award has the same force as a final judgment of a court in a Contracting State.[39] As such it can readily be enforced against an investor, if the investor refuses to comply with the terms of the award. So far, this issue has not arisen. The situation might be different if the state party to the dispute refused to comply with the award. The reason is that the ICSID Convention does not derogate from the rules of immunity from execution that may prevail in a Contracting State.[40] However, it should be recalled that failure by a Contracting State to honor an ICSID award would be contrary to its obligation under the ICSID Convention to comply with the award and would expose that state to various sanctions set forth in the ICSID Convention.[41] Second, and possibly more important than considerations of a strictly legal nature, refusal by the state involved to comply with an ICSID award could deprive it of credibility in the international business community.

It should be recalled that out of 26 ICSID proceedings, 4 of which are currently pending, only 8 have ended with final awards on the merits and 14 have been settled and/or otherwise discontinued by the parties.[42] This high proportion of settlements is consistent with the objectives of ICSID and should increase as a result of the availability of new procedures intended to facilitate such settlements. The ICSID Arbitration Rules, which were revised in 1984,[43] now offer a "pre-hearing conference" facility, which may be called by the Secretary-General or by the President of an ICSID arbitral tribunal, or may be requested by the parties. One of the objects of such a conference is to increase the efficiency of the ICSID machinery by permitting early identification of undisputed facts, thereby limiting the proceedings to the real areas of contention.[44] However, the conference is also intended to further promote amicable settlements following candid reappraisals by the parties of the merits of their respective claims.[45] Such settlements may take the form of agreements between the parties or be recorded in awards in accordance with the ICSID Rules.[46]

The effectiveness of ICSID cannot, at any rate, be assessed only on the basis of the number of disputes that have been submitted to or settled under the auspices of that institution. When an ICSID clause provides for compulsory arbitration, it is to be assumed that the prospect of involvement in such proceedings will work as a deterrent to the actions which give rise to the institution of proceedings and as an incentive to amicable settlement through negotiations.

ICSID and the Calvo Doctrine

In addition to providing a mechanism for the settlement of investment disputes that is voluntary, flexible, and effective, the ICSID Convention takes into account specific concerns which, in an earlier era, prompted the formulation of the Calvo Doctrine. An examination of the ICSID Convention's provisions on the exhaustion of local remedies, the application of domestic law, and diplomatic protection should show that the ICSID Convention indeed offers developing countries benefits that may not be obtained even from a wider application of the Calvo Clause.

Exhaustion of local remedies. The ICSID Convention gives investors direct access to an international forum and assures them that the refusal or abstention of the state party to a dispute to participate in the proceedings after it has given its consent cannot frustrate the arbitral process. But the ICSID Convention (Article 26) also provides that a Contracting State may, as a condition of its consent to ICSID arbitration, require prior exhaustion of local remedies. This condition may be specified in various ways. It could, for instance, be stipulated in the investment agreement, as has been done in agreements concluded by Latin American countries.

The *Model Clauses,* prepared by the ICSID Secretariat to assist investors and states in drafting ICSID arbitration clauses, acknowledge this option by suggesting the following language for possible insertion in an ICSID clause:

> Before [name of investor] institutes an arbitration proceeding in accordance with the provisions of this Agreement, [name of the investor] must exhaust [all local

remedies] [the (following) (administrative/ judicial) reme-
dies] [, unless (name of the Host State) waives that
requirement in writing].[47]

The condition regarding exhaustion of local remedies might also
be set forth in a bilateral treaty between the country concerned and
the country of the foreign investors.[48] Another way to accomplish the
same objective might result from a declaration made by a Contracting State at the time of signature or ratification of the ICSID Convention that it intends to avail itself of the provisions of Article 26
and will require, as a condition of its consent to ICSID arbitration, the
exhaustion of its local remedies. It should be added, however, that
among the 97 Contracting States, only one (Israel) has made such a
declaration and moreover has subsequently withdrawn it (in 1990).

Application of domestic law. The practice of Latin American
countries to stipulate in investment agreements that their relationship with foreign investors will be governed by the law of the host
country concerned is also compatible with the ICSID Convention.
Under Article 42 of the ICSID Convention, an arbitral tribunal must
decide a dispute in accordance with the rules of law agreed by the
parties. In fact, many ICSID clauses in investment agreements com-
municated to the Secretariat provide for the application of the host
state's law.[49] In the absence of a specific agreement on this matter,
the ICSID Convention (Article 42(1)) explicitly stipulates that the
law of the host state would apply, along with such rules of international law as may be applicable.

Diplomatic protection. As to diplomatic protection, the ICSID
Convention takes a radical position. It was recognized at the time
the ICSID Convention was finalized that

> When a host state consents to the submission of a dispute
> with an investor to the Centre, thereby giving the investor
> direct access to an international jurisdiction, the investor
> should not be in a position to ask his state to espouse his
> case and that state should not be permitted to do so.[50]

This fundamental consideration, which is another aspect of the
exclusivity of the ICSID system, finds its expression in Article 27 of the
ICSID Convention. That provision expressly prohibits a Contracting
State from giving diplomatic protection, or bringing an international
claim, in respect of a dispute which one of its nationals and another
Contracting State have consented to submit to ICSID arbitration.[51]

Thus, in addition to allowing for the exhaustion of local remedies in the host state and for the application of the domestic law of that state, the ICSID Convention prohibits the investor's state from espousing its national's claim, and therefore from exercising its right of diplomatic protection, as long as the matter is being or could be considered by an ICSID tribunal. These basic features of the ICSID Convention may not have been fully appreciated by Latin American countries in the past. The ICSID Convention pays considerable respect to the considerations which lie behind the Calvo Doctrine, but complements them by solutions acceptable to the investors' states. Yet, it seems that ICSID's fundamental objective to "depoliticize" the resolution of investment disputes (by affording both states and investors access to a truly neutral forum and precluding the investors' countries from intervening in the meanwhile) passed unnoticed in the negative votes cast in 1964 by all Latin American countries in respect of the formulation of the ICSID Convention.[52]

The situation is changing, however. Chile, Ecuador, El Salvador, Honduras, and Paraguay are now ICSID Contracting States. Some of them are also parties to investment treaties with such countries as France or the United Kingdom containing provisions for the arbitral settlement of investment disputes under ICSID's auspices.[53] In addition, Argentina, Bolivia, Costa Rica, and Peru have signed though not yet ratified the ICSID Convention. Finally, Brazil has not signed the ICSID Convention, but the ICSID Secretary-General has been named the "appointing authority" of arbitrators in connection with foreign loans to Brazilian public entities whose obligations are guaranteed by Brazil.[54]

MIGA as a Buffer against Diplomatic Intervention and Politicization

Concept and Features of MIGA

The Convention Establishing the Multilateral Investment Guarantee Agency (the MIGA Convention) was opened for signature on October 11, 1985, and came into force on April 12, 1988.[55] At the date of writing, 112 countries (including 95 developing ones) have signed the MIGA Convention; of these 85 have also ratified the Convention. The countries that have signed and ratified the MIGA Convention include six Latin American countries—Argentina, Bolivia, Chile, Ecuador, El Salvador, and Peru. A further seven countries from the region (Brazil, Colombia, Costa Rica, Guatemala, Honduras,

Nicaragua, and Uruguay) have signed but not yet ratified the MIGA Convention.[†] MIGA aims to stimulate the flow of resources to its developing member countries by (i) issuing guarantees for investments against noncommercial risks, and (ii) carrying out a wide range of promotional activities.[56] Although the idea of a multilateral investment guarantee facility emerged in the 1950s and was discussed at some length in the 1960s and 1 970s in the World Bank and other international forums,[57] five fundamental innovations distinguish MIGA from earlier schemes:

- While previous concepts focused exclusively on guarantee operations, MIGA provides a broader forum for international policy cooperation among capital-importing countries, capital-exporting countries, and foreign investors. In this context, it is authorized to provide technical and advisory services.
- Earlier proposals focused on investment flows from developed countries, but MIGA also takes part in the promotion of investment flows among developing countries,
- Unlike previous schemes, which envisaged an agency closely linked with the World Bank, MIGA is designed to be an autonomous institution which will operate on its own account and within its own responsibility while maintaining a significant linkage with the Bank. In accordance with Articles 32(b) and 33(b) of the MIGA Convention, the President of the Bank is *ex officio* Chairman of MIGA's Board. He has also been elected by the Board as MIGA's President.
- Political oversight of and financial responsibility for MIGA is shared by both home and host countries, with the possibility being opened of the latter eventually subscribing 40 percent of the capital and having one-half of the votes. By contrast, previous proposals envisaged an agency controlled and financed only by investors' home countries.
- More than in the previously conceived instruments, the MIGA Convention contains a number of safeguards which ensure the host governments' control over investment activities in their territories while requiring MIGA to work on the improvement of investment conditions and standards in agreement with these governments.

[†]Please see appendix II to this volume for a comprehensive list of MIGA member countries (editor).

Operations. In general terms, MIGAs objective is to stimulate the flow of resources for productive purposes among its member countries and, in particular, to and among its developing member countries.[58] It is meant to enhance the mutual understanding and confidence between host governments and foreign investors and to increase information, expertise, and skills related to the investment process. Toward this end, MIGA issues guarantees for investments against noncommercial risk and carries out promotional activities. Article 11 of the MIGA Convention provides for coverage of four broad categories of noncommercial risk: (i) the transfer risk resulting from host government restrictions on currency conversion and transfer; (ii) the risk of loss resulting from legislative actions or administrative actions and omissions of the host government which have the effect of depriving the foreign investor of his ownership or control of, or a substantial benefit from, his investment; (iii) the repudiation of government contracts in the cases where the investor has no access to a competent forum, faces unreasonable delays in such a forum, or is unable to enforce a final judicial or arbitral decision issued in his favor; and (iv) the armed conflict and civil unrest risk. At present the "transfer risk" is probably the most relevant from the viewpoint of investors. Cases of outright expropriation have become infrequent, and this is reflected in ICSID's experience. To be eligible, investments have to be new, medium or long term, and must be judged by the Agency to be sound investments which contribute to the development of the host country.[59]

MIGA is authorized to provide coverage not only for equity interests and other forms of direct investment[60] but also in respect of other medium- or long-term forms of investment, including various forms of industrial cooperation such as management and service contracts, licensing and franchising agreements, turnkey contracts as well as arrangements concerning the transfer of technology and know-how where the investor assumes a stake in the performance of the venture.[61] This enables MIGA to service several new types of investment, especially among developing member countries, which take nonequity forms. Investors, to be eligible for the Agency's guarantee, must be nationals of a member country or, in the case of juridical persons (corporate investors), must either be incorporated and have their principal place of business in a member country, or the majority of their capital must be owned by a member or members of the Agency or by their nationals.[62] In this context another innovative feature of the MIGA Convention should be noted: eligibility may, under certain conditions, be extended to nationals of the host country if they transfer the assets to be invested from abroad.[63] MIGA is therefore able to assist member countries in their efforts to reverse the increasingly menacing capital flight phenomenon. This feature of the MIGA Convention also emphasizes that MIGA's guarantee protection relates primarily to the transfer of funds into the host country for development purposes rather than merely to the foreign nationality of the investors.

In recognition of host governments' sovereign control over the admission of foreign investment into their territories and the treatment of such investment, Article 15 of the MIGA Convention provides that the Agency "shall not conclude any contract of guarantee before the host government has approved the issuance of the guarantee by the Agency against the risks designated for cover." The approval must hence extend both to MIGA's involvement, that is, the issuance of a guarantee, and to the scope of MIGA's involvement, that is, the risks designated for cover.[64] A member government may, if it wishes, limit its use of MIGA's services to the coverage of investments by its nationals in foreign member countries without necessarily allowing it to cover foreign investments in its own territory. In short, MIGA's facilities, like those of ICSID, are only available where there is consent by all concerned.

In addition to its guarantee operations, MIGA carries out a variety of promotional activities such as performing research, providing information on investment opportunities to foreign investors and policy advice to member governments, and such technical assistance as may be required in this field. The MIGA Convention provides that in its promotional efforts, MIGA "shall give particular attention ... to the importance of increasing the flow of investments among developing member countries."[65]

Organization, membership, and voting. MIGA has full juridical personality and is both legally and financially separate from the World Bank. Like other international financial institutions, MIGA has a Council of Governors composed of one representative of each member (and his alternate), a Board of Directors elected by the Council, and a chief executive officer selected by the Board and responsible for the ordinary business of the Agency.[66] Membership in MIGA is open to all members of the World Bank and Switzerland on a voluntary basis[67] As in the case of ICSID, every country is free to join without any effect on its position in the World Bank or any other organization. The distribution of voting rights represents a further innovation. The management of the World Bank had originally proposed that voting power be shared on an equal basis between home countries and host countries as groups, with countries initially classifying themselves as members of one of the two groups, subject to approval of the Agency's Council.[68]

During the discussions among the World Bank's Executive Directors, this proposal was challenged on the grounds that it could not be foretold how many countries of either group would join MIGA from the outset and that in view of the unpredictable relative size of each of the two groups it would be inequitable to allocate equal voting power to them before knowing the actual membership structure. However, the basic tenet of the management's proposal was generally accepted, namely that both groups should receive equal voting power when all members of the World Bank become members of MIGA.[69] In the first three years of its operations, the minority group has furthermore been guaranteed 40 percent of the total votes (through supplementary votes), and all decisions have been required to be taken by the special majority of two-thirds of the total votes representing not less than 55 percent of subscriptions in the Agency's capital.[70]

Financing: Self-sustenance and joint responsibility. MIGA is expected to meet its liabilities from premium income and other revenues such as return on its investments. Accordingly, Article 25 of the MIGA Convention directs the Agency to carry out its activities in accordance with sound business and prudent financial management practices. Under Article 26 of the MIGA Convention, MIGA is able to vary its premiums in accordance with the actual risks assumed under its guarantees, but such variations are based on the specifics of the investment and risks involved—and do not simply reflect a political judgment regarding the host country.

Directed to operate on a financially viable basis, MIGA, after it pays a claim, assumes such rights as the indemnified investor might have acquired against the host country as a result of the event giving rise to his claim.[71] Such subrogation—a generally accepted principle of insurance law—provides nothing more than the assignment of an existing claim from the investor to MIGA and, substantively, gives MIGA no greater rights than had been acquired by the investor.

Disputes between MIGA and a host country with respect to such rights would normally be settled by negotiation. Failing negotiation, it is envisaged that either party to the dispute will have access to international arbitration unless both parties agree to resort first to conciliation.[72] However, MIGA is authorized under Article 57(b) of the MIGA Convention to enter with individual host countries into bilateral agreements on the resolution of disputes according to alternative mechanisms if such countries so request. Such agreements would supersede the dispute settlement mechanism provided in the MIGA Convention and would presumably be satisfactory to the Agency and consistent with the constitutional requirements of the country concerned. They must, however, be concluded before the Agency initiates operations in such a country.[73]

The principle of self-sustenance is supported by arrangements to ensure the Agency's viability even when losses exceed reserves at a given moment. These arrangements include a combination of capital subscriptions and "sponsorship." The Agency's initial authorized share capital is SDR [special drawing rights]1 billion.[74]

Shares are subscribed by member countries in accordance with their relative economic strength as measured in their allocation of shares in the World Bank's capital. Only 10 percent of the subscriptions are paid in cash. An additional 10 percent is paid in the form of nonnegotiable, non-interest-bearing promissory notes to be encashed only if needed by MIGA to meet its financial obligations.[75] The rest of the subscribed capital is subject to call.[76] While developed member countries must make all payments in freely usable currencies, developing member countries may make up to 25 percent of the paid-in cash portion of their subscriptions in their own currencies.[77] The amount of guarantees which MIGA may issue may not now exceed one and one half times the amount of the subscribed capital plus reserves plus a portion of MIGAs reinsurance coverage (a 1.5:1 ratio).[78] Once MIGA accumulates a balanced risk portfolio and gains further experience, it might increase this ratio up to a maximum of 5:1.[79]

In addition to the guarantee operations based on the Agency's capital and reserves, MIGA is able to underwrite investments sponsored by member countries as trustee for these countries, as detailed in Annex I to the MIGA Convention. Revenues from sponsorship operations are to be accumulated in a "Sponsorship Trust Fund" kept separate from the Agency's own assets, with claims and other expenses resulting from sponsorship operations paid out of this fund. Upon its depletion, remaining liabilities are to be shared only by all sponsoring countries, each in the proportion which the guarantees sponsored by it bear to the total guarantees sponsored by all countries.

The combination of capital subscription and sponsorship is another factor which distinguishes MIGA from the international investment insurance schemes previously discussed in the World Bank. These schemes relied chiefly on sponsorship by investors' home countries (with some suggesting an initial contribution from the World Bank). Yet, adoption of this concept would have made the

Agency dependent to a great extent on one group of members. By contrast, MIGA relies primarily on capital subscriptions from all member countries and has the necessary independence to carry out its development mandate in the common interest of all its members.[80]

MIGA and Domestic Jurisdiction

As an international organization, MIGA is not addressed by the Calvo Doctrine, but it might appear in certain situations to be in a position similar to that of an investor's home state. It should be noted, however, that MIGA's institutional interests and its very composition can have a bearing on its behavior and distinguish such behavior from that of a state.

For the investor's home country, the interest in the protection of the economic welfare of its nationals investing abroad competes with a multiplicity of other state interests. The decisions of such country on the exercise of diplomatic protection will therefore tend to reflect a host of political considerations, including those unrelated to the merits of the investor's case.[81] In fact, the cases which gave rise to the Calvo Doctrine were characterized in several instances by the use of diplomatic protection as a pretext for a home country's intervention in the affairs of the host country for different purposes. MIGA, on the other hand, has only one institutional objective: the promotion of greater flows of foreign investment. It is explicitly prohibited from interfering in the political affairs of its members.[82] In the absence of such political interest, it can be expected to focus on the merits of the claim to which it has been subrogated.

MIGA has a financial interest in the recoupment from the host country of a payment which it has made to an insured investor. However, in its pursuit of this interest, MIGA must be mindful of the fact that its risks will be located in developing countries. Its interest in financial survival therefore requires MIGA to abstain from experiments which could jeopardize its good relations with its developing member countries. In addition, the control of MIGA is exercised collectively by many countries so that it must act in the common interest of all of its members, as reflected in the MIGA Convention. In particular, since control is shared by capital-exporting and capital-importing countries on an ultimately equal basis, the Agency can be anticipated to strike a proper balance in its approach between the interests and expectations of both groups. MIGA's management and staff are also composed of nationals of both capital-importing and capital-exporting countries.[83] Both the control exercised by its members and its internal decision-making processes help to prevent MIGA from pursuing divisive policies. The abuse of diplomatic protection of which states have often been accused cannot therefore extend to MIGA even if its intervention is to be assimilated to the fundamentally different concept of diplomatic protection. A more detailed discussion of some of the issues raised by the MIGA Convention will further explain this point.

Subrogation, international arbitration, and host countries' sovereignty. Under the MIGA Convention, the Agency, upon paying or agreeing to pay a claim to an insured investor, succeeds to the investor's rights against the host country; disputes between MIGA and a host country with respect to such rights may ultimately be submitted to international arbitration.[84] As explained earlier, the Calvo Doctrine as well as Latin American constitutions and several subregional agreements[85] reflect reservations against subrogation and international arbitration with respect to foreign investment.

The rationale behind the prohibition of subrogation under these instruments is apparent: investment disputes should not be allowed to give rise to political confrontations between governments. In accordance with this rationale, the principle of subrogation is not challenged as such; it is only the subrogation of a sovereign state to the claims of private foreign nationals that many Latin American countries refuse in principle. One may note in this context that at least 28 "executive agreements" concluded by the United States with Latin American and Caribbean countries recognize, with some variations in detail, the subrogation of the U.S. Overseas Private Investment Corporation (OPIC) to the rights of indemnified U.S. investors.[86] There is no reason why an international institution such as MIGA should be accorded less favorable treatment. A dispute involving MIGA is basically a conflict between an international organization and a member country of that organization. The submission to international arbitration of disputes of this type is established in international practice and is, for instance, embodied in the World Bank's General Conditions Applicable to Loan and Guarantee Agreements,[87] as well as those of the regional development banks, including the Inter-American Development Bank. In the case of the only other existing multilateral investment insurance program,‡ the Inter-Arab

---

‡Since this paper was published, the Asian Development Bank, the African Trade Insurance Agency, and the Islamic Corporation for the Insurance of Investment and Export Credit have all begun offering investment insurance (editor).

Investment Guarantee Corporation, disputes between that agency, acting as a subrogee, and any of its members are also referred to international conciliation and arbitration.[88] As the private investor will not be a party to the arbitration proceedings between MIGA and a host government, the envisaged arbitration by no means contravenes the several Latin American instruments which refuse to give foreign corporations direct access to international tribunals.[89]

Furthermore, the MIGA Convention refers to arbitration, in an annex, as a mechanism which may be used only in the unlikely event that a dispute between the Agency and the host country cannot be resolved through negotiation or conciliation. It also gives the host country and the Agency the option to agree on alternative methods of settlement of disputes.[90] Through the exercise of this option, MIGA may, prior to undertaking operations in a given country, enter into a bilateral agreement with it, thereby adjusting the dispute settlement mechanism to the peculiar legal and political situation of such a country. For instance, it may agree to exhaust local remedies in the host country as a condition precedent or as an alternative to resorting to arbitration under Annex II to the Convention. The issue of international arbitration has been resolved in the OPIC agreements between most Latin American countries and the United States.[91] For stronger reasons, suitable solutions should not be difficult to reach in agreements between an international organization such as MIGA and its member states.

Discrimination against host countries' national investors. One of the main tenets associated with the Calvo Doctrine is that foreign investors should not be granted any treatment more favorable than that granted to national investors.[92] As MIGA focuses on foreign investment, it could be argued that it accords foreign investors a protection which is not otherwise available to local investors, thereby discriminating against the latter.

Unlike a typical local investor, foreign investors usually convert their freely usable currencies into that of the host country and must therefore rely on their ability to repatriate their capital and transfer their profits. As noted above, MIGA's protection attaches to this peculiar situation of the investors rather than to their nationality: to the extent that they transfer assets from abroad, local investors can also qualify for coverage. The investment must be foreign but not necessarily the investor. By contrast, Decision 220 of the Andean Pact Commission guarantees foreign investors, and foreign investors only, repatriation of the invested capital, including capital gains.[93]

This justification for the distinction between foreign and local investment extends to other risk coverages offered by MIGA, notably the risks of expropriation and of breach of government contract. MIGA's guarantee does not accord a foreign investor legal protection against the occurrence of an expropriatory action or of a violation by the host government of its contractual obligations; it just guarantees him adequate compensation in a freely usable currency for a loss sustained as a result of such actions. From the viewpoint of the investor, MIGA's guarantee is not different from the guarantee available under a national investment guarantee program[94] or by a private political risk insurer.[95] Latin American countries have not objected to national or private political risk insurance covering investment in their territories. On the contrary, most Latin American countries have, as explained earlier, manifested their approval through the conclusion of agreements with the United States facilitating OPIC's operations.

The Alleviation of Political Confrontations through MIGA

Not only is MIGA compatible with the objective of the Calvo Doctrine, it may even further such objective in a more effective manner than that achieved by a typical Calvo Clause. By providing guarantees against political risks, MIGA rolls over these risks, and the losses resulting from them, from the investor and the economy of his home country to an international institution and thus reduces or even eliminates the potential of a conflict between the investor's home country and the host country.[96]

MIGA's stake in conflict avoidance and the amicable settlement of disputes. MIGA's viability and continuity depend in no small part on the good terms it must establish with its capital-importing member countries. It has every incentive to alleviate and, whenever possible, avoid conflicts with these countries. From the beginning, the MIGA initiative aimed at the creation of "a synergism of cooperation" between capital-exporting and capital-importing countries.[97] MIGA's operations, much as the discussions which led to agreement on the text of its Convention, are generally based on the consensus of both groups of countries. As every conflict with a member country might weaken this consensus, it is natural that MIGA should try to avoid conflict and, when it arises, to facilitate its amicable settlement. In fact, the MIGA Convention (Article 23(b)(i)) goes a step further and directs MIGA to encourage the amicable settlement of disputes between investors and host countries, as such disputes constitute the seeds of conflicts between the Agency and its capital-importing members.

MIGA's contribution to conflict avoidance. While the aforementioned institutional imperatives require MIGA to avoid and alleviate conflicts with host countries, its contractual obligations and its very business require it to pay justified claims. If MIGA failed to do so, it could not sell its guarantees to investors and would be stripped of revenues. The competing pressures force MIGA to underwrite risks with a view to the avoidance of claims and, where claims of guaranteed investors are justified, to assess and settle them on their legal merits and, in turn, seek recovery on the same basis.

The origins of an investment conflict can often be traced to the investment terms and conditions. If these turn out to be unfair to either party or if they lack the flexibility to be smoothly adjusted to changing circumstances, a party, especially a host government, might later feel tempted to remedy the arrangement by unilateral action. Also, if a project runs into financial or technical difficulties, a host government might interfere in order to protect its interests or those of its nationals. MIGA therefore carefully screens every investment project to make sure it is economically sound, will contribute to the development of the host country, and is consistent with its laws and declared development objectives.[98] It can be expected to deny coverage when it finds deficiencies in the investment arrangement. The MIGA Convention (Article 15) provides a second safeguard against conflicts with respect to guaranteed investment by requiring the host government's approval for both the issuance of MIGA's guarantee and the risks designated for cover.

MIGA's facilitation of amicable settlements. Where a conflict arises nevertheless, MIGA may become involved in the process in a way that will place it in a unique position to facilitate an amicable settlement. If an investor files a claim, MIGA will have to assess this claim and possibly defend itself against it. In doing this, MIGA will find itself in a similar position to that of a host government when confronted with the investor's demands. In many cases, however, MIGA will be in a better position to assess the investor's claim. MIGA's assessment, based on the broad information available to it and its worldwide experience, is likely to moderate the conflicting claims of the investor and his host country and increase the likelihood of a settlement.

Another way in which MIGA may induce host governments and investors to arrive at amicable settlements is the alleviation of the financial burden of such settlements on the governments. For example, MIGA might accept the local currency of the host country on a temporary basis and pay the investor out of its own funds in freely usable currency. MIGA might then, under an agreement with the host country, sell the local currency to the World Bank or other international institutions, to companies importing goods from the host country, or to the host government itself over a period of time and recover its position accordingly. MIGA might also finance the settlement by paying the investor in cash and accepting debt instruments from the government as recoupment. As a variant of this approach, MIGA could persuade the investor to accept installments rather than insisting on a cash payment by backing the government's commitments with its guarantee. Finally, where the views of the investor and the host government with respect to an adequate compensation cannot be completely reconciled, MIGA might pay all or part of the difference and in this way facilitate a settlement. In view of its developmental mandate and institutional interests, MIGA can be anticipated to use its potential for the facilitation of amicable settlements at least as actively as some of the national agencies, especially OPIC, have successfully done.[99]

Conclusion

Abuses of diplomatic protection in the last century led some developing countries to insist that disputes with foreign investors be settled exclusively before their domestic courts and according to their domestic law. By virtue of the Calvo Clause, Latin American countries required foreign investors to waive appeal to diplomatic protection by their states. Such a clause has, however, been deemed by other countries inapplicable to the government of the foreign investor, on the basis that diplomatic protection, being a state's right under customary international law, can only be waived by the state itself. The Calvo Doctrine, though an understandable reaction to past abuses, therefore did not succeed in preventing political intervention by the states of foreign investors in defense of their interests. Nor did it put a halt to the espousal by such states of the claims of their investors before international tribunals. Moreover, as developing countries, especially in the Latin American region, became hard pressed to obtain funds from abroad, they found themselves accepting, in the context of investment disputes, the jurisdiction of domestic courts of foreign states, including those of their creditors, in spite of conflicting provisions in their own legislation. On both counts, the Calvo Doctrine has proved to be an inadequate response to the present needs of those developing countries which, mainly for historical reasons, still attach great importance to it.

New international instruments have meanwhile developed whereby developing countries can attain their objective of encouraging foreign financial flows while avoiding the politicization of investment disputes and the espousal by foreign states of the claims of their nationals in the exercise of their own right of diplomatic protection. ICSID, operating since 1966, affords to its members the benefits of submitting an investment dispute between a member and the national of another member to a forum of their choice which operates under truly international rules approved by a Council where all members have the same voting power. Resort to ICSID precludes the investor's state from exercising diplomatic protection or instituting an international claim unless the host state fails to comply with the award rendered in such dispute. The latter state may also request the investor to exhaust first the local remedies. And an ICSID tribunal would apply the domestic law of the host state, and such rules of international law as may be applicable, unless the state itself agrees with the investor that the tribunal would apply other rules of law or decide the dispute *ex aequo et bono*. In all these respects, the ICSID machinery seems to provide developing countries with a response which, compared to the Calvo Doctrine, is both more adequate in the depoliticization of disputes and more effective in the encouragement of foreign investment, without inviting the abuses of diplomatic protection. It should also be more reassuring, from the viewpoint of these countries, than the acceptance of the jurisdiction of the courts of another state, which seems to be the pattern in recent financial agreements between foreign banks and Latin American states. Resort to ICSID becomes all the more appealing in view of its relatively low cost and the inherent safeguards which ensure the integrity of its facilities.

Likewise, MIGA's mandate, its character as an international organization, and its own internal dynamics bring it to work for the avoidance of disputes between foreign investors and their host countries and for the facilitation of the amicable settlement of such disputes when they arise. MIGA's involvement will ensure that matters are discussed with host countries on the basis of legal and economic criteria only. Under Article 34 of the MIGA Convention, "the Agency, its President and Staff shall not interfere in the political affairs of any member," "shall not be influenced in their decisions by the political character of the member or members concerned," and "considerations relevant to their decisions shall be weighed impartially in order to achieve the purposes" of the MIGA Convention. An investor covered by MIGA's guarantee would rather resort to the Agency requesting its prompt compensation than invoke the lengthy and uncertain process of diplomatic protection by his state. MIGA also has a vested interest in the improvement of investment conditions and in developing smooth relationships between investors and their host governments. The depoliticization of investment disputes should be a necessary byproduct of its day-to-day activities.

ICSID and MIGA thus represent modern responses which enable developing countries to encourage larger flows of foreign investments for the purposes of their development, and also protect them from the intervention of the usually more powerful states of the investors. If properly used, these modern instruments may well represent much more adequate tools than the politically appealing, but often counterproductive, insistence on traditional attitudes which find their justification more in the unfortunate experiences of the past than in the realities of the present and the requirements of the future.

Notes

1. An example is the famous "Jecker" claim, relating to a loan to Mexico from a Swiss-French banking firm for a nominal amount of 75 million francs, of which Mexico received less than 4 million francs. Nonpayment of 100 percent of this loan was one of the justifications used by the French government for armed intervention in Mexico in 1861–62. See D. Shea, The Calvo Clause 14 (1955).
2. The basis of the Drago Doctrine is a note sent in 1902 by Foreign Minister Drago of Argentina to the United States House of Representatives. For the text of this note, see U.S. Foreign Rel. 1 (1903). See also Drago, State Loans in their Relation to International Policy, I AJIL 692 (1907).
3. The Calvo Doctrine has its source in a number of statements made by the Argentine diplomat and international law writer, Carlos Calvo (1824–1906) in his major work, *Le droit international théorique et pratique* (5th ed. 1896). See also C. Calvo, *Manuel de droit international public et privé* 134–37 (1884).
4. Shea, *supra* note 1, at 28.
5. *Id.* at 21–27. For examples of constitutional provisions, see Bolivia Constit., Article 24; Honduras Constit., Article 33; Venezuela Constit., Article 127. The texts of these and other Latin American constitutions are available in Constitutions of the Countries of the World (A. Blaustein & G. Flanz eds. looseleaf service). See also F. Dawson and I.

Head, International Law, National Tribunals, and the Rights of Aliens 113–22 (1974).

6. Approved December 31, 1970, and effective June 30, 1971. U.S. Dept. of State translation at 11 ILM 126 (1972). Article 51 of the Decision provided that "[i]n no instrument relating to investments or the transfer of technology shall there be clauses that remove possible conflicts or controversies from the national jurisdiction and competence of the recipient country or allow the subrogation by states to the rights and actions of their national investors." *Id.* at 141. However, Decision 24 has been superseded and the replacement decision of the Andean Pact Commission, Decision 220 of May 11, 1987 (reprinted in 2 ICSID Rev.-FILJ 519 (1987)), leaves to member states the determination of which fora shall be made available for disputes of foreign investors. See Carl, The New Approach to Latin American Integration and its Significance to Private Investors, 2 ICSID Rev.-FILJ 335, 338 (1987).

7. "Transnational enterprises and the corporations comprising them are not persons under international law and lack *jus standi* in international courts. The American states should abstain from adhering to conventions which in any way grant those enterprises or the corporations comprising them direct access to international courts, including arbitration courts, because this would justifiably place transnational enterprises in an advantageous position over national enterprises. The questions posed by transnational enterprises could eventually be heard by international courts through agreements entered into by the states to resolve their disputes. International courts receive their competence by express consent of the states." Work Accomplished by the Inter-American Juridical Committee During its Regular Meeting Held from January 12 to February 13, 1976, at 147, OAS Doc. OEA/Ser.Q/IV.12 CJI-27 (May 1976).

8. Article 2(2)(c) of the Charter provides that: [Each state has the right to] nationalize, expropriate or transfer ownership of foreign property, in which case appropriate compensation should be paid by the state adopting such measures, taking into account its relevant laws and regulations and all circumstances that the state considers pertinent. In any case where the question of compensation gives rise to a controversy, it shall be settled under the domestic law of the nationalizing state and by its tribunals, unless it is freely and mutually agreed by all states concerned that other peaceful means be sought on the basis of sovereign equality of states and in accordance with the principle of free choice of means. G.A. Res. 3281, 29 U.N. GAOR Supp. (No. 31) at 50, U.N. Doc. A/9631 (1974). The Resolution was adopted by a large majority (120 states), but the United States and five Western European countries voted against it, while 10 other states, including Canada and Japan, abstained.

9. *North American Dredging Company of Texas (U.S.A.) v. United Mexican States,* 4 R. Int'l Arb. Awards 26 (1926).

10. In the North American Dredging Company case itself, the Claims Commission, commenting on the investor's waiver of diplomatic protection, asked whether: Under the rules of international law may an alien lawfully make such a promise, and answered that: The Commission holds that he may, but at the same time holds that he cannot deprive the government of his nation of its undoubted right of applying international remedies to violations of international law committed to his damage. *Id.* at 29. See also 1. Brownlie, Principles of Public International Law 546 (1979); L. Oppenheim, I International Law 345 (H. Lauterpacht ed., 1955); M. Sorensen, Manual of Public International Law 592 (1968); American Law Institute, Restatement (Third) of Foreign Relations Law § 713 cmt. g (1987).

11. See *supra* note 3.

12. Convention on the Settlement of Investment Disputes between States and Nationals of Other States, Mar. 18, 1965, 17 U.S.T. 1270, 575 U.N.T.S. 159 [the ICSID Convention]. The ICSID Convention, along with the text of the World Bank Executive Directors' Report thereon, is reprinted in 4 ILM 524 (1965).

13. See Executive Directors' Report, *supra* note 12, at para. 13. See also Broches, The Experience of the International Centre for Settlement of Investment Disputes, in International Investment Disputes: Avoidance and Settlement 75,77 (S. Rubin & R. Nelson eds., 1985); Soley, ICSID Implementation: An Effective Alternative to International Conflict 19 Int'l Law. 521 (1985).

14. See Contracting States and Measures taken by them for the Purpose of the Convention 1, Doc. ICSID/8-D (Nov. 1991). With respect to Jamaica's declaration, see also note 36 *infra.* In addition to the declarations referred to in the text, Guyana and Israel had made, but subsequently withdrew, declarations similar to, respectively, those of Jamaica and Turkey.

15. See cases referred to *infra,* note 36.

16. *Liberian Eastern Timber Corp., Letco Lumber Industry Corp. v. Liberia* (ICSID Case No. ARB/83/2).

17. *AGIP SpA v. Congo* (ICSID Case No. ARB/77/1); *Tesoro Petroleum Corp. v. Trinidad and Tobago* (ICSID Case No. CONC/83/1); *Occidental of Pakistan Ltd. v. Pakistan* (ICSID Case No. ARB/87/4).

18. *Adriano Gardella SpA v. Côte d'Ivoire* (ICSID Case No. ARB/74/1).

19. *S.A.R.L. Benvenuti & Bonfant v. Congo* (ICSID Case No. ARB/77/2). See *infra* note 38. See also Rambaud, Premiers Enseignements des Arbitrages du C.I.R.D.I., 23 Annuaire Français de Droit International 471 (1982)

20. *Guadalupe Gas Products Corp. v. Nigeria* (ICSID Case No. ARB/78/1); *Mobil Oil Corp. et al. v. New Zealand Government* (ICSID Case No. ARB/87/2).

21. *Swiss Aluminium Ltd. and Icelandic Aluminium Co. Ltd. v. Iceland* (ICSID Case No. ARB/83/1).

22. *Asian Agriculture Products Ltd. v. Sri Lanka* (ICSID Case No. ARB/87/3).

23. *Holiday Inns S.A., Occidental Petroleum Corp. et al. v. Morocco* (ICSID Case No.ARB/72/1); *Amco Asia Corp., Pan American Development Ltd. and P.T. Amco Indonesia v. Indonesia* (ICSID Case No. ARB/81/1). The Holiday Inns case is reported in Lalive, The First "World Bank" Arbitration (Holiday Inns v. Morocco)–Some Legal Problems, 51 Brit. Y. B. Int'l L. 123 (1980). As in the Klockner case detailed in *infra* note 26, the Amco Asia case has witnessed two awards, one of which was partially annulled, and two annulment proceedings, the second of which is currently pending. The award that is the subject of the present second annulment proceeding is reprinted in 5 Int'l Arb. Rep., No. 11 at sec. D (Nov. 1991).

24. *SPP (Middle East) Ltd. v. Egypt* (ICSID Case No. ARB/84/3); *Dr. Ghaith R. Pharaon v. Tunisia* (ICSID Case No. ARB/36/1). The SPP case was previously the subject of an ICC arbitral proceeding. The ICC tribunal's award was rendered on February 16, 1983, but was subsequently successfully challenged before the Court of Appeal of Paris by the respondent. The decision of the latter court was in turn confirmed by the French Court of Cassation.

25. *Société Ouest Africaine des Betons Industriels v. Sénégal* (ICSID Case No. ARBI/82/1). The award in this case is reprinted in 6 ICSID Rev.-FILJ 125 (1991) with an introductory note by N. Ziade at 119.

26. *Klockner Industrie-Anlagen GmbH, Klockner Belge, S.A., and Klockner Handelsmaatschappij B.V. v. Cameroon and Société Camerounaise des Engrais* (ICSID Case No. ARB/81/2). See Paulsson, The ICSID Klockner v. Cameroon Award: The Duties of Partners in North-South Economic Development Agreements, I J. Int'l Arb. 145 (1984); Niggemann, The ICSID Klockner v. Cameroon Award: The Dissenting Opinion, I J. Int'l Arb. 331 (1984). The claimants in this case successfully applied to have the award (rendered October 21, 1983) annulled by an ad hoc Committee constituted under the ICSID Convention, art. 52(3). Following the Committee's decision, an English translation of which appears at I ICSID Rev.- FILJ 89 (1986), the case was resubmitted to ICSID arbitration. The resubmission led to a second award (rendered January 26, 1988), which was then made the subject of a second annulment proceeding, which, however, resulted in the upholding of the award concerned.

27. *SEDITEX Engineering Beratungsgesellschaft für die Textilindustrie mbH v. Madagascar* (ICSID Case No. CONC/82/1).

28. *Atlantic Triton Co. Ltd. v. Guinea* (ICSIL) Case No. ARB/84/1. See *infra*, note 37 and accompanying text.

29. *Colt Industries Operating Corp., Firearms Division v. Republic of Korea* (ICSID Case No. ARB/84/2).

30. *Manufacturers Hanover Trust Company v. Egypt and General Authority for Investment and Free Zones* (ICSID Case No. ARB/89/1).

31. See Delaume, ICSID and the Banker, Int'l Fin. L. Rev. 9 (October 1983).

32. The only mandatory provisions of the ICSID Convention in this respect are those according to which (i) an arbitral tribunal composed of more than a sole arbitrator must include an uneven number of arbitrators (art. 37(2)); (ii) arbitrators must possess certain basic qualities, such as independence, integrity, and recognized competence in relevant fields (arts. 14(1) and 40(2)); and (iii) the majority of the arbitrators must be nationals of a state other than the Contracting State party to the dispute or whose national is a party to the dispute (art. 39). This last-mentioned provision will not, however, apply if the sole arbitrator or each individual member of the tribunal has been appointed by agreement of the parties.

33. See Rule 20 of the Rules of Procedure for Arbitration Proceedings as revised on September 26, 1984, reproduced in ICSID Basic Documents 61, Doc. ICSID/15 Jan. 1985 [hereinafter Arbitration Rules]. It may, however, be useful to recall that, in the context of ICSID arbitration, the place of the proceedings does not have the same significance that it has in regard to other types of arbitration, be it ad hoc or institutional arbitration, which remain subject to a greater or lesser extent to domestic law. In fact, in the case of ICSID, the place of arbitration is (at least so long as it is in an ICSID Contracting State) legally immaterial and its determination is one of pure convenience. The reason for this is that the ICSID rules are truly international and insulated against domestic law in Contracting States.

34. ICSID Convention, *supra* note 12, at art. 38 and Arbitration Rules, *supra* note 33, at Rules 4 and 11.

35. ICSID Convention, *supra* note 12, at art. 45(2).

36. In 1974, in spite of a provision regarding the "stabilization" of the relevant tax system, Jamaica decided to increase significantly the taxes payable by the investors. One month before that decision was published, Jamaica notified ICSID that disputes arising out of an "investment relating to minerals or other natural resources" would not be subject to ICSID jurisdiction and sought to give to that notification retrospective effect. Immediately after the enactment of the new tax legislation, the investors affected by it instituted ICSID arbitration proceedings. The arbitral tribunal considered whether they could be

deprived of jurisdiction by the ratification of Jamaica and held that the consents to ICSID arbitration given in the investment agreements could not be unilaterally withdrawn through such a notification or otherwise: *Alcoa Minerals of Jamaica, Inc. v. Jamaica* (ICSID Case No. ARB/74/2); *Kaiser Bauxite Co. v. Jamaica* (ICSID Case No. ARB/74/3); *Reynolds Jamaica Mines, Ltd., Reynolds Metals Co. v. Jamaica* (ICSID Case No. ARB/74/4). See Schmidt, Arbitration Under the Auspices of the International Centre for Settlement of Investment Disputes (ICSID): Implications of the Decision on Jurisdiction in Alcoa Minerals of Jamaica, Inc. v. Government of Jamaica, 17 Harv. Int'l L. J. 90 (1976).

37. See, for example, *Atlantic Triton Co. Ltd. v. Guinea,* Court of Appeal, Rennes decision of October 26, 1984, 24 ILM 340 (1985) and *Maritime International Nominees Establishment v. Guinea,* Tribunal of First Instance, Antwerp, decision of September 27, 1985, 1 ICSID Rev.-FILJ 380 (1986) and Tribunal of First Instance, Geneva, decision of March 13, 1986, 1 ICSID Rev.-FILJ 383 (1986). But by a decision of November 18, 1986, the Court of Cassation of France (reprinted in 2 ICSID Rev.-FILJ 182 (1987)), reversing the decision of the Court of Appeal of Rennes in the Atlantic Triton case, held that the Convention did not preclude provisional measures which could only be excluded by express consent of the parties or by implied consent resulting from the adoption of arbitration rules containing such an exclusion. The 1968 Arbitration Rules of ICSID, which contained no clear exclusion of this type, applied to the arbitration in the Atlantic Triton case. However, the revised Arbitration Rules of 1984 (*supra* note 33) provide in Rule 39(5) that "[n]othing in this Rule shall prevent the parties, provided that they have so stipulated in the agreement recording their consent, from requesting any judicial or other authority to order provisional measures, prior to the institution of the proceeding, or during the proceeding, for the preservation of their respective rights and interests." Examples of provisions retaining the option of seeking judicial assistance for provisional measures are found primarily in financial agreements between banks and foreign governmental borrowers. A suggested text of such a provision may be found in ICSID Model Clauses cl. XVI, at 13. ICSID Doc. ICSID/5/Rev.1 July 1981.

38. *S.A.R.L. Benvenutti [Benvenuti] et Bonfant v. Gouvernement de la République du Congo,* Judgment of June 26, 1981, Cour d'appel, Paris, at 108 Journal du Droit International 843 (1981). For an English translation of the judgment, see 20 ILM 877 (1981). The Court stated that: [The] provisions [of the ICSID Convention] offer a simplified procedure for recognition and enforcement (*exequatur simplifie*) and restrict the function of the court designated for the purposes of the Convention by each Contracting State to ascertaining the authenticity of the award certified by the Secretary-General of the International Centre for Settlement of Investment Disputes.... *Id.* at 881. Following

recognition of the award, Congo complied with it. See I News from ICSID, No. 2 (1984) at 8. The award itself is published in English translation at 21 ILM 740 (1982), with a correction at 21 ILM 1478 (1982). In a second ICSID case, *Societe Ouest Africaine des Betons Industriels v. Sénégal,* the Paris Court of Appeal, invoking rules on sovereign immunity from execution, in December 1989 reversed a decision of the President of the *Tribunal de grande instance* of Paris granting exequatur of the award rendered in the case in early 1988. This ruling of the court, has, however, since been quashed by the French Court of Cassation. See Ziade, Some Recent Decisions in ICSID Cases, 6 ICSID Rev.-FILJ 514 (1991).

39. ICSID Convention, *supra* note 12, at art. 54(1).

40. *Id.* at Article 55. Thus in *Liberian Eastern Timber Corp. v. Liberia,* the respondent state successfully invoked sovereign immunity from execution to have vacated attachments issued in execution of an ICSID award against it. See U.S. District Court decisions reprinted at 2 ICSID Rev-FILJ 188 (1987) and 3 ICSID Rev.-FILJ 161 (1988).

41. Including the resumption of diplomatic protection (*id.* at art. 27) and the right of the Contracting State whose national is a party to the dispute to bring an international claim against the noncomplying state (*id.* at art. 64).

42. An ICSID brochure entitled ICSID Cases, Doc. ICSID/16/Rev.2 (November 15, 1991), gives information, with regard to each case, on the nature of the dispute, its outcome, and the publications in which the case was reported. The same brochure also contains data regarding the composition of ICSID arbitral tribunals and conciliation commissions. This brochure is available from the Centre on request.

43. The text of the ICSID Convention and that of the revised Regulations and Rules are consolidated into a new brochure entitled ICSID Basic Documents; see *supra* note 33.

44. Arbitration Rules, *supra* note 34, at Rule 21(1) provides: At the request of the Secretary-General or at the discretion of the President of the Tribunal, a pre-hearing conference between the Tribunal and the parties may be held to arrange for an exchange of information and the stipulation of uncontested facts in order to expedite the proceeding.

45. *Id.* at Rule 21(2) provides: At the request of the parties, a prehearing conference between the Tribunal and the parties, duly represented by their authorized representatives, may be held to consider the issues in dispute with a view to reaching an amicable settlement.

46. *Id.* at Rule 43. This was the case in *Guadalupe Gas Products Corp. v. Nigeria* (ICSID Case No. AR1/78/1).

47. ICSID Model Clauses, *supra* note 37, cl. XIV, at 13.

48. This is the solution adopted in, for example, Agreement on the Mutual Promotion and Guarantee of Investments, Feb. 9, 1981,

Romania-Sri Lanka, Article 7(2), 2 Investment Treaties (ICSID) Year 1981 1 (1983).

49. See G. Delaume, Transnational Contracts, ch. 15, para. 15.24 (1982 updating).

50. Executive Directors' Report, *supra* note 12, at para. 33.

51. Under the ICSID Convention, *supra* note 12, at art. 27, diplomatic protection is suspended from the date of consent to ICSID arbitration (possibly subject to exhaustion of local remedies) until an award is rendered. It is only when the state party to the dispute, assuming that the award is rendered against it, fails to comply with the award, that the right of diplomatic protection is revived.

52. See ICSID, 2 Convention on the Settlement of Investment Disputes between States and Nationals of Other States–Documents Concerning the Origin and the Formulation of the Convention 606 (Doc. 39, 1968).

53. See Agreement for the Promotion and Protection of Investments, June 4, 1981, United Kingdom-Paraguay, Article 8, 2 Investment Treaties (ICSID) Year 1981, 71 (1983). See also Convention sur l'encouragement et la protection réciproques des investissements, Sept. 20, 1978, France-El Salvador, Article 8, 2 Investment Treaties (ICSID) Year 1978, 39 (1983).

54. See Delaume, *supra* note 31, at 13.

55. The Convention Establishing the Multilateral Investment Guarantee Agency, Oct. 11, 1985 [the MIGA Convention], along with the Commentary thereon, appears at I ICSID Rev.-FILJ 145 (1986). The MIGA Convention's formulation is described in detail in 1. Shihata, MIGA and Foreign Investment 61–106 (1988).

56. See MIGA Convention, *supra* note 55, at arts. 2 and 23.

57. The idea of a multilateral investment guarantee scheme was first studied by the then Development Assistance Group (now the Development Assistance Committee (DAC) of the Organisation for Economic Co-operation and Development, or OECD) in the late 1950s and early 1960s. In 1961, DAC requested the World Bank to prepare a report on this matter which was published in 1962. In 1964, the United Nations Conference on Trade and Development (UNCTAD) asked the World Bank to resume its efforts toward the establishment of a scheme. In the same year, the OECD transmitted to the World Bank a "Report on the Establishment of a Multilateral Investment Guarantee Corporation," setting forth the principal features of a scheme. During the following years, the initiative was discussed by the World Bank's Executive Directors on the basis of draft conventions prepared by the staff. UNCTAD in 1968 adopted a resolution endorsing the establishment of a scheme, but the World Bank suspended its work on this initiative indefinitely in 1973. At that time, many developing countries

were questioning the merits of foreign investment in general, and several OECD countries were just launching their national investment guarantee programs and not interested in the simultaneous establishment of an international scheme. During the 1970s, there were also suggestions to establish regional investment guarantee schemes, notably in the Inter-American Development Bank and the European Community. While none of these initiatives succeeded, the Arab countries established in 1974 the Inter-Arab Investment Guarantee Corporation which has been in operation since then. The European Community has since resumed its study of an investment guarantee facility to operate within the framework of its cooperation with African, Pacific, and Caribbean countries. See Shihata, *supra* note 55, at ch. 1 on the previous efforts of the World Bank toward the establishment of an International Investment Insurance Agency, and Shihata, Arab Investment Guarantee Corporation-A Regional Investment Insurance Project, 6 J. World Trade L. 185 (1972) on the establishment of the Inter-Arab Investment Guarantee Corporation.

58. MIGA Convention, *supra* note 55, at art. 2.

59. *Id.* at art. 12.

60. *Id.* IMF Balance of Payments Manual 136, para. 408 (4th ed. 1977) defines foreign direct investment as "investment that is made to acquire a lasting interest in an enterprise operating in an economy other than that of the investor, the investor's purpose being to have an effective voice in the management of the enterprise"; see also OECD, Detailed Benchmark Definition of Foreign Direct Investment (1983).

61. See MIGA Convention, *supra* note 55, at art. 12(b) and Operational Regulations of MIGA (reprinted at 3 ICSID Rev.-FILJ 364 (1988)), at para.1.05. For a survey and discussion of the new forms of investment, see C. Oman, New Forms of International Investment in Developing Countries (1984).

62. MIGA Convention, *supra* note 55, at art. 13(a).

63. *Id.* at art. 13(c), which requires a decision by MIGA's Board, acting by special majority, upon a joint application of the investor and his country.

64. It may be added that under Article 13(c) of the MIGA Convention, the host government must even apply for the guarantee jointly with the investor in the case of a host country national investing funds transferred from abroad.

65. MIGA Convention, *supra* note 55, at art. 23(c).

66. *Id.* at art. 30.

67. *Id.* at art. 4(a).

68. For the text of the Convention as proposed by the management of the World Bank, see 24 ILM 688 (1985). The principle of equal representation of groups of countries which have distinct interests in the

activities of the institution is reflected in most international commodity agreements. For example, the International Coffee, Cocoa and Jute Agreements (647 U.N.T.S. 3; 882 U.N.T.S. 67; UNCTAD Doc. TD/JUTE/11/Rev. 1 (1983)) distinguish between member countries which are primarily exporters of the commodity concerned and those which are primarily importers; each group is allotted 1,000 votes, which are then divided among the members of the group under various keys. Under the system of weighted voting which prevails in most international lending institutions, voting rights are tied to capital subscriptions (one vote per share) while each member receives also an equal amount of membership votes. The Articles of Agreement of the International Bank for Reconstruction and Development, Dec. 27, 1945, 60 Stat. 1440, 2 U.N.T.S. 134, for instance, accord to each member country 250 basic votes as well as one additional vote per share held in the Bank's capital stock, each share being worth $100,000 (Article V, Section 3(a)). But compare, Agreement Establishing the International Fund for Agricultural Development, June 13, 1976, 28 U.S.T. 8435, 15 ILM 922 (1976), where members are divided in three groups each having one-third of the total votes.

69. See MIGA Convention, *supra* note 55, at art. 39(a) and sched. A.

70. *Id.* at arts. 3(d), 39(b), and 39(d). On March 13, 1991, the Board of Directors of MIGA agreed to expand by two years the period in which nonsignatory countries may subscribe to the shares initially allocated to them, and, in the meantime, to continue to adopt decisions by the special majority, if not by consensus.

71. *Id.* at art. 18.

72. *Id.* at art. 57(b) and Annex I.

73. *Id.* at art. 57(b).

74. See *id.* at art. 5(a).

75. *Id.* at art. 7(i).

76. *Id.* at art. 7(ii).

77. *Id.* at art. 8(a).

78. *Id.* at art. 22(a).

79. *Id.*

80. It should be noted that decisions with respect to sponsorship operations are also to be made by MIGA's Board or Council, as the case may be, under the Agency's normal voting structure, except that sponsoring countries and host countries of sponsored investments will receive additional votes which they may cast only for decisions related to sponsored investments. See *id.* at annex I, art. 7.

81. Compare Martin, Multilateral Investment Insurance: the OECD Proposal, 8 Harv. Int'l LJ. 280, 318 (1966).

82. MIGA Convention, *supra* note 55, at art. 34

83. Compare id., at art. 33(d).

84. *Id.* at arts. 18 and 57(b).

85. See *supra* notes 5 and 6.

86. See, for example, Agreement relating to investment guaranties, July 29, 1960, United States-Chile, 405 U.N.T.S. 127; Agreement relating to the guaranty of private investments, Dec. 22, 1959, United States-Argentina 411 U.N.T.S. 41; Agreement relating to investment guaranties, Nov. 26 and 29, 1962, United States-Venezuela, 474 U.N.T.S. 107; Investment Guaranty Agreement, Feb. 6, 1965, United States-Brazil, 719 U.N.TS. 3.

87. IBRD, General Conditions Applicable to Loan and Guarantee Agreements, Article X Jan. 1, 1985).

88. See Article 35 (1) and annex to the Convention Establishing the Inter-Arab Investment Guarantee Corporation, published by that Corporation in Arabic and English. See also Shihata in J. World Trade L., *supra* note 57, at 201.

89. The 1979 Constitution of Peru is an example for a new trend. Article 136 of this Constitution provides that "[t]he State and persons under public law can submit disputes stemming from agreements with foreigners to judicial or arbitral tribunals constituted in accordance with international agreements to which Peru is a party."

90. MIGA Convention, *supra* note 55, at art. 57(b).

91. Differing in details, some of these agreements provide for the prior exhaustion of local remedies and confine international arbitration to "questions of public international law."

92. See Decision 220 of the Andean Pact Commission, *supra* note 6, at art. 33.

93. *Id.* at arts. 7 and 15.

94. At present almost all OECD countries, as well as the Republic of Korea and India, operate such a program. For a survey, see OECD, Investing in Developing Countries (5th ed. 1983).

95. Private political risk coverage is available from Lloyd's of London and U.S. underwriters. See Svensk, The Role of Private Sector Insurance, in Managing International Political Risk: Strategies and Techniques 114 (F Ghadar et al. eds., 1983).

96. Compare Meron, The World Bank and Insurance, 47 Brit. YB. Int'l L. 301, 312 (1974-1975): "[T]he very raison d'être of the establishment of a multilateral insurance agency was to make subrogation into a non-political, technical, non-confrontation issue"; Martin, *supra* note 81, at 318–19 (1967): "With an international Agency it is more likely that the claim will be treated as the legal issue that it should be."

97. Compare Address of World Bank President A. W. Clausen, 1981 Joint Annual Meetings of The World Bank and International Monetary Fund Summary Proceedings 15, 23 (1982).

98. MIGA Convention, *supra* note 55, at art. 12(d).

99. According to unpublished figures obtained from OPIC, that Corporation had by 1986 settled claims in the total amount of $96 million by paying compensation in cash to the investor while accepting installments from the host government; and claims totalling some $292 million, by persuading investors to accept host government commitments backed by OPIC guarantees or by a combination of cash payment and guarantees.

The Global Financial Crisis
and the Future of
International Financial Institutions

James Bond

The financial and economic crash of 2008 is turning out to be the worst financial crisis since the 1930s. Its global reach has left practically no country untouched, and it is erasing the past decade of development gains in the emerging world. World industrial production fell by an unprecedented 20 percent in the fourth quarter of 2008 (annualized rate), and is expected to continue to contract in the first half of 2009. GDP fell in all industrial countries in the last quarter of 2008, and several large developing economies are also showing GDP compression for late 2008 and early 2009. Estimates are that around 100 million people have been put out of work worldwide. The worldwide destruction of wealth through declines in equity—housing values and corporate stock—is on the order of the GDP of the United States. The Wall Street investment banking sector, as we knew it, has all but disappeared. And commodity prices, recently at an all-time high, have plummeted. By the time the crisis is over, the geopolitical and economic landscape will be quite different from what it was at the beginning of the century.

This chapter looks at the underlying causes of the crisis and the likely effect on foreign direct investment (FDI), and makes some

---

James Bond is Chief Operating Officer of MIGA.

observations concerning the provision of political risk insurance (PRI) in the new environment. The crisis itself is multidimensional: like Russian Matryoshka dolls that fit inside one another, the unfolding of each facet of the crisis reveals another imbalance and correction that adds to the misery.

The Financial Crisis

The innermost doll of the unfolding drama is the financial crisis. Conventional wisdom attributes this to the "subprime mess"—the collapse of the subprime mortgage market and housing prices in the United States. But at the heart of the financial crisis is a toxic cocktail of loose monetary policy in the United States and Europe resulting from the cut in interest rates following the September 11, 2001, terrorist attacks (the U.S. Federal Reserve lowered interest rates to close to 1 percent at the end of 2001, and kept them low for three years); a global savings glut resulting from the enormous surpluses in countries like China and the oil producers in the Gulf; and unfettered financial sector innovation, unchecked by financial regulators, leading to a slew of new financial products that seemed to provide the chimera of high yields at low or close to zero risk.

In this crisis, excess liquidity did what excess liquidity has always done in past financial crises: it led to massive, unsustainable leverage—excessive levels of debt—throughout the United States and the European economies. At the collapse of Bear Stearns and its sale to JP Morgan at $2 per share on March 16, 2008, the investment bank's leverage (the ratio of its outstanding loans to its capital) stood at 38; and when Lehman Brothers filed for bankruptcy under Chapter 11 on September 15, 2008, its leverage was around 35. A good prudential regulation rule of thumb is that banking leverage should not exceed a ratio of about 10 or 12 (depending on the nature of its capital). This leverage was spread throughout the economy: firms had borrowed excessively to maximize returns to equity holders; and households had bought houses beyond their means, taken out home equity lines of credit, and racked up excessive credit card debt.

When the unwinding of excess liquidity commenced, its effects snowballed throughout the economy. In early 2007, home prices started to fall in key markets like the United States and the United Kingdom. The first telltale sign of the impending crisis was on June 22, 2007, when Bear Stearns bailed out two of its hedge funds. The snowball started to roll in August, 2007: on August 9, BNP Paribas suspended three of its funds and Countrywide Financial (the largest U.S. mortgage lender) exhausted its lines of credit; and on September 14, 2007, Northern Rock turned for help to the Bank of England. By the third and fourth quarters of 2007, mortgage defaults were rising sharply in the United States, particularly in the subprime mortgage segment of the market. In late November, Citigroup obtained an injection of capital amounting to $7.5 billion from the Abu Dhabi Investment Authority. In January 2008, global equity markets were reeling; the Fed made its biggest interest cut ever. On March 16, 2008, Bear Stearns went under and was sold to JP Morgan. Between late July and early September 2008, Fannie Mae and Freddie Mac (U.S. government–sponsored enterprises created to support mortgage finance) were placed in government conservatorship of the Federal Housing Finance Agency. September was the "winter of discontent" for the markets; investors started to lose confidence and firms started to have difficulty raising finance. Mid-September was a key turning point: on September 15, Merrill Lynch sold itself to Bank of America, Lehman Brothers filed under Chapter 11, and later in the week AIG (the largest insurance company in the world) needed to be bailed out by the U.S. Federal Reserve. The financial crisis was in full swing.

The Credit Crisis

If the financial crisis is the first nested doll, the second is the credit crisis. And whereas the financial crisis unfolded over time, the commencement of the credit crisis can be dated quite precisely, to September 15, 2008, when the Fed decided not to bail out Lehman Brothers and allowed it to go under. This decision was probably made by the Fed to reduce the risk of moral hazard in the rest of the financial sector. However, the collapse of a major Wall Street player deemed by the markets to be "too interconnected to fail" rattled banks and financial operators throughout the economy. This act brought home the reality of counterparty risk: what are the consequences if the counterparty of a valid transaction suddenly fails? On the news of the Lehman Brothers collapse, interbank credit markets froze and interbank rates rose to unprecedented levels. The TED spread (the difference between the London Interbank Offer Rate [LIBOR] and the U.S. Treasury bill rate at the same maturity), which is an indicator of confidence in the credit markets, rose from its normal 0.5 percent to 4.5 percent in October 2008 (figure 2.1). Since that

FIGURE 2.1 TED SPREAD

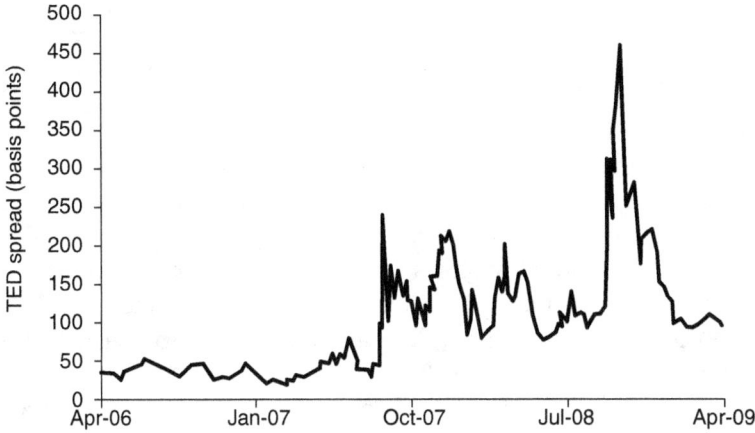

Source: Bloomberg April, 2009.

time, the availability of credit throughout the economy (trade finance, bank syndications, availability of lines of credit for firms) has declined sharply throughout the United States and Europe, and margins over central bank lending rates have risen sharply. To date, credit markets have not yet fully returned to normal despite massive programs of support from governments providing guarantees for commercial paper issued by banks and large corporations; but there has clearly been an overall improvement since October 2008.

The credit crisis is a powerful multiplier from the financial crisis to the rest of the economy. Nearly all firms rely on credit to function; if this credit becomes more expensive the firm becomes less profitable and reins in production at the margin. If credit disappears, the firm goes under. The massive deleveraging in the financial sector has already made credit much scarcer and more expensive in the economy. But the credit crisis, which has led to lines of credit to firms not being renewed, supplier credit being curtailed, and projects not being financed, has triggered a tsunami throughout the economy.

Governments have reacted to the credit crisis by providing guarantees for paper issued by banks and large corporations to reduce the perception of counterparty risk. This has, for the most part, been quite successful. But as banks scale back their lending to adjust to their reduced capital base, the decrease appears to have hit trade credit disproportionately hard, which is having a significant impact on global trade.

The Economic Crisis

The third nested doll is the economic crisis, which is unfolding as this is being written. The massive reduction in demand has led to the biggest single-quarter decline in rich-country GDP in a quarter century in fourth quarter 2008. In rich countries automobile sales have plummeted, housing starts are at an all-time low, and discretionary consumer spending has frozen as households take a prudent stance on consumption. Unemployment has started to rise as factories lay off workers or shutter their doors.

The economic crisis in industrial countries has had a rapid impact on developing countries, as demand for manufactures and commodities has plummeted, and import volumes have declined in response to lower consumer demand. Containers of unsold goods have piled up in both exporting and importing ports and charter rates for shipping have declined. By the fourth quarter 2008, this increase in inventories triggered a fall in world industrial production of an unprecedented 20 percent, and GDP fell in all industrial countries.

The economic crisis is having an impact on everyone everywhere, even in countries whose financial sectors have conservative leverage ratios and relatively modest recourse to private financial flows. It is leading to higher unemployment, cuts in public spending on social programs, and loss of household wealth. The social impact is difficult to estimate at this point, but without a doubt, the curtailment of programs worldwide is leading to an increase in poverty and a decline in living standards.

Private Financial Flows to Developing Countries

These nested crises have not left financial flows to the developing world untouched. In 2007, private financial flows to developing countries were close to $1 trillion. Developing country investments were seen as having better yields than those in industrial countries, and just as excess liquidity pumped money into real estate and exotic synthetic financial products, it fueled a significant expansion of investment in the emerging world. High liquidity and an abundance of capital compressed sovereign risk premiums and brought the cost of financing to emerging markets down to hitherto unseen levels, as overall volumes of financing were rising.

The combination of the financial and credit crises reversed this phenomenon. Flows from private creditors and banks to emerging markets have stopped; creditors and banks are now pulling money out of the developing world as they deleverage in an effort to shore up their balance sheets. At the same time, direct investment in the developing world is declining, following the reduction in cross-border debt financing, because projects—such as infrastructure and extractive industries—that rely on syndicated loans and other complex debt structures can no longer close financing deals. These trends have led to a massive decline in private sector financing for development. The Institute of International Finance estimates that private flows to emerging economies will decline to no more than $165.3 billion in 2009, compared with $465.8 billion in 2008 and $928.6 billion in 2007 (see table 2.1).

Also, as private financing for projects in emerging economies has dried up, the cost of this financing has risen dramatically. This increase is partly due to a shift of the supply-demand curve for finance as supply has become scarcer, but also to the rediscovery of

TABLE 2.1 EMERGING MARKET ECONOMIES' EXTERNAL FINANCING
US$ BILLIONS

	2006	2007	2008e	2009f
Current account balance	383.9	434.0	387.4	322.8
External financing, net				
Private flows, net	564.9	928.6	465.8	165.3
Equity investment, net	222.3	296.1	174.1	194.8
Direct investment, net	170.9	304.1	263.4	197.5
Portfolio investment, net	51.5	-8.0	-89.3	-2.7
Private creditors, net	342.6	632.4	291.7	-29.5
Commercial banks, net	211.9	410.3	166.6	-60.6
Nonbanks, net	130.7	222.2	125.1	31.1
Official flows, net	-57.5	11.4	41.0	29.4
IFIs	-30.4	2.7	16.6	31.0
Bilateral creditors	-27.1	8.7	24.3	-1.6
Resident lending and other, neta	-336.5	-425.3	-449.8	-271.6
Reserves (- = increase)	-554.8	-948.7	-444.3	-245.9

Source: Institute of International Finance 2009.
Note: e = estimate; f = forecast; IFI = international financial institution.
a. Including net lending, monetary gold, and errors and omissions.

risk and more rational pricing. Thus, developing countries are being hit by a triple effect: a decline in exports to rich countries; a decline in financial flows from rich countries; and more expensive financing.

Effects on the Political Risk Insurance Sector Going Forward

Recent months have seen two diametrically opposed trends in the PRI sector: first, an overall decline in demand for PRI as financial flows have dried up; and second, a significant increase in rates as the reality of risk has returned with a vengeance. How these will play out over the coming months is not yet clear, although for MIGA itself, we can see a clear decline in overall volumes of PRI provided, resulting directly from the difficulty in closing financing on complex investments in developing countries, with a significant shift away from support to infrastructure toward banking recapitalization.

Going forward, we expect that FDI growth will resume, probably starting from a lower base than seen in recent years. We also expect that perceptions of risk will return to their historical averages. These two trends will translate into increased demand for PRI, probably associated with higher premiums. On the opposite side of the coin, history teaches that severe economic disruption triggers political turmoil; the 1930s is a stark case in point. It is therefore to be expected that the number of events leading to potential claims will rise in coming months and years.

References

Bloomberg. April 2009. http://www.bloomberg.com/apps/quote?ticker=.TEDSP%3AIND

Institute of International Finance. 2009. "Capital Flows to Emerging Market Economies." January 27. http://www.iif.com/press/press+90.php.

Principles and Development of Islamic Finance

Zamir Iqbal

Islamic finance is a rapidly growing part of the global financial sector. Indeed, it is not restricted to Islamic countries and is spreading wherever there is a sizable Muslim community. More recently, it has caught the attention of conventional financial markets. According to some estimates, more than 250 financial institutions in over 45 countries practice some form of Islamic finance, and the industry has been growing at a rate of more than 15 percent annually for the past five years. The market's current annual turnover is estimated to be $350 billion, compared with a mere $5 billion in 1985.[1] Since the emergence of Islamic banks in the early 1970s, considerable research has been conducted, focusing mainly on the viability, design, and operation of "deposit-accepting" financial institutions, which function primarily on the basis of profit- and loss-sharing partnerships rather than the payment or receipt of interest, a prohibited element in Islam.

Although the emergence of Islamic banks in global markets is a significant development, it is dwarfed by the enormous changes

Zamir Iqbal is a Lead Investment Officer in the World Bank. This chapter was orginally published in *Risk Analysis for Islamic Banks*, 2007, eds. Hennie van Greuning and Zamir Iqbal. Washington, DC: World Bank.

taking place in the conventional banking industry. Rapid innovations in financial markets and the internationalization of financial
flows have changed the face of conventional banking almost beyond
recognition. Technological progress and deregulation have provided
new opportunities, increasing competitive pressures among banks
and nonbanks alike. The growth in international financial markets
and the proliferation of diverse financial instruments have provided
large banks with wider access to funds. In the late 1980s, margins
attained from the traditional business of banking diminished. Banks
responded to these new challenges with vigor and imagination by
forging into new arenas. At the same time, markets expanded, and
opportunities to design new products and provide more services
arose. While these changes occurred more quickly in some countries
than in others, banks everywhere developed new instruments, products, services, and techniques. Traditional banking practice—based
on the receipt of deposits and the granting of loans—was only one
part of a typical bank's business and often the least profitable. See
box 3.1 for a summary of the critical points of this chapter.

Box 3.1 Key Messages

- Institutions offering financial instruments and services compatible with the principles of Islam are emerging rapidly in
  domestic and international financial markets.
- The basic framework for an Islamic financial system is a set
  of rules and laws, collectively referred to as *Shariah*, governing economic, social, political, and cultural aspects of Islamic
  societies.
- Prohibition of *riba*—a term literally meaning "an excess" and
  interpreted as "any unjustifiable increase of capital whether
  in loans or sales"—is the central tenet of the system. Such
  prohibition is applicable to all forms of "interest" and therefore eliminates "debt" from the economy.
- Efforts to develop financial intermediation without interest
  started in the 1960s. Several Islamic banks were established
  in the 1970s, and their number has been growing since then.
- The last decade has witnessed rapid developments in the
  areas of financial innovation, risk management, regulation,
  and supervision.

New information-based activities, such as trading in financial markets and generating income through fees, became a major source of a bank's profitability. Financial innovation also led to the increased market orientation and marketability of bank assets, which entailed the use of assets such as mortgages, automobile loans, and export credits as backing for marketable securities, a process known as securitization. A prime motivation for innovation was the introduction of prudential capital requirements, which led to a variety of new financial instruments. Some instruments were technically very complicated and poorly understood except by market experts, while many others posed complex problems for the measurement, management, and control of risk. Moreover, profits associated with some of these instruments were high and, like the financial markets from which they were derived, were highly volatile and exposed banks to new or higher degrees of risk.

These developments increased the need for and complicated the function of risk measurement, management, and mitigation (control assessment). The quality of corporate governance of banks was a hot topic, and the approach to regulation and supervision changed dramatically. Within an individual bank, the new banking environment and increased market volatility necessitated an integrated approach to asset-liability and risk management. Rapid developments in conventional banking also influenced the reshaping of Islamic banks and financial institutions. There was a growing realization among Islamic financial institutions that sustainable growth requires the development of a comprehensive risk management framework geared to their particular situation and requirements. At the same time, policy makers and regulators were taking serious steps to design an efficient corporate governance structure as well as a sound regulatory and supervisory framework to support development of a financial system conducive to Islamic principles.

This chapter provides a comprehensive overview of topics related to the assessment, analysis, and management of various types of risks in the field of Islamic banking. It is an attempt to provide a high-level framework (aimed at nonspecialist executives) attuned to the current realities of changing economies and Islamic financial markets. This approach emphasizes the accountability of key players in the corporate governance process in relation to the management of Islamic financial risk.

Principles of Islamic Financial Systems

The Islamic financial system is not limited to banking; it also covers capital formation, capital markets, and all types of financial intermediation and risk transfer. The term "Islamic financial system" is relatively new, appearing only in the mid-1980s. In fact, earlier references to commercial or mercantile activities conforming to Islamic principles were made under the umbrella of either "interest-free" or "Islamic" banking. However, interpreting the Islamic financial system simply as free of interest does not capture a true picture of the system as a whole. Undoubtedly, prohibiting the receipt and payment of interest is the nucleus of the system, but it is supported by other principles of Islamic doctrine advocating social justice, risk sharing, the rights and duties of individuals and society, property rights, and the sanctity of contracts.

An Islamic economic system is a rule-based system formulated by Islamic law, known as *Shariah*. The *Shariah* consists of constitutive and regulative rules according to which individual Muslims, and their collectivity, must conduct their affairs. The basic source of the law in Islam is the Qur'an, whose centrality in Islam and influence on the life of Muslims cannot be overemphasized. Its chapters constitute the tissues out of which the life of a Muslim is tailored, and its verses are the threads from which the essence of his or her soul is woven. It includes all the necessary constitutive rules of the law as "guidance for mankind." However, it contains many universal statements that need further explanation before they can become specific guides for human action. Hence, after the Qur'an, the Prophet Muhammad's sayings and actions are the most important sources of the law and a fountainhead of Islamic life and thought.

The philosophical foundation of an Islamic financial system goes beyond the interaction of factors of production and economic behavior. Whereas the conventional financial system focuses primarily on the economic and financial aspects of transactions, the Islamic system places equal emphasis on the ethical, moral, social, and religious dimensions, which seek to enhance equality and fairness for the good of society as a whole. The system can be fully appreciated only in the context of Islam's teachings on the work ethic, distribution of wealth, social and economic justice, and the role of the state. The Islamic financial system is founded on the absolute prohibition of the payment or receipt of any predetermined, guaranteed rate of return. This closes the door to the concept of interest and precludes the use of debt-based instruments.

Given an understanding of the role of institutions, rules, the law, and ideology of Islam, one can make the following propositions regarding the economic system:[2]

- The foremost priority of Islam and its teaching on economics is *justice and equity*. The notion of justice and equity, from production to distribution, is deeply embedded in the system. As an aspect of justice, social justice in Islam consists of the creation and provision of equal opportunities and the removal of obstacles equally for every member of society. Legal justice, too, can be interpreted as meaning that all members of society have equal status before the law, equal protection of the law, and equal opportunity under the law. The notion of economic justice, and its attendant concept of distributive justice, is characteristic of the Islamic economic system: rules governing permissible and forbidden economic behavior on the part of consumers, producers, and government, as well as questions of property rights and the production and distribution of wealth, are all based on the Islamic concept of justice.
- The Islamic paradigm incorporates a spiritual and moral framework that values human relations above material possessions. In this way, it not only is concerned about material needs but also establishes a balance between the material and spiritual fulfillment of human beings.
- Whereas conventional thinking focuses on the individual, society, or community and appears as a mere aggregate having no independent significance, the Islamic system creates a balanced relationship between the individual and society. Self-interest and private gains of the individual are not denied, but they are regulated for betterment of the collectivity. Maximizing an individual's pursuit of profit in enterprise or satisfaction in consumption is not the sole objective of society, and any wasteful consumption is discouraged.
- The recognition and protection of the property rights of all members of society are the foundation of a stakeholder-oriented society, preserving the rights of all and reminding them of their responsibilities.

To ensure justice, the *Shariah* provides a network of ethical and moral rules of behavior for all participants in the market and requires that these norms and rules be internalized and adhered to by all (see box 3.2). This concept of market is based on the basic

BOX 3.2 PRINCIPLES OF AN ISLAMIC FINANCIAL SYSTEM

The basic framework for an Islamic financial system is a set of
rules and laws, collectively referred to as *Shariah*, governing economic, social, political, and cultural aspects of Islamic societies.
Shariah originates from the rules dictated by the Qur'an and its
practices and explanations rendered (more commonly known as
Sunnah) by the Prophet Muhammad. Further elaboration of the
rules is provided by scholars in Islamic jurisprudence within the
framework of the Qur'an and Sunnah. The basic principles of an
Islamic financial system can be summarized as follows.

- **Prohibition of interest.** Prohibition of *riba*—a term literally
  meaning "an excess" and interpreted as "any unjustifiable
  increase of capital whether in loans or sales"—is the central
  tenet of the system. More precisely, any positive, fixed, predetermined rate tied to the maturity and the amount of principal (that is, guaranteed regardless of the performance of
  the investment) is considered *riba* and is prohibited. The general consensus among Islamic scholars is that *riba* covers not
  only usury but also the charging of "interest" as widely practiced. This prohibition is based on arguments of social justice, equality, and property rights. Islamic law encourages the
  earning of profits but forbids the charging of interest because
  profits, determined ex post, symbolize successful entrepre-
  neurship and creation of additional wealth, whereas interest,
  determined ex ante, is a cost that is accrued irrespective of
  the outcome of business operations and may not create
  wealth. Social justice demands that borrowers and lenders
  share rewards as well as losses in an equitable fashion and
  that the process of accumulating and distributing wealth in
  the economy be fair and representative of true productivity.
- **Money as "potential" capital.** Money is treated as "potential" capital—that is, it becomes actual capital only when it
  joins hands with other resources to undertake a productive
  activity. Islam recognizes the time value of money, but only
  when it acts as capital, not when it is "potential" capital.

(continued)

BOX 3.2 CONTINUED

- *Risk sharing.* Because interest is prohibited, suppliers of funds become investors instead of creditors. The provider of financial capital and the entrepreneur share business risks in return for a share of the profits. The terms of financial transactions need to reflect a symmetrical risk-return distribution that each party to the transaction may face. The relationship between the investors and the financial intermediary is based on profit- and loss-sharing principles, and the financial intermediary shares the risks with the investors.
- *Prohibition of speculative behavior.* An Islamic financial system discourages hoarding and prohibits transactions featuring extreme uncertainties, gambling, and risks.
- *Sanctity of contracts.* Islam upholds contractual obligations and the disclosure of information as a sacred duty. This feature is intended to reduce the risk of asymmetric information and moral hazard.
- *Shariah-approved activities.* Only those business activities that do not violate the rules of *Shariah* qualify for investment. For example, any investment in businesses dealing with alcohol, gambling, or casinos is prohibited.
- *Social justice.* In principle, any transaction leading to injustice and exploitation is prohibited. A financial transaction should not lead to the exploitation of any party to the transaction. Exploitation entails the absence of information symmetry between parties to a contract.

principle forbidding any form of behavior leading to the creation of instantaneous property rights without commensurate equity created by work. In this context, market imperfection refers to the existence of any factor considered not to be permissible by the *Shariah*, such as fraud, cheating, monopoly practices, coalitions and all types of combinations among buyers and sellers, underselling, speculative hoarding, and bidding up of prices without the intention to purchase. The freedom to enter into a contract and the obligation to fulfill it; consent of the parties to a transaction; full access to the market for all buyers and sellers; honesty in transactions; and provision of full information regarding the quantity, quality, and prices of factors and products to buyers and sellers before the start of negotiation and bargaining are prescribed.

Beginning with the notion of property as a sacred trust, as well as prohibitions also present in other monotheistic religions, *Shariah* protects property from any exploitation through unjust and unfair dealings. Prohibition of *riba* (interest), elimination of *gharar* (contractual ambiguity), and restrictions on other forms of exploitation are some of the implications of this core principle. (See annex 3A at the end of this chapter for a glossary of Islamic terms.) The significance of contracts and the related obligations cannot be overstated. In this context, financial transactions are no different from any other set of contracts subject to compliance with *Shariah* principles. Primarily, a financial transaction is considered valid if it meets the basic requirements of a valid legal contract and does not contain certain elements, such as *riba, gharar, qimar* (gambling), and *maysur* (games of chance involving deception). While the prohibition of *riba* is the most critical and gets the most attention, one cannot dispute the criticality of *gharar* and other elements. Historically, jurists or *Shariah* scholars did not interfere unnecessarily in economic activities and gave economic agents full freedom to contract as long as certain basic requirements—that is, the prohibition of *riba*—were met.

Prohibition of interest is not due to any formal economic theory as such but is directly prohibited by the divine order in the Qur'an. Verses of the Qur'an clearly prohibit dealing with *riba* but do not define it precisely. Such omission is often attributed to the fact that the concept was not vague at the time of prohibition, so there was no need to provide a formal definition. Defining the term in any language other than Arabic adds further complexity. For example, no single English word captures the essence of *riba*. This has caused much of the confusion in explaining the concept both to the lay person and to scholars.

Literally, the Arabic term *riba* refers to excess, addition, and surplus, while the associated verb implies "to increase, to multiply, to exceed, to exact more than was due, or to practice usury." E. W. Lane's Arabic-English Lexicon presents a comprehensive meaning that covers most of the earlier definitions of *riba*:[3]

> To increase, to augment, swellings, forbidden "addition," to make more than what is given, the practicing or taking of usury or the like, an excess or an addition, or an addition over and above the principal sum that is lent or expended.

While the original basis for the prohibition of interest was divine authority, Muslim scholars recently have emphasized the lack of a theory to justify the use of interest. Muslim scholars have rebutted the arguments that interest is a reward for savings—a productivity of capital—and constitutes the difference between the value of capital goods today and their value tomorrow. Regarding interest being a reward for savings, they argue that interest could be justified only if it resulted in reinvestment and subsequent growth in capital and was not a reward solely for forgoing consumption. Regarding interest as productive capital, modern Muslim scholars argue that the interest is paid on the money and is required regardless of whether capital is used productively and thus is not justified. Finally, regarding interest as an adjustment between the value of capital goods today and their value tomorrow, they argue that this only explains its inevitability and not its rightness: if that is the sole justification for interest, it seems more reasonable to allow next year's economic conditions to determine the extent of the reward, as opposed to predetermining it in the form of interest (Mirakhor 1989).

After *riba*, contractual ambiguity is the most important element in financial contracts. In simple terms, *gharar* refers to any uncertainty created by the lack of information or control in a contract. It can be thought of as ignorance in regard to an essential element in a transaction, such as the exact sale price or the ability of the seller to deliver what is sold. The presence of ambiguity makes a contract null and void.

Gharar can be defined as a situation in which either party to a contract has information regarding some element of the subject of the contract that is withheld from the other party or in which neither party has control over the subject of the contract. Classic examples include transactions involving birds in flight, fish not yet caught, an unborn calf in its mother's womb, or a runaway animal. All such cases involve the sale of an item that may or may not exist. More modern examples include transactions whose subject is not in the possession of one of the parties and over which there is uncertainty even about its future possession.

Keeping in mind the notion of fairness in all Islamic commercial transactions, *Shariah* considers any uncertainty as to the quantity, quality, recoverability, or existence of the subject matter of a contract as evidence of *gharar*. However, *Shariah* allows jurists to determine the extent of *gharar* in a transaction and, depending on the circumstances, whether it invalidates the contract. By prohibiting *gharar*,

Shariah prohibits many pre-Islamic contracts of exchange, considering them subject to either excessive uncertainty or opaqueness to one or both parties to the contract. In many cases, *gharar* can be eliminated simply by stating the object of sale and the price. A well-documented contract eliminates ambiguity as well.

Considering *gharar* as excessive uncertainty, one can associate it with the element of "risk." Some argue that prohibiting *gharar* is one way of managing risks in Islam, because a business transaction based on the sharing of profit and loss encourages parties to conduct due diligence before committing to a contract. Prohibition of *gharar* forces parties to avoid contracts with a high degree of informational asymmetry and with extreme payoffs; it also makes parties more responsible and accountable. Treating *gharar* as risk may preclude the trading of derivative instruments, which is designed to transfer risks from one party to another.

Another area where prohibition of *gharar* has raised concerns in contemporary financial transactions is the area of insurance. Some argue that writing an insurance (*takaful*) contract on the life of a person falls within the domain of *gharar* and thus invalidates the contract. The issue is still under review and not fully resolved.

Development and Growth of Islamic Finance

Islamic finance was practiced predominantly in the Muslim world throughout the Middle Ages, fostering trade and business activities with the development of credit. Islamic merchants in Spain, the Mediterranean, and the Baltic states became indispensable middlemen for trading activities. In fact, many concepts, techniques, and instruments of Islamic finance were later adopted by European financiers and businessmen. An interest in the Islamic mode of banking emerged in several Muslim countries during the postcolonial era as part of an effort to revive and strengthen an Islamic identity. Independent but parallel attempts in the Arab Republic of Egypt and Malaysia led to the establishment of financial institutions in the early 1960s that were designed to operate on a noninterest basis so as to comply with Islamic economic principles.[4] The first wave of oil revenues in the 1970s and the accumulation of petrodollars gave momentum to this idea, and the growth of Islamic finance coincided with the current account surpluses of oil-exporting Islamic countries. The Middle East saw a mushrooming of small commercial banks competing for surplus funds. At the same time, interest grew in undertaking theoretical work and research to understand the functioning of an economic and banking system without the institution of "interest." The first commercial bank was established in 1974 in the United Arab Emirates, followed by establishment of the Islamic Development Bank in 1975.

Western analysts quickly challenged the feasibility of a financial system operating without interest and debt. Here, we summarize their arguments in six propositions:[5]

- Zero interest would mean infinite demand for loanable funds and zero supply.
- Such a system would be incapable of equilibrating demand for and supply of loanable funds.
- Zero interest would mean no savings.
- Zero savings would mean no investment and no growth.
- There could be no monetary policy because instruments for managing liquidity could not exist without a predetermined, fixed rate of interest.
- In countries adopting such a system, there would be one-way capital flight.

By 1988 these arguments were countered when research, based on modern financial and economic theory, showed the following:

- A modern financial system can be designed without the need for an ex ante positive nominal fixed interest rate. In fact, as Western researchers showed, no satisfactory theory could explain the need for an ex ante positive nominal interest rate.
- The failure to assume an ex ante positive nominal fixed interest rate—that is, no debt contract—does not necessarily mean that there has to be zero return on capital.
- The return on capital is determined ex post, and the magnitude of the return on capital is determined on the basis of the return to the economic activity in which the funds are employed.
- The expected return is what determines investment.
- The expected rate of return—and income—is what determines savings. Therefore, there is no justification for assuming that there will be no savings or investment.
- Positive growth is possible in such a system.
- Monetary policy would function as in the conventional system, its efficacy depending on the availability of instruments designed to manage liquidity.

■ Finally, in an open-economy macroeconomic model without an ex ante fixed interest rate, but with returns to investment determined ex post, the assumption of a one-way capital flight is not justified.

Therefore, a system that prohibits an ex ante fixed interest rate and allows the rate of return on capital to be determined ex post, based on returns to the economic activity in which the funds are employed, is theoretically viable.

In the process of demonstrating the analytical viability of such a system, research also clearly differentiated it from the conventional system. In the conventional system, which is based on debt contracts, risks and rewards are shared asymmetrically, with the debtor carrying the greatest part of the risk and with governments enforcing the contract. Such a system has a built-in incentive structure that promotes moral hazard and asymmetric information. It also requires close monitoring, which can be delegated to an institution acting on behalf of the collectivity of depositors and investors; hence the need for banking institutions.

In the late 1970s and early 1980s, it was shown, mostly by Minsky (1982), that such a system is inherently prone to instability because there will always be maturity mismatch between liabilities (short-term deposits) and assets (long-term investments). Because the nominal value of liabilities is guaranteed, while the nominal value of assets is not, when the maturity mismatch becomes a problem, banks will attempt to manage liabilities by offering higher interest rates to attract more deposits. There is always the possibility that this process will not be sustainable but instead will erode confidence and lead to a run on banks. Such a system, therefore, needs a lender of last resort and bankruptcy procedures, restructuring processes, and debt workout procedures to mitigate the contagion.

During the 1950s and 1960s, Lloyd Metzler of the University of Chicago proposed an alternative system in which contracts are based on equity rather than debt and in which the nominal value of liabilities is not guaranteed, since this is tied to the nominal value of assets.[6] Metzler showed that such a system does not have the instability characteristic of the conventional banking system. In his now classic article, Mohsin Khan showed the affinity of Metzler's model with Islamic finance (Khan 1987). Using Metzler's basic model, Khan demonstrated that this system produces a saddle point and is, therefore, more stable than the conventional system.

By the early 1990s, it was clear that an Islamic financial system not only is theoretically viable, but also has many desirable characteristics. The phenomenal growth of Islamic finance during the 1990s demonstrated the empirical and practical viability of the system (see table 3.1).

The 1980s proved to be the beginning of a period of rapid growth and expansion of the Islamic financial services industry. This growth became steady through the 1990s. The major developments of the 1980s included continuation of serious research at the conceptual and theoretical level, constitutional protection in three Muslim countries, and the involvement of conventional bankers in offering *Shariah*-compliant services. The Islamic Republic of Iran, Pakistan, and Sudan announced their intention to make their financial systems compliant with *Shariah*. Other countries such as Bahrain and Malaysia introduced Islamic banking within the framework of the existing system. The International Monetary Fund (IMF) initiated research in understanding the macroeconomic implications of an economic system operating without the concept of interest. Similar research was conducted to understand the issues of profit- and loss-sharing partnership contracts and the financial stability of such a system.

During the early growth of Islamic financial markets in the 1980s, Islamic banks faced a dearth of quality investment opportunities, which created business opportunities for conventional Western banks to act as intermediaries, deploying Islamic banks' funds according to guidelines provided by the Islamic banks. Western banks helped Islamic banks to place funds in commerce and trade-related activities by arranging for a trader to buy goods on behalf of the Islamic bank and resell them at a markup.

Gradually, Western banks recognized the importance of the emerging Islamic financial markets and started to offer Islamic products through "Islamic windows" in an attempt to attract clients directly. Islamic windows are not independent financial institutions; rather, they are specialized setups within conventional financial institutions that offer *Shariah*-compliant products. Meanwhile, as a result of the growing demand for *Shariah*-compliant products and fear of losing depositors, non-Western conventional banks also started to offer Islamic windows. In general, Islamic windows are targeted at high-net-worth individuals who want to practice Islamic banking: approximately 1–2 percent of the world's Muslim population.

The number of conventional banks offering Islamic windows is growing, and several leading conventional banks, such as the Hong

TABLE 3.1 DEVELOPMENT OF ISLAMIC ECONOMICS AND FINANCE IN
MODERN HISTORY

Time period	Development
Pre-1950s	■ Barclays Bank opens its Cairo branch to process financial transactions related to construction of the Suez Canal in the 1890s. Islamic scholars challenge the operations of the bank, criticizing it for charging interest. This criticism spreads to other Arab regions and to the Indian subcontinent, where there is a sizable Muslim community. ■ The majority of *Shariah* scholars declare that interest in all its forms amounts to the prohibited element of riba.
1950s–1960s	■ Initial theoretical work in Islamic economics begins. By 1953, Islamic economists offer the first description of an interest-free bank based on either two-tier *mudarabah* (profit- and loss-sharing contract) or *wakalah* (unrestricted investment account in which the Islamic bank earns a flat fee). ■ Mit Ghamr Bank in Egypt and Pilgrimage Fund in Malaysia start operations.
1970s	■ The first Islamic commercial bank, Dubai Islamic Bank, opens in 1974. ■ The Islamic Development Bank (IDB) is established in 1975. ■ The accumulation of oil revenues and petrodollars increases the demand for *Shariah*-compliant products.
1980s	■ The Islamic Research and Training Institute is established by the IDB in 1981. ■ Banking systems are converted to an interest-free banking system in the Islamic Republic of Iran, Pakistan, and Sudan. ■ Increased demand attracts Western intermediation and institutions. ■ Countries like Bahrain and Malaysia promote Islamic banking parallel to the conventional banking system.
1990s	■ Attention is paid to the need for accounting standards and a regulatory framework. A self-regulating agency, the Accounting and Auditing Organization of Islamic Financial Institutions, is established in Bahrain. ■ Islamic insurance (takaful) is introduced. ■ Islamic equity funds are established. ■ The Dow Jones Islamic Index and the FTSE Index of *Shariah*-compatible stocks are developed.
2000–the present	■ The Islamic Financial Services Board is established to deal with regulatory, supervisory, and corporate governance issues of the Islamic financial industry. ■ Sukuks (Islamic bonds) are launched. ■ Islamic mortgages are offered in the United States and the United Kingdom.

Sources: Khan 1996; IDB and IFSB 2005.

Kong and Shanghai Banking Corporation (HSBC), are pursuing this market very aggressively. HSBC has a well-established network of banks in the Muslim world and, in 1998, launched HSBC Global Islamic Finance with the objective of promoting Islamic asset securitization, private equity, and banking in the industrial countries. The list of Western banks keeping Islamic windows includes, among others, ABN Amro, American Express Bank, ANZ Grindlays, BNP-Paribas, Citicorp Group, and Union Bank of Switzerland (UBS). The leading non-Western banks with a significant presence of Islamic windows are National Commercial Bank of Saudi Arabia, United Bank of Kuwait, and Riyadh Bank. Citibank is the only Western bank to have established a separate Islamic bank: Citi Islamic Investment Bank (Bahrain) in 1996. By the early 1990s, the market had gained enough momentum to attract the attention of public policy makers and institutions interested in introducing innovative products. The following are some of the noteworthy developments.

Recognizing the need for standards, a self-regulatory agency—the Accounting and Auditing Organization for Islamic Financial Institutions (AAOIFI)—was established. AAOIFI was instrumental in highlighting the special regulatory needs of Islamic financial institutions. AAOIFI defined accounting and *Shariah* standards, which were adopted or recognized by several countries. However, as the market grew, the regulatory and supervisory authorities, with the help of the IMF, established a dedicated regulatory agency, the Islamic Financial Services Board (IFSB), in the early 2000s to address systemic stability and various governance and regulatory issues relating to the Islamic financial services industry. IFSB took on the challenge and started working in the areas of regulation, risk management, and corporate governance.

Further progress was made in developing capital markets. Islamic asset-backed certificates, *sukuks*, were introduced in the market. Different structures of *sukuks* were launched successfully in Bahrain, Malaysia, and other financial centers. Among the issuers were corporations, multilaterals, and sovereign entities such as the IDB, the International Bank for Reconstruction and Development (World Bank), and the governments of Bahrain, Pakistan, and Qatar. During the equities market boom of the 1990s, several equity funds based on *Shariah*-compatible stocks emerged. Dow Jones and Financial Times launched Islamic indexes to track the performance of Islamic equity funds.

Several institutions were established to create and support a robust financial system, including the International Islamic Financial Market, the International Islamic Rating Agency, the General Council of Islamic Banks and Financial Institutions, and the Arbitration and Reconciliation Centre for Islamic Financial Institutions. Today, Islamic finance is no stranger to leading financial centers of the world. With the recent wave of high oil revenues in the Middle East, demand for *Shariah*-compliant products on both the buy and sell sides has increased sharply. It is expected that as leading market makers embrace and begin to practice Islamic finance, the market will grow further, and new products and services will be introduced in the near future.

Annex 3A

Gharar. Any uncertainty created by the lack of information or control in a contract; ignorance in regard to an essential element in a transaction.

Maysur. Games of chance involving deception.

Qimar. Gambling.

Riba. Interest. Literally it means excess, addition, and surplus, while the associated verb implies "to increase, to multiply, to exceed, to exact more than was due, or to practice usury."

Sukuk. Islamic asset-based certificates.

Takaful. *Shariah*-compliant mutual insurance; literally, a mutual or joint guarantee.

Notes

1. A billion is 1,000 million.
2. For further details see Mirakhor (1989); Iqbal and Mirakhor (2007).
3. www.studyquran.co.uk/LLhome.htm.
4. In Malaysia, a pilgrimage fund was established in the late 1950s to facilitate savings to pay for the pilgrimage trip to Makkah. The Pilgrimage Fund became a full-fledged, interest-free investment bank in 1962. Around the same time, a cluster of small, interest-free savings banks emerged in northern rural Egypt, starting in Mit Ghamr in 1963.
5. For further details, see Iqbal and Mirakhor (2007).
6. See http://cepa.newschool.edu/het/profiles/metzler.htm.

References

IDB (Islamic Development Bank) and IFSB (Islamic Financial Services Board). 2005. Ten Year Master Plan for Islamic Financial Industry Development : Ten Year Framework and Strategies. Jeddah, Saudi Arabia.

Iqbal, Zamir, and Abbas Mirakhor. 2007. *Introduction to Islamic Finance: Theory and Practice.* Asia: John Wiley and Sons.

Khan, Mohsin. 1987. "Islamic Interest-Free Banking: A Theoretical Analysis." In *Theoretical Studies in Islamic Banking and Finance,* ed. M. Khan and A. Mirakhor. Houston, TX: IRIS Books.

Minsky, Hyman. 1982. *Inflation, Recession, and Economic Policy.* London: Wheatsheaf Books.

Mirakhor, Abbas. 1989. "General Characteristics of an Islamic Economic System." In *Essays on Iqtisad: The Islamic Approach to Economic Problems,* ed. Baqir Al-Hasani and Abbas Mirakhor, 45–80. Silver Spring, MD: Nur Corporation.

Sovereign Wealth Funds, Financial Crisis, and Management of Noncommercial Risk

Roxanna Faily, Kevin W. Lu, and Shuilin Wang

Sovereign wealth funds (SWFs), together with other sovereign investors such as public pension funds and a few state-owned enterprises, have emerged as major players in international finance in recent years. The current financial crisis, which has severely weakened many private sector financial institutions, brought further prominence to sovereign investors. However, the financial crisis has also led to new waves of protectionism, which has increased the noncommercial risks in cross-border investing. This issue is particularly pertinent among SWFs because of their public sector nature and the perception of possible noncommercial considerations in their investments. This chapter presents the landscape of SWFs; assesses existing and potential impacts of the financial crisis on SWFs; examines how SWFs are coping with the new international environment, including two case studies of SWFs facing noncommercial risk; and concludes with recommendations on ways SWFs can manage these noncommercial risks.

The opinions and conclusions expressed here are entirely the views of the authors and do not represent the organizations with which they are affiliated. Roxanna Faily is an Investment Officer and Kevin Lu is Chief Financial Officer of the Multilateral Investment Guarantee Agency. Shuilin Wang is Management Director of the Public Relations and International Cooperation at China Investment Corporation.

SWFs: The Landscape

SWFs have attracted more attention in recent years with their increased global presence and the growth of foreign assets under their control. Interest in SWF activity has been further amplified by their seeming lack of transparency as state-owned entities. Most provide limited access to their investment strategies, portfolios, structure, and decision-making processes. Thus, significant speculation has occurred, particularly in the media, about the role of SWFs in the global financial marketplace, their intentions, and their potential impact. Although information on SWFs continues to be sparse, it is important to focus on that which is known. Indeed, key facts are available on their genesis, mandates, and even aspects of their investment behavior.

History and Market Characteristics

SWFs have existed for more than 60 years. The first known SWF was the Kuwait Investment Authority, which was established in 1953 to invest Kuwait's oil revenue surpluses for the future and reduce its reliance on a single nonrenewable resource. Outside of the oil-rich countries, formation of SWFs remained limited. In the last 20 years, however, high commodity prices and increased export revenues spurred expansion of SWFs. While the five largest SWFs were established in 1990 or before, including Kuwait's, these sovereign funds have now been joined by newer entrants, with almost half of the top 15 founded since 2000. A significant feature of these newer funds is their origins, with almost 90 percent of them having originated in emerging economies. With the exception of the Norwegian Government Pension Fund (NBIM), the Alaska Permanent Fund, and the Australian Government Future Fund, the majority of the largest sovereign funds originated in the Middle East and Asia (figure 4.1).

Current estimates place the number of SWFs at more than 60, with assets under management of approximately $3.6 trillion (Deutsche Bank 2008). These funds vary significantly in size, but capital is concentrated in the hands of a few, with the top 10 funds controlling more than 80 percent of total SWF assets (Sovereign Wealth Fund Institute 2009, http://www.swfinstitute.org/). The Abu Dhabi Investment Authority is widely recognized to be the largest among its peers, with estimates putting its total size somewhere between $675 billion and $875 billion. Each of the top 10 SWFs has $100 billion or more in assets under management (Merrill Lynch 2008; Deutsche Bank 2008). Middle Eastern and Asian SWFs hold the majority of these assets and control more than three-quarters of total SWF assets (table 4.1).

SWFs vary significantly in mandate, management model, and investment behavior. To date, there is still no standard acceptable definition for SWFs. According to the Santiago Principles, a set of generally accepted principles and practices concerning SWFs (and discussed in greater detail later in this chapter), sovereign wealth funds are "special purpose funds or arrangements, owned by the general government. Created by the general government for varying macroeconomic purposes, SWFs hold, manage, or administer assets to achieve financial objectives, and employ a set of investment strategies which include investing in foreign financial assets. The SWFs are commonly established out of balance of payments surpluses, official foreign currency operations, the proceeds of privatizations, fiscal surpluses, and/or receipts resulting from commodity exports" (International Working Group of Sovereign Wealth Funds 2008, 27). Key features common to SWFs are (i) ownership by sovereigns or subsovereigns, (ii) an explicit ability to own foreign assets, (iii) higher risk tolerance, and (iv) long-term investment horizons.

FIGURE 4.1 SWF ASSETS BY REGION

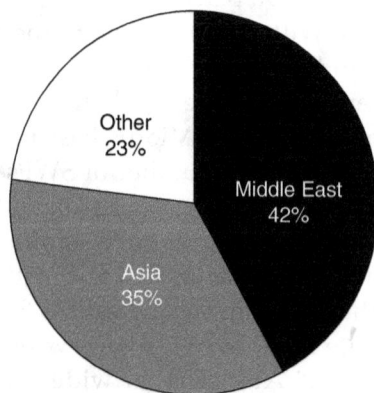

Source: Hawkpoint and Sovereign Wealth Fund Institute 2009.

TABLE 4.1 LARGEST SOVEREIGN WEALTH FUNDS

Country	Fund	Assets under management ($ billions)
United Arab Emirates	Abu Dhabi Investment Authority (ADIA)	875
Norway	Norges Bank Investment Management (NBIM)	401
Saudi Arabia	Various funds (including Saudi Arabian Monetary Authority)	350
Singapore	Government of Singapore Investment Corporation (GIC)	330
Kuwait	Kuwai Investment Authority (KIA)	264
China	China Investment Corporation (CIC)	200
Hong Kong, China	Hong Kong Monetary Authority Investment Portfolio	152
Russian Federation	Reserve Fund	141
Singapore	Temasek Holdings Ltd.	131
Libya	Libyan Arab Foreign Investment Company (LAFICO)	100
United Arab Emirates	Investment Corporation of Dubai	82
Qatar	Qatar Investment Authority (QIA)	60
Australia	Australian Government Future Fund (AGFF)	59
Russian Federation	National Wealth Fund	49
Algeria	Fonds de Régulation des Recettes de l'Algérie	47
United States	Alaska Permanent Reserve Fund Corporation (APRF)	40
Brunei	Brunei Investment Agency (BIA)	35
Ireland	National Pensions Reserve Fund (NPRF)	31
Republic of Korea	Korea Investment Corporation (KIC)	30
Kazakhstan	Kazakhstan National Fund (KNF)	26

Source: Deutsche Bank 2008.

Investment Objectives and Management

SWFs are also typically classified by their source of funds—commodity or noncommodity—and by their purpose. Whether single purpose or oriented toward multiple goals, three main categories of SWF objectives emerge: (i) commodity revenue stabilization, (ii) savings for future generations, and (iii) strategic diversification and development. Excess capital in reserves has meant that sovereigns have had the flexibility to use SWFs to seek out higher-yielding investments and to manage their assets strategically—allowing for future planning for savings, aging populations, and national development as well as allowing diversification of country revenues, which is especially relevant for commodity-reliant economies.

SWFs are generally free to take on more risk and invest in a broader spectrum of assets than are traditional reserves, which are typically managed with the aims of liquidity and safety (Bahgat 2008). The lure of higher returns provided an impetus to many sovereigns that sought to participate in the high gains being realized in stocks and alternative assets. Historically, SWFs have opted to use external fund managers to achieve their strategic allocation objectives and their risk-adjusted return goals. This strategy has been useful for a variety of reasons, foremost being the lack of knowledge and experience among the SWF fund managers themselves. However, in recent years funds have increasingly built up their internal capacity, with a few even relying solely on their in-house operations. Abu Dhabi's Mubadala Development Company and Singapore's Temasek Holdings are key examples of SWFs that manage investments internally. Their investment portfolios even include some majority or complete ownership stakes, a role that is not customary among SWFs, which generally hold minority ownership stakes.

SWFs characteristically invest the majority of their holdings in publicly traded enterprises and favor the largest public companies. Recent analysis shows that their average investments tend to be in companies that have total asset values of $229 million, are tracked by 13 analysts on average, and generate 32 percent of their sales from the international market (Fernandes and Bris 2009). Overall, a typical asset allocation for SWFs is estimated to be 35–40 percent fixed income, 50–55 percent public equity, and 8–10 percent alternative assets for those funds that invested across all these asset classes.

Alternative assets, which include real estate, private equity, and emerging-markets investments, are an interesting and potentially growing part of SWF portfolios. The current decline in Western real estate prices makes such investments increasingly attractive for sovereign investors. For instance, the Libyan Investment Authority indicated that its $70 billion fund will be targeting property markets in the United States and Europe. Meanwhile, other funds are taking a strong interest in Africa, Asia, and Latin America. A recent survey of SWFs observed continued interest in investment opportunities in the United States and Western Europe, but respondents identified Brazil, Mexico, and China as the most attractive markets (Financial Dynamics International 2009). It is estimated that of those SWFs investing in alternative asset classes, their allocation to these classes will increase 5–12 percentage points to be in the range of 10–15 percent of overall investment portfolios.

Geographic and Sectoral Investment Behavior

With regard to investment behavior, SWFs tend to invest in Europe and the United States, economies that they perceive as low risk and attractive. These markets have offered a broad spectrum of opportunities, with high levels of asset liquidity. Some estimates suggest 37 percent of total SWF transactions are in North America, 32 percent in Europe, and 28 percent in Asia. Sector dispersion significantly favors the financial sector with a reported $109.8 billion in investments, a trend that reflects the recent high-profile and sizeable investments by SWFs in entities such as Merrill Lynch, Citigroup, Morgan Stanley, and UBS.

With regard to foreign direct investment (FDI), although SWFs have been expanding their roles as direct investors, their impact has been limited. In 2007, FDI by SWFs was worth $10 billion representing just 0.2 percent of SWF total assets and accounting for only 0.6 percent of global FDI flows (UNCTAD 2008). However, many of these SWF investments were acquisitions that made up less than 10 percent of outstanding ownership shares and thus cannot technically be categorized as FDI. There is a trend toward increased FDI among SWFs evidenced by the high levels of recent activity; almost 80 percent of the $39 billion SWF FDI flows over the last 20 years occurred over 2005 through 2007 (UNCTAD 2008). Overall sector exposure for SWF FDI seems to be more balanced than that of their overall portfolios (figure 4.2), but geographic exposures are still weighted significantly toward Europe and the United States (figure 4.3). Developing country SWF FDI represented 25 percent of total

FIGURE 4.2 SWF INVESTMENTS BY SECTOR, 1995–JULY 2008

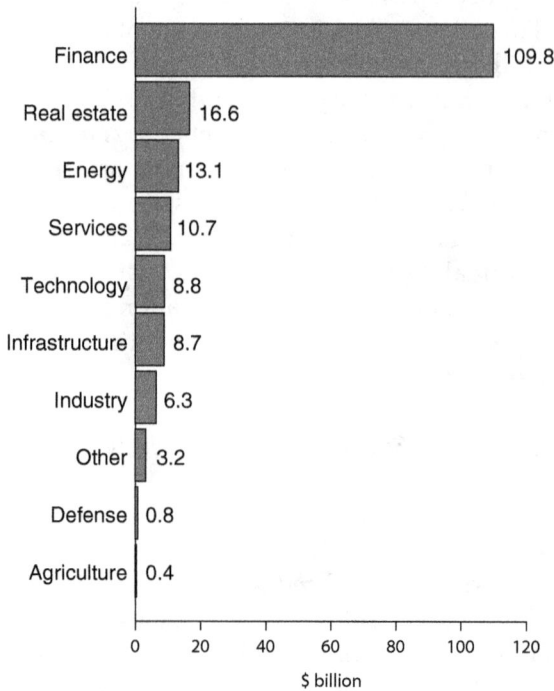

Sector	$ billion
Finance	109.8
Real estate	16.6
Energy	13.1
Services	10.7
Technology	8.8
Infrastructure	8.7
Industry	6.3
Other	3.2
Defense	0.8
Agriculture	0.4

Source: Deutsche Bank 2008.

SWF FDI and constituted a mere 0.5 percent of the 2007 peak levels of $500 billion in global FDI flows to developing countries achieved that same year (UNCTAD 2008).

Interest in investing in neighboring markets varies from fund to fund. Intraregional investment among Asian SWFs has grown more active. Among those that have invested significantly across the region, several have shown a preference for China as an investment destination, representing approximately 10 percent of these intraregional flows (Deutsche Bank 2008). This trend, however, is occurring more slowly among some Gulf SWFs. Gulf sovereigns, which have tended to invest in developed economies, are now increasingly focusing on building their economies. In fact, Gulf states are

FIGURE 4.3 VALUE OF DEALS BY REGION, 1975–2008

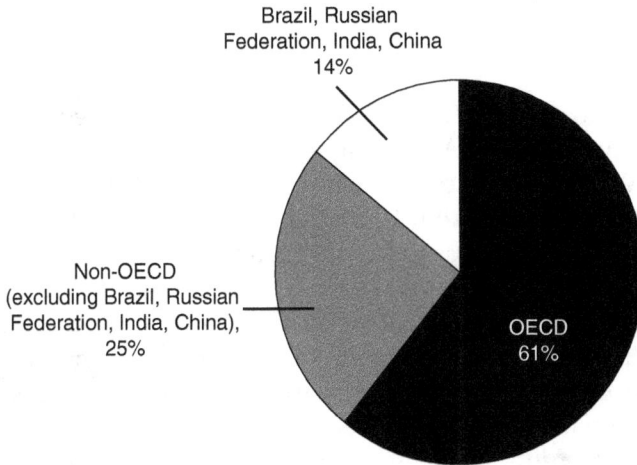

Brazil, Russian
Federation, India, China
14%

Non-OECD
(excluding Brazil, Russian
Federation, India, China),
25%

OECD
61%

Sources: Hawkpoint, Monitor, JPMorgan (May 2008); De Boer, Farrell, and Lund (2008). Based on publicly reported deals between 1975 and March 2008 (about $250 billion).

expected to put more than $3 trillion into local projects by 2020 (De Boer, Farrell, and Lund 2008). The financial crisis has only intensified the need to support domestic markets, with governments calling on SWFs to step in and provide needed support and liquidity.

Impact of the Global Financial Crisis

The global financial crisis has had a few notable implications for SWFs, including their ability to commit capital, their investment behavior, and the changing political environment confronting them. SWFs are still projected to grow, albeit at a slower rate; SWF assets under management are expected to reach between $5 trillion and $8.5 trillion by 2012 (Merrill Lynch 2008). The SWFs are a welcome source of funding, especially during the financial crisis and because of their typical long-term investment horizons. However, it has also become clear that SWFs are not unlimited sources of global financing. Like other investors, SWFs are held accountable for performance and can face future funding issues, changing market environments, and increased pressure from constituents.

Investment Losses

The global economic and financial downturn has affected SWF assets and future funding. According to some assessments, SWFs have endured a drop in asset value in the range of $700 billion to $850 billion, representing about a 25 percent loss in wealth. The effects on SWFs have varied as a result of individual fund exposures. For instance, NBIM's performance dropped 23 percent in 2008, resulting in a significant loss of $118 billion. Meanwhile, fund losses of the Saudi Arabian Monetary Agency were reported to be minimal because of its conservative asset allocation strategy (Bloomberg 2009). In addition to the substantial decline in assets, SWFs may also be facing reduced funding as their governments no longer see the considerable capital surpluses of years past. In fact, sovereigns are facing low oil prices, a drop in trade, and increased stress on reserves. Thus, the outlook for SWFs appears to be one of less flexibility and lower levels of capital support.

Investment Targets: Organisation for Economic Co-operation and Development (OECD) Countries vs. Emerging Markets

The implications of the global financial turmoil are significant as SWFs reevaluate their capacity and corresponding investment strategies in light of the changing risk-reward environment. Having suffered dramatic losses from their financial sector investments, many SWFs reduced their investment activity in the second half of 2008, particularly through their decision to limit OECD exposure. SWF investment in OECD markets declined to $8 billion during the third quarter of 2008, a fraction of the $37 billion invested in the first quarter (Monitor Group 2008). However, emerging markets benefited and were the recipients of 54 percent of SWF investment flows during the second and third quarters of 2008 (Monitor Group 2008). Consequently, SWFs have been under pressure to reconsider their investment strategies, including their asset allocations and their sector and country exposures. In some cases, SWFs have taken strong cash positions as they reevaluate investment risk and wait out market volatility.

Changing International Environment: Elevated Noncommercial Risks

The global investment environment is clearly changing, with potential opportunities arising from undervalued or distressed assets and liquidity-seeking enterprises. Economic and political risks are perceived to be on the rise as nations face the crippling effects of tight credit environments, destabilized financial markets, and real economic downturn. The desire to be opportunistic is offset by the caution with which SWFs view the moving global landscape. The stress on liquidity and the economic downturn have added political pressure in several countries, particularly in emerging Europe. Analysts have downgraded the political ratings for numerous countries, highlighting the increased exchange and transfer, sovereign default, and civil disturbance risks in some countries.

SWFs have witnessed a broad range of reactions from the international community, which has both criticized and courted them. SWFs have dealt with higher levels of protectionist rhetoric and face increased government market intervention in countries such as the United States, Germany, Belgium, and Australia. At the same time, expectations have grown among those who view SWFs as stabilizing forces and sources of global liquidity. Japan, Tanzania, and France are among the governments vying for the attention and capital of SWFs for the benefit of their constituents and their national economies.

Changing Domestic Environment

Such high expectations are mirrored among domestic constituents of sovereigns who view helping local economies as a key responsibility of SWFs, particularly during this downturn. Likewise, many are progressively more critical of fund performance regardless of market conditions. Thus, SWFs face significant domestic pressure to support local markets and to provide much needed liquidity through the financial crisis. In fact, governments are calling upon SWFs to step in. Recently, the Kuwait Investment Authority allocated a $1 billion fund to purchase shares in Kuwaiti companies and support the Kuwait Stock Exchange. Similarly, the Qatar Investment Authority is recapitalizing its commercial banking sector by buying public equity in seven banks (Hadfield 2009). The local flow of capital has been evident—domestic investment during the third quarter of 2008 constituted 46 percent of reported deals by SWFs (Monitor Group 2008).

At the same time, the international holdings of SWFs are also being assessed by their various constituents. Public criticism and indignation have been observed in countries such as the Republic of Korea, China, and Singapore following disappointing investment returns on key transactions. As a result, many SWFs have begun to adjust their investment appraisal processes and revise their strategies in response to the increased demand for accountability.

Overall Implications of Global Financial Crisis

The implications of the global financial crisis for SWFs are manifold. With regard to their internal assessment processes and overall strategies for investment and risk management, several observations merit close consideration. First and foremost, the importance of risk management cannot be overstated. With huge absolute losses from financial sector investments, the risks of being overweighted in a sector or region have become apparent. Second, the perception of "safer" markets is changing as heightened political risks and protectionist behaviors are observed in many OECD countries. Third, the crisis has implications for accountability and how investments and risks are managed and appraised. Whether SWFs continue to build their in-house capacity or use external fund managers remains in flux. Before the crisis, conventional wisdom within the SWF community had been that the use of professional fund managers would not only provide investment expertise but also political protection when investments underperformed. That assumption has been proven inaccurate. Regardless of how much of the assets are externally managed, shareholders continue to hold fund management accountable for investment performance. This highlights the importance of internal capacity. Finally, SWFs should reconsider their traditional stance of being passive investors, especially in a distress or crisis situation in which the interests of different shareholders vary and passive minority shareholders tend to be overlooked.

The Changing International Political Risk Environment: How Sovereign Wealth Funds are Coping

These various implications point to the importance of managing noncommercial risks in SWF investments. The crisis highlights the inherent links between financial risks and government risks. Potential financial failures of major banks triggered government interventions. In some cases, ownership structures are being overhauled, and various shareholders, including SWFs, could fare differently depending on their level of operational control. Passive investors have less say in such circumstances and could lose out. Another consideration is systemic risk in a country's financial system that could trigger capital flight, which in turn could force the government to establish capital control. For SWFs, these problems are even more acute because they are government owned themselves.

Major Types of Political Risks

Investors face a variety of risks, both commercial and noncommercial, when they directly invest internationally in companies. Commercial risks are commonly considered part of the normal hazards of doing business and can include fluctuations in foreign currency rates, changes in the competitive landscape, difficulties in supply chain management, and volatility in product demand. Noncommercial risks, also called political risks, are beyond the control of firms or their investors and result from actions taken (or inaction) by governments that threaten a firm's well-being or ability to conduct business. These political actions can also hinder an investor's ability to access or use their assets.[1]

Political risks are traditionally classified into several categories:

- *Expropriation or nationalization* includes acts of government that result in investors being unable to exercise their rights of ownership or use of assets with no fair compensation for the denial of these rights. Examples of such actions include seizure of physical assets and could even include intellectual property rights. Also generally included in this category is "creeping expropriation," which refers to a series of acts that over time have an expropriatory effect. Implicit in expropriation is the discriminatory nature of the acts against the investor.

- *Transfer restrictions or inconvertibility* typically refers to the inability to access funds, whether arising from an investor's inability to convert local currency into foreign exchange for transfer out of the country or from host country actions (or inaction) resulting in excessive delays in acquiring foreign exchange. This class of risk does not include currency devaluation.

- *War or civil disturbance* generally encompasses the disappearance or destruction of physical assets caused by politically motivated acts of war or civil disturbance, which include revolution, insurrection, and coups d'état. These risks also span the events that result in the complete inability to conduct operations, resulting in business interruption and jeopardizing an investment's financial viability. Terrorism and sabotage fall under this class of risk.
- *Breach of contract* includes a host government's repudiation or breach of a contractual agreement with an investor. Such acts can result in a considerable loss to the investor. Guarantee coverage often requires the use of a dispute resolution mechanism, which then assesses fault and determines awards for damages, and host-government denial of the award. The strength of the contract that has been violated is critically important.

These political risks are historically associated with investment in developing countries and have been a deterrent for trade and investment. Multiple tools can be enlisted to manage political risk once it is determined that specific political risks pose a significant and real threat to an investment or project. These risk management techniques run the gamut from "soft" techniques to more robust and precise risk mitigation tools; examples include incorporating political risk into financial equations, in-depth due diligence, stress scenario preparation, portfolio diversification, key relationship building and management make-up, strong contract drafting, and guarantee coverage or insurance. Bilateral agencies, multilateral institutions, and private insurers have sought to provide coverage for political risks to facilitate trade and investment. Multiple programs exist and political risk insurance (PRI) has been an effective tool for investors and banks that are looking for guarantees to cover this type of noncommercial risk.

The opportunity for SWFs to protect against these traditional political risks is growing. A series of trends indicates rising potential for the mitigation of political risks for SWF transactions. First, SWFs are increasingly acting as direct investors. Although strategies differ between funds, SWFs have been increasing internal capacity and have been acting as principal investors. Second, SWFs have, on an anecdotal basis, started to use leverage in some cases, making tools such as PRI potentially interesting as a mechanism to reduce their cost of capital. Third, interest in natural resources may expose

SWFs to higher levels of political backlash in addition to the typical political risks facing commodity investments. Fourth, SWFs might increase their investments in developing countries as a result of the location of key resources markets, the changing economic and financial risks resulting from the financial crisis, and the protectionist rhetoric and behavior witnessed in many OECD countries. Finally, SWFs could benefit from the use of coverage such as PRI by their portfolio companies that invest internationally.

Increasingly Unfriendly Global Investment Environment

SWFs have been subject to growing global concerns about their investment activities, particularly since their high-profile financial sector transactions in 2007. The media and research coverage of SWFs grew to new levels, and new groups of analysts and experts in the area of sovereign investments were established in recognition of the importance and force of this new set of investors. Scrutiny and political concerns accompanied the new-found fame of these funds and was intensified by the general lack of information on the SWF community, their practices, and holdings. Of paramount concern was the intention of the SWFs, with commentators making nationalistic and protectionist critiques of their behavior.

Concerns about SWFs originate in apprehension of state capitalism and focus on three main areas. First, there is an inherent suspicion that SWFs are agents of their governments and a growing concern that investment decisions are made with political objectives. Second, SWFs are deemed to benefit from their access to government officials and networks and thus represent unfair competition to private sector investors. Third, national security interests are often at the center of the controversy, with protectionist unease about foreign ownership of national treasures or assets of importance to the strategic and security interests of a country. The backlash has been so severe in some instances that the viability of projects has become questionable as waves of public sentiment and government debate jeopardize the feasibility of investments.

This controversy can most widely be seen in, but is not limited to, the developed world where investment from SWFs and other sovereign entities has been hotly debated in countries such as Australia, the United States, and Germany. It is unclear, however, if these concerns are founded on the evidence of past behavior. Attempts have been made to alleviate concerns with increased transparency and greater communication of fund information, such as investment objectives. Assessment of SWF activity produced a single example of an investment in a defense-related firm; in fact, some funds can be praised for their moral responsibility, with NBIM actively blocking investments over the past few years because of social responsibility considerations. Overall, SWFs have sought to maintain their positions as passive investors who do not take controlling stakes, and they surrender their board seats. This behavior, although potentially reassuring to some, has not succeeded in extinguishing the political outcry and media mania surrounding their activities.

Case Studies

Examples of how sovereign wealth funds and their supported investments manage and deal with political risk can more clearly be seen by looking at specific examples. In the following case studies, you will see how two entities, Temasek and Dubai Investment Company, have faced increased political backlash and risk in their investments.

Temasek Holdings in Indonesia. Through a series of investments made by subsidiaries, Singapore's Temasek Holdings has faced a turbulent political risk environment in Indonesia. Since 2006, Temasek has been fighting Indonesian authorities' allegations of monopoly power and anticompetitive behavior. In fact, Indonesia's courts have ruled that Temasek is guilty of these charges but the decision has been appealed to the country's Supreme Court with final ruling pending.

Temasek faces the real possibility of forced divestiture in its Indonesian telecommunications investments even though initial risk management would not have predicted this outcome. The initial acquisitions were approved by Indonesian authorities in 2001 and 2002 with Temasek's subsidiaries participating in a highly subscribed-to bidding process. A changed interpretation of laws resulted in the monopoly allegations, which were not prevented by the more subtle risk management techniques used by Temasek and its subsidiaries. In an effort to avoid firm-specific discriminatory actions by the government itself, Temasek gave company control to the government of Indonesia and maintained majority government-appointed boards in these companies.

However, these techniques have not proven effective in protecting Temasek and its subsidiaries from exposure to the risk of doing business in Indonesia. The presence of government-appointed management in these companies reflected either a lack of competence among these officials or support for the nonmonopolistic intention of Temasek's activities. Indonesian investments were made during a time when assessments of political risk and business environment by independent research organizations would have highlighted the potential need for mitigation instruments.[2] Whether Temasek could have protected itself by using more formal risk mitigation tools can be debated, but it is clear that the fund is facing a potential loss because issues of forced divestiture and resulting share price at time of exit remain uncertain.

Dubai Investment Company (DIC) holdings in the United States. DIC and the government of Dubai were highly scrutinized by U.S. public officials in 2005 and 2006 as a result of the investment activities of their subsidiary, Dubai Ports World (DP World). DP World's status as a sovereign entity wholly owned by DIC led to heavy political backlash in the United States for its acquisition of British interests with significant holdings of American port facilities in the United States.

Although DIC's subsidiary had engaged in the appropriate processes and complied with national regulatory requirements, DIC and DP World were not spared from exceptional media frenzy and political backlash. In fact, DP World had even engaged the Committee on Foreign Investment in the United States (CFIUS) on the prospect of the potential acquisition. While the deal was reviewed and approved by authorities, negative reaction remained high. Opponents to the deal cited the national security concerns resulting from foreign ownership of U.S. ports and the debate engulfed Congress; in March 2006, the House of Representatives voted to block the deal. DP World's response came before the U.S. government's actions were conclusive; just 24 hours after the vote, the firm announced its decision to sell off its U.S. port holdings.

The overwhelming international attention and controversy and opposition felt in the United States clearly were motivating factors for DP World's decision to sell off these U.S. assets. Their initial attempts to work within the regulatory framework in the U.S. system failed to protect them from political backlash, and they were unable to benefit from strong relationships between nations—the United Arab Emirates being a key ally of the United States in the Middle East. In the end, it is unclear whether the firm was able to obtain a fair market value for these U.S. assets, but the devastating effects of political risk and protectionist reactions were clearly demonstrated in this example of international sovereign investment.

Managing Noncommercial Risk

Three focus areas would help SWFs manage noncommercial risks. First, improvements in their own governance and transparency could lower the anxiety level in investment-recipient countries, thus minimizing potential adverse government intervention. Second, SWFs can improve their internal risk management systems and make use of various risk mitigation instruments available in the marketplace. Third, SWFs could improve their internal processes and ensure that investment projects are socially and environmentally responsible.

The concerns that came to the forefront of the SWF debate since 2008 are closely connected to stakeholders' understanding of the funds. Historically, SWFs have lacked visibility and have not proactively engaged with external audiences or built key stakeholders' understanding of SWFs' nature, structure, or objectives. However, in an effort to build trust, increase understanding, and combat political backlash, SWFs have started to engage more directly with the global community and are more proactive with regard to communication and transparency.

A prime example of this movement toward increasing transparency and building stakeholder confidence is the development of the Generally Accepted Principles and Practices (GAPP) for SWFs. The GAPP, also known as the "Santiago Principles," was issued in October 2008 and is a set of voluntary principles agreed to by the International Working Group of Sovereign Wealth Funds (IWG).[3] The GAPP is a significant document that details principles designed to govern the nature, objectives, governance, investment, and risk management of SWFs. The Santiago Principles recommend that SWFs operate as economically and financially oriented entities, and the principles are drawn from related international principles and practices that have already gained wide acceptance in related areas. Furthermore, the IWG meetings have served as a catalyst for the coming together of SWFs as an industry to openly discuss issues and engage with international organizations, such as the IMF, and different governments.

The GAPP sought to address a few key concerns that had been raised about SWFs, such as investment policy, institutional integrity, transparency, and respect for host-country rules. Regarding investment policies, the GAPP states that investment decisions be based solely on economic and financial grounds. On governance, the SWFs have agreed to abide by world-class standards for institutional integrity, including public disclosure, risk management, governance, and internal controls. On transparency, the GAPP calls on SWFs to maintain transparent legal structures, investment policies, sources of funding and withdrawal policies, and disclosure concerning relevant financial information. And, with respect to host countries, the GAPP requires SWFs to conduct their operations in compliance with all applicable regulations where they invest. Though the GAPP is a voluntary set of principles, the members of the IWG, as well as the broader SWF community, have either implemented or voiced their intention to implement these principles. Also noteworthy, the GAPP was not only created by the SWFs, but endorsed by their home governments.

While the Santiago Principles are of significant to the future of SWFs, it is important to reflect on the entire process. The process allowed open and meaningful dialogue. This collective effort was extremely effective at addressing the negative mystique that shrouded many groups' impressions of SWFs, and demonstrated that SWFs do not undermine national security or national economic security. The process demonstrated, instead, that SWFs are a positive component in a multifaceted investment environment, and that they abide by the laws of the nations in which they invest to achieve financially risk-adjusted returns.

It only makes sense that the expectation for reciprocity is high as SWFs look for guarantees of fair and nondiscriminatory treatment from investment-recipient countries after the SWFs have made assurances on transparency and openness. Attention will be focused on the protectionist debates through the OECD Freedom of Investment project and its reinforcement of its recipient-country investment codes, which highlight the importance of (i) nondiscrimination, (ii) transparency and predictability, (iii) regulatory proportionality, and (iv) accountability.

In addition to transparency and governance, SWFs should also strengthen their risk management capacity, especially in the area of noncommercial risk, and be familiar with available risk mitigation instruments. Traditional financial risk management capacity is easier to acquire because the vast majority of these risks are quantifiable, with existing financial models to deploy. In contrast, noncommercial risk is harder to quantify and requires more qualitative judgment, which can be supplemented with quantitative analysis. This capacity is particularly important for SWFs' direct investment portfolios, which are now more prominent. Noncommercial risk management capacity can be further divided into three categories: country risk assessment, project-level risk evaluation, and portfolio analysis. A number of tools can be used to mitigate noncommercial risk through contractual arrangements, such as political risk insurance, certain derivatives, contract carve-outs, and so forth.

Finally, SWFs may want to focus on the nonfinancial aspects of their direct investments, especially the social and environmental impacts of companies and projects in which they invest. Investments with positive social and environmental impacts on the recipient country or community tend to be less vulnerable to political factors and are inherently less risky.

Conclusion

The global economic dynamics over the last decade, including the rising significance of oil and other commodities and growing exports from many countries, especially those in East Asia, have brought visibility to SWFs, an expanding new class of investors, even though technically SWFs have existed for much longer. After resolution of the global financial crisis, SWFs and other sovereign investors will inevitably play an even bigger role in global finance and the worldwide economy. The crisis has also affected SWFs in a number of ways, prompting them to reevaluate where they will invest, how they will invest, and what risks need to be managed. In that context, management of noncommercial risk in SWF investments is key to their success. SWFs need to deploy soft approaches, such as enhancing transparency and governance, as well as hard contractual approaches, and in this process need to improve their capacity to evaluate and mitigate such risks.

Notes

1. According to the PRS Group, political risks are associated with government actions that deny or restrict the rights of an investor or owner to use or benefit from his or her asset; or which actions reduce the value of the firm.

2. According to Friedrich Wu's analysis of the Temasek investments in Indonesia, EIU gave Indonesia a political risk rating of "D" and a low business environment rating of 5.09 (Wu 2008). Business Monitor International was also cited as giving Indonesia ratings

(43.0 for the long term and 53.0 for the short term) below regional averages for political risk.

3. The International Working Group of Sovereign Wealth Funds was established in April 2008 and includes representation from 26 International Monetary Fund (IMF) member countries with SWFs. This initiative is part of an ongoing process of engagement with SWFs to increase understanding of the issues for investors and recipients of SWF funds. The IMF has been responsible for facilitating the process and did so at the request of the International Monetary and Financial Committee (a committee of the board of governors of the IMF that typically comprises representatives, normally ministers of finance and central bank governors, of all 185 IMF member countries).

References

Bahgat, Gawdat. 2008. "Sovereign Wealth Funds: Dangers and Opportunities." *International Affairs* 84 (6): 1189–1204.

Bloomberg Business News. 2009. "Plunging Equity Markets Hit Norway Investments." March 12.

De Boer, Kito, Diana Farrell, and Susan Lund. 2008. "Investing the Gulf's Oil Profits Windfall." *McKinsey Quarterly* 4: 20–3.

Deutsche Bank. 2008. "SWFs and Foreign Investment Policies— An Update." October 22. Deutsche Bank Research, Frankfurt, Germany.

Fernandes, Nuno, and Arturo Bris. 2009. "Sovereign Wealth Revalued." *Financial Times*, FT.com, February 12. http://www.ft.com/cms/s/0/2c8e3874-f7d0-11dd-a284-000077b07658.html?nclick_check=1.

Financial Dynamics International. 2009. "Sovereign Wealth Funds Remain Cautious toward Current Market Valuations and Re-iterate Their Status as Passive Long Term Investors." Press Release, February 15, FTI Consulting, London and New York.

Hadfield, Will. 2009. "Sovereign Funds Come to the Rescue." *Middle East Economic Digest* 53 (5): 20–1.

International Working Group of Sovereign Wealth Funds. 2008. "Sovereign Wealth Funds: Generally Accepted Principles and Practices, 'Santiago Principles.'" International Working Group of Sovereign Wealth Funds. http://www.iwg-swf.org/pubs/eng/santiagoprinciples.pdf.

Merrill Lynch. 2008. "Sovereign Wealth Funds: One Year On." November 11. Merrill Lynch Global Economics.

Monitor Group. 2008. "Assessing the Risks: The Behaviors of Sovereign Wealth Funds in the Global Economy." Monitor Group, Cambridge, MA.

Stein, Robert. 2009. Sovereign Wealth Funds Forum. Presentation deliv-
     ered in London, UK, February 24. http://www.oxan.com/Events/
     Other/SovereignWealthFundsForum.aspx.
UNCTAD (United Nations Conference on Trade and Development).
     2008. *World Investment Report: Transnational Corporations and the Infra-
     structure Challenge.* New York: United Nations Publications.
Wu, Friedrich. 2008. "Singapore's Sovereign Wealth Funds: The Politi-
     cal Risk of Overseas Investments." *World Economics* 9 (3): 97–122.

The Changing Face of Political Risk

Patrick Garver

Multinational corporations active in the global resources sector face a number of challenges when looking to expand their operations into new territories. Four key questions come to mind:

- How have political risks for global natural resources companies changed over the last three to five years?
- How have recent changes in the global economy affected the political risks we face?
- How has Barrick's appetite for political risk insurance (PRI) evolved?
- Apart from PRI, what tools are available to today's investor to manage political risk?

Patrick Garver is Executive Vice President and General Counsel of Barrick Gold Corporation. Barrick Gold Corporation, headquartered in Toronto, is the world's largest gold mining company. Barrick currently operates 27 mines and 10 new projects in various stages of development on four continents. The views expressed in this chapter are those of the author and do not necessarily represent those of Barrick Gold Corporation.

The Changing Face of Political Risk

For large multinational resources companies, risks of a noncommercial nature have evolved substantially in the last five years. While the three main traditional political risks—expropriation, political violence, and currency inconvertibility—are still of concern, significant new risks have emerged alongside them.

The principal emerging risks for a foreign investor in many parts of the developing world are those associated with the empowerment of local, regional, and nongovernmental interests—including local and regional governments, cultural or religious interests, and nongovernmental organizations.

Some portion of this growing area of risk is due to the formal devolution of political power from national governments to local or regional subdivisions of government, as has been demonstrated, for example, in Indonesia and Peru. But most of this risk is more a function of new technology and globalization than of changes in government structure, namely, the more informal empowerment of certain interests that only recently have gained dramatically improved access to information, communications, and the media, including the global media. These interests now have a global voice, in real time, and are becoming increasingly sophisticated at asserting their considerable political will. As a consequence, local and regional interests and certain special interests now share power with national governments to a degree unheard of in recent history. In short, in most jurisdictions the support of a national government may be necessary to ensure political stability, but it is no longer sufficient.

Today, local, regional, and special interests often assert themselves in connection with what is colloquially known as the "social license to operate." The political risk associated with such interests first becomes apparent when, for example, the local community organizes a "referendum" regarding a project; a local magistrate suddenly revokes zoning approval; the local parish priest and 100 *campesinos* block the road to the operations; or a provincial official arbitrarily bans some commercial activity that is essential to the operations. One then finds that the national government, which seemed to have on some level committed to support the investment, is conspicuously absent or ineffective.

A second significant genre of evolving threats facing international investors is that associated with transnational crime, corruption, and certain nontraditional competitors who do not operate by the Marquess of Queensberry rules. In some developing countries, criminals and criminal networks may constitute the most powerful interests confronting a government, national or local, often with resources, capabilities, and tenure that exceed those of the government itself.

In that context, it is not surprising that illicit businesspeople can create an unlevel playing field to affect an investment in a natural resources project. It is not surprising that they can cause a government bureaucrat to revoke an operating license or cancel a concession agreement and cause it to be issued to another "friendly" party. It is not surprising that they can cause national or local governments to use their regulatory powers—tax, immigration, police, environmental, or the like—to undermine an investor's interest in a property or project or favor the interests of a local partner.

In fact, in some jurisdictions it is increasingly difficult to differentiate between criminal elements and the political interests with which they appear to be aligned. The lines between "traditional" political violence or terrorism and such criminal activity and corruption are also increasingly blurred.

Whether speaking of old risks or new, today the specific nature of political risks faced by a global company can be quite different from region to region. For example, and speaking generally:

- Risks attendant to *public corruption* are typically much more prevalent in certain regions or countries that do not traditionally score well for transparency or the rule of law, for example, countries in the Commonwealth of Independent States, Kazakhstan, or Indonesia.
- Risks attendant to *resource nationalism* are most prevalent in Latin America and Africa, where populist politics often drive a country's political agenda to seek a greater piece of the mineral resources pie. Obviously, resource nationalism is alive and well in other countries (such as the Russian Federation) and regions, but it appears to be more contagious in certain parts of Latin America and Africa.
- In contrast to resource nationalism, risks attendant to *criminal behavior* (for example, piracy, kidnapping, industrial sabotage, theft of intellectual property) are far less sensitive to a country's prevailing political leanings. Such risks are more pronounced in failed or failing states (for example, Sudan,

Somalia, the Democratic Republic of Congo) with either limited institutional will or limited law enforcement capacity to
protect investors or prosecute prominent criminal elements.

■ In contrast, in the last several years political risks attendant to
the *empowerment of local or regional interests* have increased virtually everywhere in the world where Barrick does business.

Today's Economy and Political Risk

By its nature, political risk is a transitory phenomenon. At any given
time, political risk is, after all, simply an expression of current social,
political, and economic pressures. For the last several years political
risks in the natural resources industries have been dominated by
developments in the global economy. Until mid-2008, record-high
global commodity prices and booming emerging markets put political pressure on governments all over the world—both in developing and developed economies—to cancel or renegotiate contracts
and concessions or impose new taxes and royalties to dramatically
change the economics of natural resources development. While
countries such as República Bolivariana de Venezuela and Russia
may have led the charge to change the ground rules for existing
investors in the resources sector, the common perception of "windfall profits" accruing to foreign investors was an irresistible target
for politicians worldwide.

Despite recent dramatic decreases in commodity prices, there has
not yet been a corresponding reduction of the political pressure to
extract more revenue from foreign investors. It appears that the
politicians and their constituents in many developing countries are
simply not as responsive to the recent changes in the investment climate as are the worldwide capital and debt markets.

This disconnect between significantly lower commodity prices
and continuing political pressure to tap investors for more revenue
occurs, in part, because the average person on the street in La Paz
or Ulan Bator is likely to oversimplify foreign investment in natural
resources projects. It is not uncommon for people to simply assume
that resources development is inherently profitable. Consequently,
political pressure mounts to increase the size of the government's
share of the proceeds of the sale of production, largely without
regard to considerations of profitability or other developmental benefits (such as employment, training, technology transfer, infrastructure development, and so forth) that flow from the underlying
investment. In any event, the pressure for more revenue from

foreign investors continues. And this pressure may be slow to abate in many countries because government officials see precious few other options to meet their revenue needs in a weakening global economy.

In the last two or three years, high commodity prices empowered a new wave of emerging market competitors, such as parastatal resources companies, sovereign wealth funds, Russian oligarchs, and other private equity of indeterminate origin. These competitors were often flush with petrodollars or other proceeds of a booming global economy (and not always the mainstream economy). For a variety of reasons, these competitors significantly increased the political risk profile faced by more established global resources companies. The recent retreat in oil prices from US$130 per barrel to less than $50 per barrel, and the dramatic softening of the global economy, will surely slow that trend. But whatever the short-term economic situation, nontraditional competitors in many industries such as natural resources, power, and infrastructure appear to be here to stay. Their potential impact on the evolving landscape for political risk and PRI should not be underestimated.

Case Study: Barrick's Appetite for Political Risk Insurance

Barrick is frequently asked about the company's perspective regarding PRI. While the company believes that PRI has an important place in its risk management portfolio, the overall appetite for PRI has been tempered by a number of concerns.

It should first be noted that Barrick recently put in place a new global PRI policy covering 11 mines and projects in six different countries—Argentina, Chile, Papua New Guinea, Peru, South Africa, and Tanzania. Rather than moving away from using PRI, the company believes that as it ventures further afield on the global stage PRI has the potential to play an even larger role. However, several issues must still be addressed.

First, a perception has arisen that available PRI coverage is increasingly too narrow and has not evolved with the changing face of political risk. Despite some recent improvements in available coverage, PRI products and the language of existing PRI policies still remain largely focused on specific elements of the traditional risks mentioned earlier. Consequently, such products and policies do not mitigate several of the risks with which Barrick is most concerned.

Second, there is also a perception among some insureds that the international financial institutions (IFIs) and export credit agencies

(ECAs) that issue PRI do not have the same "deterrence" value that they have had in the past. For many companies, deterrence was the principal attraction of such coverage. This view of the declining deterrence value of PRI is based on the judgment that many countries no longer see themselves as beholden to the IFIs because they have far less, or in some cases no, outstanding exposure to such institutions. Some countries, particularly in Latin America, have even found it politically advantageous to publicly thumb their noses at institutions such as the World Bank Group.

Last, some concern has also arisen that some of the IFIs and ECAs have become less willing to intercede with host governments to protect the interests of their clients in loss-avoidance discussions. If this estimation is correct, it may be a function of the insurer's perception of its own declining influence in certain countries, perhaps reflecting conflicting political priorities of the insurer's government sponsor in its strategic relations with a host country. (Political imperatives such as access to oil or the war on terrorism can affect a government's priorities.) Or, it may reflect an insurer's reluctance to take any action that may seem to acknowledge that a particular potential loss is covered. Whatever the reason, if the insurer is not viewed as a proactive and enthusiastic advocate to avoid a potential loss, PRI becomes far less attractive to a company like Barrick.

The recent collapse of the global credit markets may have some important implications for the demand for PRI.

First, as commercial credit dries up more companies like Barrick might rely on the IFIs and ECAs to participate in projects as *lenders* in place of commercial banks that either have no appetite or no capacity. Their participation as lenders has the potential to obviate the need to also include PRI as part of project financing.

Second, the simultaneous collapse in credit markets and commodity prices also will have a significant effect on the absolute number of new natural resources projects that are going to be undertaken. A recent Reuters article listed some 60 projects in the mining industry that had been canceled or shelved in the last three months alone of 2008. It is likely that the actual number will eventually be much higher than that. And this trend is not limited to the mining industry. It may provide a preview of what could be expected on the demand side for PRI. It will also be interesting to monitor how the current credit crisis affects both the health and the capacity of political risk insurers and reinsurers, and whether PRI can continue to be competitively priced in the private market given current credit spreads.

On a more positive note, however, circumstances have changed for many host countries. As countries now begin to look at their options for funding impending budget deficits, many may have no choice but to return to the IFIs for assistance. That, in turn, may breathe some additional vigor into the concept of deterrence.

Other Tools Available to Mitigate or Manage Political Risk

A few tools other than PRI can be used to mitigate political risk. Most of these tools are employed in an investment well before the project gets to the point at which PRI comes into play.

- First and foremost, it is essential to assess the nature of the risk comprehensively before making an investment. A company must do its homework on the country, the region, and prospective partners well before it becomes contractually committed. Ample resources are available to assess political risk—one just needs to use them. (In this regard, the task of comprehensively assessing the risk of a particular investment is not so much different than the same exercise by a political risk insurer.) Once the initial evaluation is complete, those risks, because they are not static, must be actively monitored, and mitigation strategies must be adjusted without hesitation.
- A key mitigation strategy for those investing for the long term in the natural resources industry is for companies to seize the moment and make fair deals, structured to keep the interests of the foreign investor generally aligned with those of all of the key stakeholders—including local and regional interests—over the life of an investment. To the extent possible, the deals should be structured to account for the cyclical nature of commodities prices.
- While it has been considered by many to be beneficial to include local partners or investors that are thought to bring something to the table, it is equally important to ensure that they profit only if the investment prospers.
- Investments should be structured to take advantage of investment treaties and access to international arbitration. If fiscal or tax stabilization arrangements are envisioned under local law, the time must be taken to complete such agreements before fully committing to a project. It is also important to keep in mind that with such agreements, as with PRI policies, the devil is in the details.

- Companies also need to ensure, more than ever before, that adequate capacity is committed to establishing and maintaining the company's local "social license" to operate. From a risk avoidance standpoint, this point cannot be overemphasized.
- Last, irrespective of predominant local business practices, companies must be utterly and uncompromisingly transparent.

Conclusion

A discussion of political risk at any appointed time necessarily tends to focus on events and forces that by their nature are ephemeral. Undoubtedly, today's political risk profile will change tomorrow with the global economy, global commodity prices, and global social and political winds. While the global commercial world may have gotten smaller and flatter, it has not gotten any less complicated. Consequently, assessing and managing this moving target have never been any more important to the success of our businesses than they are today.

Advancements in Recurring Issues and New Dimensions for Political Risk Insurance

Linking Political Risk Insurance Pricing and Portfolio Management with Economic Capital Modeling: A Multilateral Perspective?

Mikael Sundberg, Faisal Quraishi, and
Sidhartha Choudhury

Providers of political risk insurance (PRI) may need to consider several objectives in their pricing decisions. As laid out in its convention, the primary mandate of the Multilateral Investment Guarantee Agency (MIGA) is to offer insurance against noncommercial political risks broadly in the categories of expropriation (EX), currency inconvertibility or transfer restriction (TR), war and civil disturbance (WCD), and breach of contract by a host government (BOC). As a mono-line investment insurer and a member of the World Bank Group, MIGA aims to open frontier markets by leading syndicated efforts together with other public and private PRI providers, takes

---

The authors are responsible for the ongoing maintenance of MIGA's risk and pricing models and provide MIGA's underwriters with pricing indications. The descriptions in this chapter of MIGA's models and general objectives are factual. Interpretations of the role of pricing in PRI and the industry itself are the opinions of the authors and should not be seen as representative of the management or Board of Executive Directors of MIGA or The World Bank Group, or its owners.

advantage of reinsurance to share risks and leverage capacity, and may from time to time also act as a reinsurer for other firms.

MIGA's convention further stipulates that the agency shall sustain itself financially and pay claims as they arise, without an expectation of drawing on additional owner capital. As a result of its market position, which focuses on frontier markets and often complex projects, and its nature as a development institution, the premium MIGA charges its clients needs to reflect a multifaceted picture of low-frequency but high-severity risk—often large exposures in difficult environments, significant due diligence involvement in projects to ensure social and environmental safeguards are met, and special relationships with host governments that influence MIGA's recovery position. Consequently, in addition to the traditional pricing considerations of PRI providers, MIGA is faced with the challenge of offering the product at prices that optimize the value proposition between making a particular project viable for the betterment of a developing country's economy and compensating itself reasonably for its risk exposure.

As a development institution, MIGA aims not to maximize profit, but to manage and optimize the use of its shareholder capital to realize a measurable impact on development goals in countries that are also members of MIGA. To further complicate the picture, MIGA operates in a marketplace with private PRI providers whose objectives are to maximize profits for their shareholders and with public export credit agencies whose objectives are to support their nation's firms in cross-border transactions. In addition to meeting its own objectives, MIGA must also set its pricing at a level that avoids disrupting market-based pricing mechanisms in the larger PRI market (for example, by crowding out private insurance or leading a "race to the bottom" by persistent underpricing in market segments of particular development importance). Indeed, one of MIGA's roles is to complement the presence of private PRI providers rather than to compete with them outright. Even with these multiple considerations, MIGA, like other insurance entities, must ensure that its income from premiums covers its administrative expenses and enables payment of claims by building up its reserves and capital base to adequately match potential liabilities.

The objective of this chapter is to describe the analytical, risk-based modeling approach that the pricing team in MIGA's Finance and Risk Management Group uses to arrive at a basis for appropriate premium rates for individual projects, and how the multiple objectives have been reconciled. The nature of risk parameters that feed into the models is discussed, addressing how MIGA has tackled the issue many PRI providers face, that is, how to find meaningful data to construct robust models. Furthermore, the discussion illustrates ways in which the pricing exercise can be made an integral component of an overall portfolio risk management framework, and how the calculation of cost- and risk-based premium rates can be placed in a broader context of development objectives and a PRI market consisting of both private and public insurers. The chapter is descriptive and does not attempt to prescribe a generally applicable formula for modeling and pricing PRI. Nonetheless, some details of the approach described herein may be of use to other practitioners grappling with the difficult task of pricing PRI products.

Pricing as an Art and a Science

Given the dynamic nature of country risk and the relative absence of obvious claims patterns, the pricing of political risk guarantees has traditionally been more a qualitative rather than a quantitative exercise. The pricing process has relied to a large extent on the measured judgment of underwriters, where risk differentiation in pricing—for example, across countries or sectors—has been based more on underwriters' experience and on heuristics than on sophisticated models. This contrasts with many other lines of insurance, such as property and casualty or life insurance. While the latter markets enjoy large quantities of actuarial data on which to base their risk models, PRI providers, whose risks are typically low frequency but carry the potential to be severe, cannot easily refer to in-house or other statistical sources of claims history to model the pricing of their guarantees. As a result, PRI providers have traditionally looked at historical events as guidance for future claims activity and have used their intuition for interpretation.

Particularly in light of the global financial crisis of 2008 and 2009—by some accounts the worst since the 1930s—which has exposed serious shortcomings in risk measurement and management standards across the financial services industry, there is little doubt that now more than ever, PRI providers (like any insurance and financial services firms) need to take seriously the prospect of investing time, money, and effort in a solid quantitative approach to pricing and risk management that is based on robust risk models. However, PRI coverage constantly evolves within the industry:

tenors have been extended, and covered investment projects are often large, highly complex, and located in poor countries with rapidly changing economic and political conditions. Moreover, large-scale investments often involve collaboration between private and public insurers, who may assess risks differently depending on their strategic objectives. Finally, and potentially critically important, the current financial crisis may create some unpredictable consequences for vulnerable developing economies, where financial distress is often followed by political turmoil.

Putting the many considerations into context, the conclusion for pricing and risk management for PRI seems to be that risk models, no matter how complex and sophisticated, can never anticipate and fully quantify every element of constantly evolving risk situations. Therefore, just as for sole reliance on heuristics or individual experience (which is greatly influenced by perception), dependence on a purely quantitative approach to risk assessment and pricing is neither sufficient nor prudent. Instead, a rigorous risk management framework needs to consist of models that balance stability and flexibility in parameters and application, and that allow for quantification of risk under the best assumptions of what the world will look like under medium- and long-term outlooks. Indeed, the models need to be combined with a policy framework for experienced front-line practitioners, such as PRI underwriters, to interpret the modeled results in collaboration with risk managers who operate the models behind the scenes. Consistent with lessons being learned by numerous risk managers in the financial industries today, MIGA management's philosophy is that modeled results—for example, in the form of risk capital and guarantee premiums—should not be seen as exact economic "truths," but as guidelines and frames of reference anchored in a solid analytical framework.

Pricing as an Integrated Component of an Economic Capital–Based Risk Management Framework

Many public and private PRI providers have recently made quantitative models a part of their operational processes and pricing decisions. In an effort to undertake a more consistent approach to both pricing and risk management, MIGA implemented a risk management framework over a period of about four years built around a quantitative portfolio risk model (the Economic Capital model). With the help of an additional costing model, components of this framework are designed to contribute the analytical or "science" angle to the pricing of MIGA's guarantee products. As will be described in a later section of this chapter, this angle constitutes one part of a broader pricing approach.

MIGA has completed several stages of modeling work to incorporate quantitative measures and viewpoints into decision processes previously dominated by qualitative considerations. Development of the portfolio risk model began in 2004 with the help of external consulting firms, and was introduced beginning in 2005. At the same time, a costing model was developed, the aim of which is to calculate the premium rates to charge for individual projects such that, on a portfolio basis, the objective can be met of recovery of full administrative expenses and a charge for claims risk, allowing for necessary reserves[1] and capital build-up. The Economic Capital (EC) and costing models were fully integrated in 2007, allowing the cost of capital charged as part of the project premium to be consistent with the risk capital calculated for the portfolio and allocated to the project, proportional to the project's relative contribution to the risk of the overall portfolio.

The general financial risk management framework was developed over time, and work continues to be carried out to add applications and to integrate the parts with a particular emphasis on merging the pricing methodology with prudent portfolio risk management. Today the framework consists of the building blocks depicted in figure 6.1.

The components of the framework feed into overall financial and operational management, contribute key information to internal and external financial reporting, and constitute the platform for various types of stress testing performed on the financial outlook and capital position.

An Approach to Modeling PRI Risk and Underlying Model Parameters

The development of a modeling framework involves selecting an analytical basis for the measurement of risk from among several methodologies available, and then capturing the parameters needed to populate the model and calibrating the parameters to ensure useful model output. The source of data to generate the model parameters and the frequency with which to update the data will depend on the industry and the type of risk products that are modeled.

FIGURE 6.1 ILLUSTRATION OF COMPONENTS OF THE EC-BASED RISK
MANAGEMENT FRAMEWORK

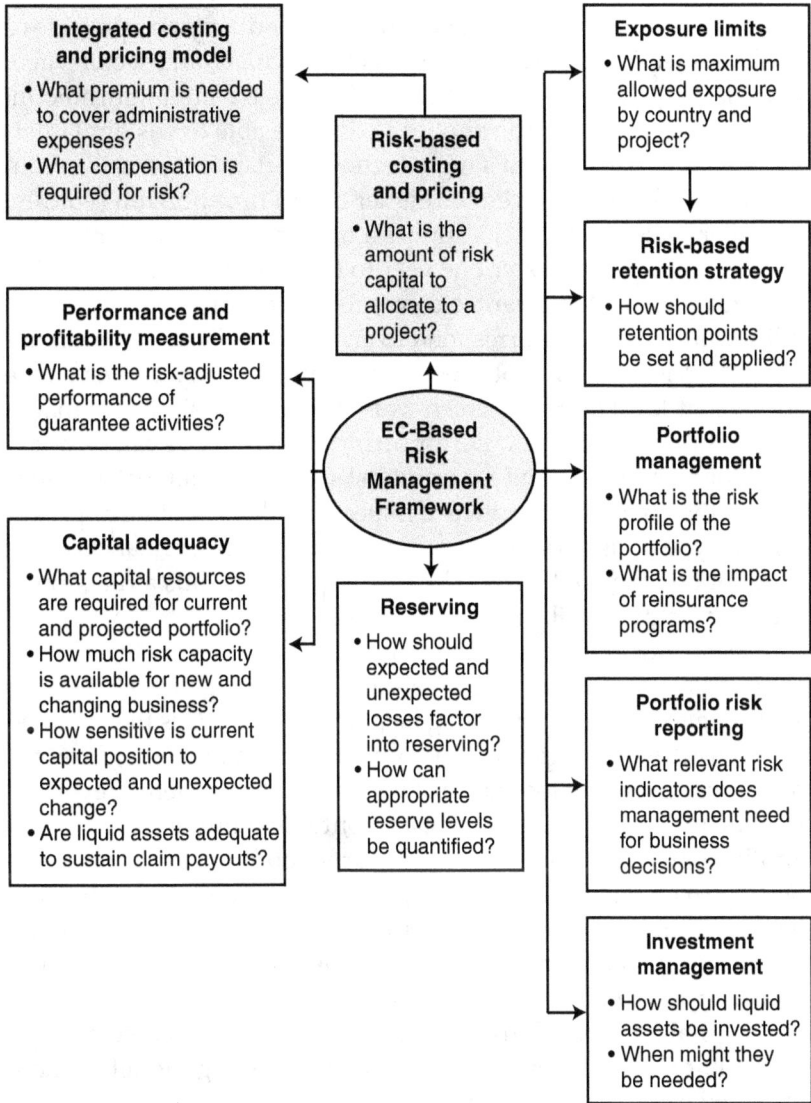

Integrated costing and pricing model
- What premium is needed to cover administrative expenses?
- What compensation is required for risk?

Exposure limits
- What is maximum allowed exposure by country and project?

Risk-based costing and pricing
- What is the amount of risk capital to allocate to a project?

Risk-based retention strategy
- How should retention points be set and applied?

Performance and profitability measurement
- What is the risk-adjusted performance of guarantee activities?

EC-Based Risk Management Framework

Portfolio management
- What is the risk profile of the portfolio?
- What is the impact of reinsurance programs?

Capital adequacy
- What capital resources are required for current and projected portfolio?
- How much risk capacity is available for new and changing business?
- How sensitive is current capital position to expected and unexpected change?
- Are liquid assets adequate to sustain claim payouts?

Reserving
- How should expected and unexpected losses factor into reserving?
- How can appropriate reserve levels be quantified?

Portfolio risk reporting
- What relevant risk indicators does management need for business decisions?

Investment management
- How should liquid assets be invested?
- When might they be needed?

Source: Authors and MIGA Finance and Risk Management Group.

Economic Capital

EC, chosen by MIGA as the basis for measurement of risk in its portfolio, is a common measure in the financial industry and provides a uniform measure of risk across projects, products, and sectors; geographical areas; and risk types. It is defined as the minimum amount of capital an organization should hold to be able to sustain larger-than-expected losses with a high degree of certainty (typically a confidence level of 99.5 percent or higher over a time horizon typically of one or three years. MIGA applies a more conservative confidence level of 99.99 percent over one year to the modeled losses resulting from claims on the guarantee contracts in its portfolio. This probability would typically correspond to an institution's target credit rating. MIGA is currently not rated by any rating agency. However, the confidence level of 99.99 percent was chosen to be similar to that of an institution rated AAA. EC for financial institutions can be calculated for market risks and for credit risks. MIGA's main risk is claims risk on the guarantee products it issues, and the modeling approach for this type of risk is similar to that of a bank or other financial institution modeling credit risk. The calculated EC is thus a function of the probability distribution of losses (see figure 6.2).

The EC model calculates the full loss distribution for the guarantee portfolio's potential loss levels and gives the probability corresponding to each level of aggregate portfolio loss. EC is then defined by subtracting the expected loss amount (mean of losses) from the maximum probable loss (at the 99.99 percent confidence level) for the portfolio. EC provides for easy contextual interpretations and applications; it is expressed as a dollar amount of capital required, which can be directly compared with available capital, and this capital "consumption" gives a measure of risk that can easily be aggregated along many different dimensions of the portfolio, such as product type, country, region, or business sector. Moreover, the modeled capital amount, along the various dimensions, can be brought into other modeling applications, such as costing models, where allocated capital is charged with a desired cost of capital.

Although the loss horizon for the definition of EC is one year, to calculate an economic value concept of risk associated with a guarantee portfolio, the EC model captures two forms of political risk: (i) claim risk, which is the risk that a claim will occur within the chosen time horizon, and (ii) nonclaim economic loss risk or value risk, which is the risk associated with changes to the economic value of

FIGURE 6.2 CONCEPT OF ECONOMIC CAPITAL

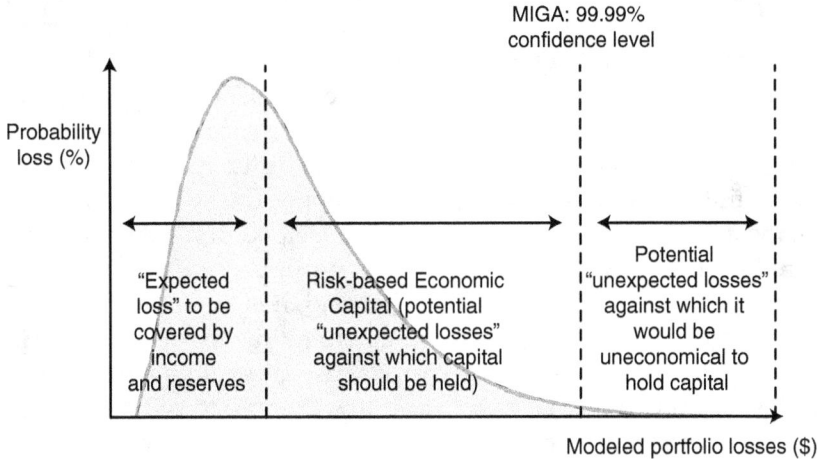

Source: Adapted from Marrison (2002).
Note: Probability of total area under line is 100 percent.

the guarantee portfolio resulting from changing future claim expectations (the "economic risk" of a country downgrade).

Parameters for Development of a PRI EC Model

The output from the EC calculations is only as good as the data inputs and assumptions that are used. Historical claims data in the PRI industry useful for modeling purposes are limited, and models are expected to predict low-frequency, high-severity events based on these data. In addition, the countries that are the recipients of foreign direct investment flows to be insured and where the perceived risk is the highest are often the countries where historical data are least available This is particularly true for multilaterals and development organizations, which have explicit goals to emphasize the least developed economies in a wide range of markets. A further complicating factor is that most private providers (which make up a large share of the market) will not publicly disclose detailed claims information; thus, public agencies' claims data become the default source.

To develop the core model parameters for claims probability, severity (loss given default), recovery, and correlations in MIGA's model, the starting point was published claims history data by the U.S. Overseas Private Investment Corporation (OPIC) over the period 1973–2000. The number of claim occurrences over this period was about 170, distributed among the various risk covers. The relatively long period, which includes a large number of PRI policies and a significant number of observed claim events, encompasses a changing political risk picture and incidences of different types of events over time, as well as general global economic conditions. Moreover, choosing this period of nearly 30 years helped prevent short-term trends from having a disproportionate impact on the resulting parameters used in the models. That said, it is important to revisit the model's underlying assumptions from time to time to factor in newer data; although MIGA's own claims history does not currently provide a rich enough data set, over time it would constitute an additional component in such future reviews of PRI claim events.

Parameter Adjustments for Unique Characteristics

OPIC's claims history data is a good starting point for modeling the risk of most PRI providers: it is probably the richest publicly available data set and it spans a long period. The modeler, however, also needs to consider the type of claim events being compared and whether recent and distant events should receive equal weights. MIGA has made some adjustments to the model's parameters to factor in perceived differences between OPIC and MIGA. The "World Bank effect" aims to capture the extent to which host countries who are also members of MIGA will be deterred from invoking measures leading to political risk claims, and the OPIC claims probability data was adjusted accordingly. The basis for the adjustments was judgmental interpretation by experienced professionals, and drew on anecdotal evidence as well. Recovery parameters were largely based on the OPIC data, plus data from the Berne Union association for export credit and investment insurers. For a measure of conservatism, recovery parameters received no adjustments for a "World Bank effect," even though MIGA would typically be in a relatively strong position to recover from a host government after paying a claim.

Enhancing the Usefulness of Historical Claims Data

The ultimate model parameters derived from the data need to have a significant level of explanatory power and to provide meaningful differentiation between countries of various risk levels. The raw

OPIC claims history data alone were not deemed to be rich enough for the type of model MIGA was building; that is, there were neither enough data points, nor did the data contain sufficient levels of detail for calculating differentiated model parameters along the dimensions of risk cover type, country risk level, and so forth. To address this need for additional "richness" in the data, intermediate "analog scoring models" were constructed as part of building MIGA's models, allowing for the actual observed claims data to be layered over econometric model–based parameter differentiation.

The analog models were developed to produce probabilities for claimable events occurring in countries with different relative risk levels for each of the risk covers MIGA offers. The resulting differentiated relative claims probabilities were calibrated along a 10-notch rating scale (A+ through D). To build the analog models for each of the risk covers (EX, TR, WCD), three papers by macroeconomic researchers were identified (Collier and Hoeffler 2000; Burton and Inoue 1987; Mulder, Perrelli, and Rocha 2002), which included the structure for the econometric models that were built. These econometric analog models are not used on an ongoing basis by MIGA—their purpose was to aid in the design of the relative differentiation of claim probabilities applied to the 10-notch rating scale as part of the development of the EC model. Risk management officers in MIGA's Economics and Policy Group rate each country for each political risk cover every quarter according to this scale, thereby attributing a particular claim probability pattern for each country and contract in the portfolio; this becomes a key input to the EC model.

Another data enhancement was the generation of a "transition matrix" along which the first-year assessed claim probabilities for each of the 10 ratings are expected to change (term structure adjustment) over a period of up to 20 years. Having the claim probabilities reflect reasonable expected changes to a country's risk level over time is an essential feature of MIGA's costing model because contracts are often for long tenors, up to 15 years and in some cases up to 20 years.

EC models typically capture claims (or loss) correlations, describing the extent to which several claims situations may be expected to occur simultaneously. Because there are relatively few actual claims events, the analog models described above were used to estimate the correlation parameters for MIGA's EC model and risk-based pricing. Correlation parameters were estimated on several levels: (i) between different claimable events covered in a contract, (ii) between similar claimable events on several contracts within a country, (iii) between several countries within a geographic region, and (iv) between different regions in the world. These calibrated correlation parameters drive the effects of risk concentration and diversification, impacting capital calculation and allocation.

MIGA's Incorporation of EC into Pricing

As indicated above, the analytical angle of MIGA's pricing involves calculating the premium rate on guarantees to fully recover incurred administrative expenses (both direct underwriting cost and general overhead) and to ensure that each contract includes a charge for claims risk, drawing on EC consumed. The objective is to price each guarantee so that premium income generated by the portfolio as a whole recovers all administrative expenses and generates enough "surplus" income to increase actual available operating capital (via retained earnings), a portion of which can be set aside in reserves to pay out claims on a recurring and long-term basis. A costing model is employed, bringing these expense and risk-compensation objectives together through several components that make up the premium charged on an individual contract. Figure 6.3 illustrates the build-up of premiums through expense and risk components.

Risk Charge via Allocated Marginal EC

The risk load component is calculated using allocated EC and a capital charge. The model calculating the EC consumed by the portfolio can also allocate a portion of the total capital to each individual contract in the portfolio. To price a new project, the project is hypothetically added to the portfolio in the model, then the new total portfolio EC consumption is calculated, as is the portion of this new EC to be allocated to the new incremental project. This allocated capital is then charged with a cost of capital (the hurdle rate).

By allocating a marginal portion of the portfolio's EC to the project, the project is thus charged with a cost commensurate with the project's contribution to the portfolio's risk, that is, the additional amount of capital that the project places at risk. Estimating the individual project's relative share or contribution to the portfolio's overall risk is necessarily a forward-looking exercise. The actual portfolio information applied in the EC model for pricing is regularly updated, so any trends or "drift" in the overall portfolio exposure profile and risk level are factored into the models and reflected in the pricing of new guarantees. MIGA's practice is for project premium rates to

FIGURE 6.3 MODEL INPUTS AND PREMIUM COMPONENTS

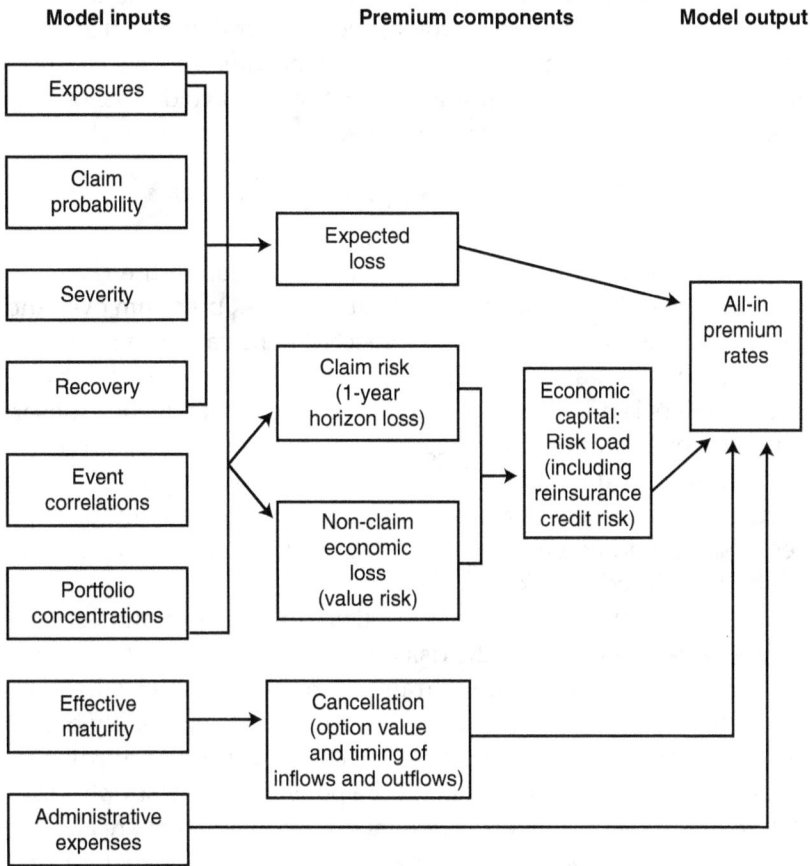

Model inputs	Premium components	Model output

Exposures

Claim probability

Expected loss

Severity

All-in premium rates

Recovery

Claim risk (1-year horizon loss)

Economic capital: Risk load (including reinsurance credit risk)

Event correlations

Non-claim economic loss (value risk)

Portfolio concentrations

Effective maturity

Cancellation (option value and timing of inflows and outflows)

Administrative expenses

Source: Authors and MIGA Finance and Risk Management Group.

remain unchanged for the life of a contract; later discovery of a different risk assessment for a project or host country does not lead to a review of the premium rates for outstanding guarantees.

The risk load premium component calculated according to EC consumption effectively captures the concentration and diversification effects in a portfolio across several potential dimensions, via the correlation parameters. If a project is added to the portfolio in a host country where MIGA's exposure is already significant, the EC consumption of the portfolio increases more than if an otherwise identical project of identical risk were added in a host country with little or no existing exposure. The new project's relatively severe contribution to the portfolio's risk also is reflected through a relatively higher amount of EC allocated by the model to the project, and the premium rate that needs to be charged is correspondingly higher. In the same way, a well-diversified portfolio, in which exposure concentration is avoided, helps keep the premium rates of new projects down.

Establishing the Cost of Capital

The hurdle rate or cost of capital used to calculate the risk load should be determined such that it includes a risk premium over and above the "risk-free" rate that is expected to be earned on any capital currently not at risk. In MIGA's case, all capital paid in by its shareholders is invested in a liquid asset portfolio, which is conservatively invested for a high degree of certainty of capital preservation, in highly liquid asset classes such as treasury and agency securities. The capital placed at risk (EC consumed) by the guarantee business should be charged at a higher rate than any capital currently not placed at risk.

The total cost of capital used in calculating the premium should compensate an insurer for the risk borne, accounting for the fact that in PRI (and other lines of insurance exposed to potentially catastrophic losses), actual loss in any year may be significantly higher than expected or average loss. So the cost of capital or hurdle rate must be enough to compensate for the potential of catastrophic loss. MIGA and its shareholders (national governments that are also the shareholders of the International Bank for Reconstruction and Development) are not seeking profit maximization. Rather, it is expected that contributed capital will be put to use for optimal development impact while emphasizing capital preservation. Specifically eschewing profit maximization can help an organization like MIGA keep its cost of capital down and focus its strategy in large part on operations in host countries with perceived high levels of political risk and on complex projects, without this leading to prohibitively high premium rates.

Generally, a PRI provider (public or private) also needs to consider whether any additional margin should be added to the cost of capital to compensate for uncertainty in parameters used in models and for the provider's capital position in light of the potential calamitous events for which capital might be needed (and taking into account the provider's other systems for mitigating risk, such as exposure limits).

Details of the Premium Rate Calculation

MIGA's costing model was designed to generate premium rates for its guarantees that take into account country or project risks and concentration effects (both current assessment and expected changes to claims probabilities over time—reversion to average country risk levels), the size and tenor of the project, complexity of underwriting, and whether the guarantee is for an equity or debt investment. Premium rates are worked out for each of the covers offered, and the client chooses the risks for which cover is desired. Several factors will affect the total premium rate. Depending on allocation rules, the size of the project will have an impact on administrative expenses allocated to the project and the premium rate needed for expense recovery. The size also impacts the concentration of risk in the host country and portfolio and may be reflected in higher premium rates for larger exposures.

In a model like MIGA's, premium rate components for administrative expenses and risk are calculated such that the net present value (NPV) of all annual premium payments (inflows) equals the NPV of the project's expected outflows. In other words, for each year of its expected life, a project is allocated a certain amount of administrative expenses based on an agreed-on set of allocation rules; some of these expenses are incurred as upfront underwriting expenses, and some occur over time in the form of contract management and overhead expenses. In MIGA's case, the premium income is generated over each year of the life of a project, through a fixed premium rate (in percent), multiplied by each year's outstanding exposure (guarantee liability), which may vary from year to year. In calculating the premium rate, the model captures expected variations in the annual exposure for debt contracts according to the expected disbursement and repayment schedules; the exposure is larger in the early years if an underlying loan disburses over time and decreases in later years as the loan is repaid.

For the purpose of calculating the premium rate components for risk for each of the different types of cover (EX, TR, WCD, and BOC), amortization of a loan also means that the risk exposure decreases over time; this is taken into consideration in the model's calculation of annual charges for risk and the calculation of equal annual premium rates. In calculating the allocated EC and the premium rates, consideration is also given to changing probabilities over time that claims will occur, that is, the model assumes a gradual reversion to the mean of the claims probabilities. Transition matrixes for annual claims probabilities reflect this, under the rationale that a host country has a certain risk rating based on a short to medium-term assessment of its situation, but will not retain this assessment indefinitely. In other words, an assessment of high risk in a country at present (as reflected in its most current country ratings) translates to a higher claim probability for the next year. If the project has survived at the end of the year, that is, there has been no claim, the claim probability for the next one-year period will be slightly lower. The reverse is true if the country risk rating at present is low; some worsening in the form of increasing claim probabilities in outer years is expected.

MIGA reflects the current risk assessment for a given project using country risk ratings, generated and updated each quarter for each of the four risk covers. The exercise of rating the countries for political risk is an in-house process; external sources and ratings are considered, but the final ratings are unique and confidential to MIGA. The country assessments are made by staff in a department separated from the department that performs the pricing exercise, to eliminate bias and to support a system of checks and balances. When calculating the risk premiums for a particular project, the host-country risks are used by default, but a project's rating may be upgraded or downgraded based on the project's own risk characteristics.

Early Cancellations of Guarantee Contracts

The calculated rates may need to be adjusted for expected early cancellations of contracts. For providers like MIGA, for which the contract is expected to generate revenue through annual premium payments that recover both upfront and ongoing incurred expenses, the timing of expenses and revenues will be mismatched. The expenses will be frontloaded in comparison with the revenues, and if the expected revenue stream is cut short by an early cancellation, a cost recovery shortfall can occur. Because early cancellations are very difficult to predict for individual projects, MIGA's remedy is to include a component in the premium for each project based on the average expected cancellation pattern for all projects. The adjustment is based on historical experience and incorporated into the costing model using contract survival ratios that decrease for each year of the project's expected life.

The early-cancellation adjustment has a moderate impact on premiums. To avoid severe mispricing and under-recovery of costs if many projects are canceled very early, MIGA's contracts include a clause that states that if a contract is canceled before its third anniversary, a penalty fee is payable by the guarantee holder. An alternative payment structure is also available to MIGA's clients; by making a substantial upfront payment, the client can reduce the annual premium. The NPV of administrative expenses and risk costs are reduced by payment of the upfront premium; the costing model calculates the alternative lower annual premium rate based on this reduced NPV.

Global Policies and the Pricing of Risk

MIGA has relatively little experience writing multicountry or "global" policies. However, the modeling framework for costing described here can accommodate this type of situation well. The fact that a significant portion of the premium charged by a multinational development agency like MIGA typically pertains to fixed expense recovery can help the process of determining the premium rate for these policies; it can be argued that some of the risk charge is "embedded" in the administrative expense charge, resulting from MIGA's risk-mitigating activities. Calculating the administrative expense component is straightforward, following the approach described above. Multicountry policies may enjoy certain economies of scale at underwriting, which can be reflected in the administrative expense allocation and charge. With regard to the risk component of the premium, if a client wants to purchase coverage for a single project that involves risks in two or more host countries (the claim event can occur in any of the countries), the risk component of the premium would typically reflect the risk of the country with the highest risk. Alternatively, if a client wants to purchase coverage for a portfolio of several projects, and the exposure of each is limited to a single host country, the EC model allows for pricing this as if it were a subportfolio added to MIGA's overall portfolio. This approach captures concentration or diversification effects within the client's subportfolio and between that subportfolio and MIGA's overall portfolio and reflects these effects in the risk premium.

Linking Pricing and Portfolio Management through EC

A project's impact on the riskiness of the portfolio is a key consideration in MIGA's pricing framework; as discussed in the section on the overall risk management framework, decisions about management of guarantee exposures in individual host countries and projects are based on the same EC measures used for the costing calculations. MIGA manages its exposures through treaty-based and facultative reinsurance programs. Treaty reinsurance agreements with a few counterpart firms were initially implemented in 1997. These firms take on ceded exposure up to certain agreed-on limits. Capacity is further augmented as needed through additional facultative reinsurance. Both programs are instrumental to MIGA's objective of leveraging its own resources to raise more capacity in the PRI marketplace and maximize its ability to encourage highly developmental investment projects.

Risk-Based Levels for MIGA's Net Retention

MIGA revised its exposure retention framework in 2007 and implemented corresponding changes to its reinsurance agreements with a view to optimizing the use of reinsurance across the portfolio to manage the dual objectives of avoiding excessive exposure concentrations while optimizing income from premiums. At the same time, limits for maximum net exposure per project and per country were revised and are now complemented by internal guidelines for exposure retention levels based on country risk groupings consisting of four categories, from low to high risk. To determine the country risk grouping, weighted averages of MIGA's country risk ratings (A, B, C, and so on) of risk covers (TR, EX, and WCD) are used. Each group corresponds to a "standard" retention level, which becomes the internal benchmark for a new project being analyzed and priced. The suggested retention levels are differentiated between the country risk groups and may further vary between projects with different risk and return characteristics. In no case may the suggested retention level be such that either the maximum per project or per country limit is exceeded (currently $180 million and $600 million, respectively).

Overall Portfolio Risk Level as the Main Gauge

MIGA's retention framework, like its pricing, is anchored in the calculation of EC. The relative differentiation between the internal risk groups in per project net retention amounts was derived by analyzing the additional marginal EC consumed for a marginal increase in the amount of net exposure. As mentioned earlier, the pricing of MIGA's guarantees involves calculating the incremental EC consumed for a potential new project in the context of the existing portfolio. With this information, relative differentiation between standard net project retention levels by risk group was established, such that the portfolio's ratio of EC/Net Exposure remained largely unchanged when a project of the size of each category's retention level was added to the respective risk groups. In other words, if an "average" project within a country risk group were underwritten and added to the guarantee portfolio at the standard retention level, it would not materially change the risk profile of the portfolio as measured by EC/Net Exposure. By following the retention guideline in broad terms since implementation in 2007, MIGA management has kept this ratio for the portfolio quite stable. It currently stands at about 7 to 8 percent. The ratio is a function of the characteristics of a PRI provider's portfolio exposure, concentration, and risk types.

Results of a Risk-Based Retention Framework

This approach has advanced MIGA's initial retention and reinsurance framework established more than a decade ago. The revised risk-based methodology has allowed more informed decisions to be made about pricing and risk retention, especially for potential transactions in countries where exposure is already substantial. Concentration risk is captured in the EC consumed by the new project and is reflected in both pricing and reinsurance decision making. The ability to share risks selectively using the treaty and facultative reinsurance programs referred to above has been instrumental in MIGA's management of exposures. If any project exceeds MIGA's standard net retention for the country risk group, an amount is ceded through the surplus treaty, up to the limit set out in the treaty agreement. Additional facultative reinsurance is then used to further manage exposure within MIGA's absolute limits and country group guidelines.

Table 6.1 illustrates a hypothetical example for a country in a risk group for which MIGA's standard retention is assumed to be $50 million. Three scenarios with varying gross guarantee amounts illustrate how each party participates in the project.

In scenario 3, MIGA would have the option to approach facultative reinsurers to syndicate $30 million of exposure. In such a case, a panel including private and public sector insurers and reinsurers, as well as the Lloyd's syndicates, would be contacted to understand their interest and capacity to participate in the proposed transaction.

TABLE 6.1 REINSURANCE FRAMEWORK EXAMPLE
(US$ MILLIONS)

Item	Scenario 1	Scenario 2	Scenario 3
Amount of guarantee	40	70	130
MIGA retains	40	50 of 70	50 of 130
Surplus treaty	0	20 of 70	50 of 130
Facultative reinsurance (optional)	0	0	30 of 130

Source: Authors.

Retention Analysis for Individual Projects

Given any constraints, such as available capacity of reinsurance partners, MIGA's senior management ultimately decides how much
exposure to retain for an individual project at its Project Review
Committee (PRC) meeting at which the project is discussed. The decision is supported by a project retention scenario analysis (see hypothetical example in table 6.2). The impact to the risk profile of the
guarantee portfolio is analyzed (as measured by the relationship
between EC and Net Exposure) at several hypothetical levels of exposure retention for the project. In the example in table 6.2, increasing
the retention level from $120 million to $160 million increases the risk
significantly, indicating that the retention of exposure would add a
disproportionate amount of risk to MIGA's overall portfolio. From a
risk compensation perspective, a commensurately higher premium
rate would need to be charged.

Additional Considerations for Pricing of
Political Risk Guarantees

In addition to the theoretical modeling aspects described in previous sections, the nature of the PRI industry and MIGA's special characteristics as a multilateral entity need be taken into consideration
for the determination of the final premium rate to charge a client for
a guarantee product.

Cost Structure

Given a multilateral's unique position in the PRI market, its mandate, and its requirements and conditions for offering a guarantee,
its pricing structure may differ at times from that in the marketplace.

TABLE 6.2 HYPOTHETICAL PROJECT EXPOSURE RETENTION ANALYSIS

Retention Scenarios
Project XYZ Financial   Region: ABC
$200 million gross exposure, Loan contract, Finance sector, 10-year tenor
Covers: EX, TR, WCD, and BOC
Portfolio EC/Net Exposure as of 12/31/2008, prior to this project: 7.5%

	Retention level 1 $40 million	Retention level 2 $80 million	Retention level 3 $120 million	Retention level 4 $160 million
Ex post portfolio EC/Net Exposure (%)	7.46	7.43	7.51	7.60
EC of project ($ million)	$4.80	$6.90	$10.20	$18.10
Ex post EC of portfolio ($ million)	$360.20	$361.80	$365.00	$374.30
Project premium rate (%)	1.00	1.05	1.12	1.20
Remaining country headroom (net exposure; $ million)	$210	$170	$130	$90

Source: Authors.

MIGA's position as both a development institution and an insurance provider has implications for its cost structure and loss expectations. Specifically, while MIGA's administrative expense ratio[2] is higher than that of private insurance firms providing similar PRI products, its loss ratio[3] is also lower than that of the private firms. On a combined ratio basis, both MIGA and its private counterparts are operating profitably so long as the sum of the two ratios is below 1. As an insurance entity assesses the adequacy of its pricing, the main measure to study is this combined ratio. In MIGA's case many of its expenses are fixed and relate to such in-house activities as thorough environmental and social studies ensuring developmental objectives are met; to activities aimed at resolution of potential claims situations before they occur; and to cost sharing with other World Bank units where the relationship allows for the deterrence effects referenced previously in this chapter.

Extrinsic Factors of Uncertainty

Notwithstanding its low historical loss ratio, MIGA's financial risk management framework recognizes that historical loss experience may not be a good predictor of future losses in the PRI segment of the insurance industry, especially in the uncertain economic environment the current financial crisis has created and in light of the weaknesses it has revealed in the predictive power of models. In particular, PRI providers need to "expect the unexpected" and be prepared for potentially catastrophic claims situations when large and interconnected nations encounter serious distress and the insurer is faced with multiple claims in rapid succession. This is the reality for insurers operating in environments of high-severity and (perceived) low-probability losses. MIGA's strategy includes using its strong capital base to position the agency directly in these markets and not to turn away from new business as conditions worsen. Complementary to a judicious underwriting approach, pricing structures should reflect such goals through return targets, administrative expense allocation, exposure management, and partnering with other financially strong entities.

When exposures are managed with the help of reinsurance, counterparty credit risk (nonperformance risk) of reinsurers is possible, which adds to the basic political risk in the model. Therefore, MIGA's EC and costing models for political risks have been extended to take into account the nonperformance probabilities of reinsurers, to capture concentrations of reliance on individual reinsurance entities, and to add this to the amount of capital needed to be held and for which MIGA needs to be compensated.

Intrinsic Relevance of the Premium Rates

The previous point is important for multilaterals, whose focus on large and complex projects in difficult markets can mean that significant amounts of reinsurance may be required (MIGA has reinsured approximately 47 percent of its aggregate portfolio exposure as of December 2008). MIGA is expected to pay any large claim in full, and in turn needs to be able to rely on its reinsurance partners to contribute their shares. Pricing thus needs to be such that these sophisticated reinsurers receive satisfactory compensation for these complex shared risks through the premium established by the original underwriter. While modeled premiums are by definition not market rates, they need to be calculated in such a way that MIGA does not price itself out of the reinsurance market it relies upon to provide the capacity that is expected by its clients.

Experience shows that other PRI providers see opportunity in reinsuring projects with MIGA involvement, drawing on MIGAs extensive due diligence efforts in the form of social and environmental studies. This rigor is important to the partnering organizations, including MIGA's role in mitigation of reputational risks. In difficult markets in which price discovery otherwise is tenuous, the price worked out by MIGA and based on a World Bank presence may take on the value of a market reference point for the reinsurers to follow. Development of an appropriate price is thus important, not only for MIGA's own financial sustainability, but also for that of the reinsurance partners and other PRI providers who may enter newly opened markets.

MIGA's Rates Relative to the Market

MIGA sometimes may play the role of a "market maker"—the facilitator or discoverer of risk-based prices—particularly in markets that are part of the agency's focus areas. However, sometimes a market price is already established. As any insurer will know, it would not be prudent to keep only one type of risk on a balance sheet or to focus a business line only on one particular geographic area or risk cover type. Thus, MIGA makes conscious efforts to maintain a well-diversified portfolio. Strategic pricing of insurance contracts may involve setting prices for some products to recover those products' costs and then generate sufficient premium income to help support other important deals, such as South-South investments. It should be noted that such decisions may stem not only from strategic considerations, but also from constraints resulting from the market's pricing practices.

A costing framework, therefore, needs to be flexible enough to accommodate considerations of differentiated return objectives and market conditions. Some projects will be expected to generate higher-than-average administrative expense recovery and produce enough premium income to make up for other projects priced with less than full administrative expense recovery. A risk-adjusted return on capital (RAROC) measure can be used to assess whether a project would be contributing a satisfactory return on capital targets. While a particular target return is the goal for the overall portfolio, this average return may not need to be achieved for each and every project; premium analysis for strategically important projects might suggest a rate yielding a below-average but still adequate RAROC.

Conclusion: MIGA's Attempt at Synthesis

As discussed above, the pricing decisions for PRI products comprise many complex and sometimes conflicting considerations, and it is safe to say that even a sophisticated model will not yield one single "correct" price for each individual project. The intuition and feel for the market of the underwriter need to be reconciled with costing results of the analytical models and with the strategic objectives articulated by management.

MIGA's approach is to use its analytical pricing framework to generate analytically derived premium rate ranges that provide a sound basis for risk differentiation in the rates quoted. The underwriter takes this information as the analytical underpinning of his or her negotiation with the client, and proposes any adjustments that are felt to be needed in light of the analyst's interpretation of current market conditions. Finally, when the project is discussed at MIGA's PRC, management has the opportunity to opine on the price and offer guidance with regard to strategic pricing considerations.

To help the underwriter in the pricing process and the pricing discussion with management at the PRC, the pricing team produces a pricing overview (see figure 6.4). The overview includes the calculated premium from the costing model (as either a point estimate or a range), information on any previous similar deals, and any pricing information from the reinsurance market. The objective is to put the calculated rate for cost recovery and risk in the context of market rates and comparables for possible adjustment. The project exposure retention analysis (discussed in the section on portfolio management) is also helpful, showing the sensitivity of the risk-based premium rates to the decision of how much to retain on MIGA's own books.

The RAROC measure is also helpful in interpreting the meaning of a range of premium rates; displayed on the right-hand axis in figure 6.4, the RAROC is produced by MIGA's models and indicates the expected impact on overall finances and return on capital at various points in a contemplated premium range.

In a "soft" market for foreign direct investment and project finance, where lending spreads are tight, less flexibility is available in pricing PRI covers. MIGA acknowledges this by monitoring spreads on current debt-financed deals in the relevant sector and country as well as current sovereign borrowing spreads. The state of these spreads will have an impact on the interpretation of the premium rate range from the costing model. To the extent this information is available, it is also included in the pricing overview chart.

The EC and costing models used by MIGA cannot capture all the nuances of the PRI market landscape (no model can do more than represent a simplified version of reality). However, the models have

FIGURE 6.4 EXAMPLE OF HYPOTHETICAL PRICING OVERVIEW

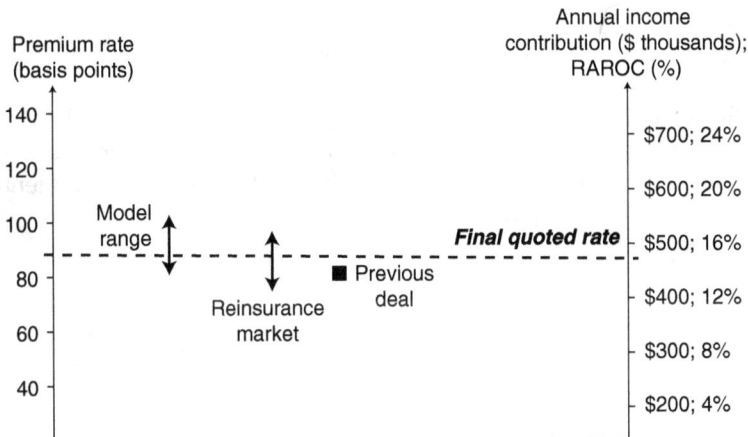

proven they can serve as important elements of a rigorous framework for risk measurement and management and make pricing fit into this larger context. The balance between market dynamics and analytics (or between "art" and "science") will continue to require constant assessment because markets evolve constantly. While they should not be blindly relied upon, EC-based models developed on sound principles provide stability, help point to important relative differences in the risks of market segments, and provide an anchor to the underwriter navigating a complex marketplace.

Notes

1. MIGA's framework for provisioning for reserves uses the same core economic capital model as for the calculation of the required size of its portfolio reserve. This ensures consistency of the risk measures used to manage and assess the adequacy of the various components on MIGA's balance sheet.

2. Measured as annual administrative expenses divided by annual net revenues.

3. Measured as annual claim payouts divided by annual net revenues.

References

Burton, F. N., and Hisashi Inoue. 1987. "A Country Risk Appraisal Model of Foreign Asset Expropriation in Developing Countries." *Applied Economics* 19 (8): 1009–48.

Collier, Paul, and Anke Hoeffler. 2000. "Greed and Grievance in Civil War." Policy Research Working Paper No. 2355, World Bank, Washington, DC.

Marrison, Chris. 2002. *The Fundamentals of Risk Measurement.* New York: McGraw-Hill.

Mulder, Christian, Roberto Perrelli, and Manuel Rocha. 2002. "The Role of Corporate, Legal and Macroeconomic Balance Sheet Indicators in Crisis Detection and Prevention." Working Paper No. 02/59, Intenational Monetary Fund, Washington, DC.

Issues Affecting Pricing in the Political Risk Insurance Market, and a Probabilistic Approach to Measuring Country Risk in a Political Risk Insurance Portfolio

Edward Coppola

This chapter addresses three related but somewhat distinct issues. First, it makes general observations about differences in the way public and private political risk insurers may approach the pricing of their products. It then links this topic to a discussion of an analytical foundation insurers could use to construct a probabilistic model to evaluate the risk in a global portfolio of political risk insurance (PRI) exposures. Finally, the chapter addresses the relevance of multicountry policies to the above topics.

Pricing Issues in the Political Risk Investment Insurance Market

Public insurers such as Export Development Canada, the Multilateral Investment Guarantee Agency (MIGA), and the Overseas Private Investment Corporation (OPIC) are authorized and funded directly by governments (and indirectly by taxpayers). They are,

Edward Coppola is Executive Vice President and Chief Underwriting Officer at Zurich Security, Credit and Risk.

therefore, accountable to the public in a number of ways. Public agencies such as these and other government-owned or -sponsored export credit agencies (ECAs) are typically held to very specific and sometimes rigid guidelines that reflect their public policy mandates (for example, environmental protection, support of small businesses). In addition, a certain level of disclosure is expected of public organizations with regard to their activities, processes, and pricing. Indeed, disclosure is in their interest to demonstrate that they are fulfilling their public service mandates.

Private PRI entities are accountable to the public as well but in somewhat different ways from public insurers. Although called private insurers to distinguish them from public (that is, government) agencies, private insurers are in many cases publicly traded. As such, they cannot ignore some of the issues that can preoccupy public insurers. Like any publicly traded company, private insurers want to sell products and services profitably and grow to increase value for their shareholders. But they also want to be good corporate citizens. For example, Zurich Financial Services launched in January 2008 a global climate change initiative to understand the emerging weather, financial, and regulatory risks associated with climate change, and to develop products and services that help customers cope with these risks. Thus, public and private insurers share some common high-level public service goals.

When it comes to pricing, however, the differences between public and private insurers become more apparent. Private PRI providers must tread carefully when participating in open pricing discussions so as not to run afoul of antitrust issues, not to mention corporate compliance guidelines related to disclosure. That statement identifies the first factor to consider when analyzing the differences between pricing in the public and private PRI markets. There is only so much a private insurer can say publicly about this subject. However, general observations can be made about the different factors that may affect private insurers' approach to pricing PRI.

Public PRI providers owned by single governments have as their primary goal the promotion of their own economies and business interests. They are, of course, also interested in helping to advance the cause of economic development in emerging markets. But that is a secondary consideration after their own internally directed goals. Therefore, they tend to measure their success by such factors as the amount of locally sourced trade and investment they have facilitated, the number of domestic jobs created, and the number of projects or transactions supported. It could be argued that multilateral organizations like MIGA are more focused on promoting global investment and economic development than are traditional ECAs, in part as a result of the dilution of individual country interests that comes with having a large and diverse base of stakeholders. Nonetheless, for both ECAs and multilateral insurers, the revenue produced from premiums, while important to ensuring their futures by procuring a reasonable return to their owners, is a secondary concern.

Private PRI providers, while seeking to provide valuable products and services, also seek to do so profitably. A key measure of any insurer's underwriting success is whether it is able to generate more income than it incurs in expenses and pays out in claims. This is referred to as the combined ratio, and if it is under 100 percent, the insurer has made a profit on its underwriting. Thus, premiums, and therefore pricing, are important to private PRI providers. Two additional factors that distinguish public and private PRI providers' approaches to pricing are that the private insurance market is decentralized in the United States, and highly regulated in the United States and in many other countries. Private insurers in different countries, and U.S. insurers that have filed their products with various state insurance regulators, are not unfettered in their product pricing.

The nature of PRI is such that underwriting and pricing the product often appears to involve a combination of art and science. It is true that an individual underwriter's experience and knowledge, policy drafting skills, as well as access to good information (the elements of the art), are important in underwriting PRI. But to underwrite PRI profitably, the private insurer must also have a sound approach to pricing. In the private insurance market, pricing is a key factor in the long-term success of the product. A prudent private insurance company will put a great number of resources into actuarial analysis, modeling, and monitoring of changes in prices over time (the science).

However, applying the science part of the pricing process to PRI is a challenge for a number of reasons, including limits on the amount of detailed information that PRI providers (and private PRI providers in particular) can disclose, especially information related to loss experience; the generally high-severity, low-frequency nature of PRI, which makes it difficult if not impracticable to perform a reliable actuarial-based analysis of loss experience; the heterogeneous nature of the product; and the role of recoveries and the insurer's recovery strategy—factors that do not apply to many traditional lines of insurance. But it would be wrong to suggest that private PRI providers do not have various tools and techniques available to them to price their products. Indeed, if those individuals in a company who are involved in overseeing the underwriting and risk management process are doing their jobs well, they will insist that underwriters have a structured approach to pricing. As with any other business, those tools and techniques must take into account such fundamentals as the product's capital intensity and acquisition cost. But for the reasons cited at the beginning of this paragraph, the tools and techniques they use will be proprietary and most likely produced internally based on each insurer's assessment of the key inputs into pricing PRI.

Does the importance to multilateral insurers and ECAs of promoting trade and investment relative to the importance of the profit motive to private PRI providers mean that pricing is of only minor significance to public insurers? Public insurers are indeed interested in making sure that their pricing processes result in at least enough revenue to cover their losses (and presumably their expenses as well); some ECAs operate under more commercial principles, while others try to compete with the private market on pricing. In addition, multilateral institutions such as MIGA use highly analytical and methodological approaches. It would appear, therefore, that pricing is not an insignificant issue for public PRI providers.

From Pricing to a Probabilistic Approach to Managing PRI Country Aggregates

The previous section suggests that one of the challenges in pricing PRI is the limited amount and the quality of publicly available information related to losses in the PRI market.[1] Such information could provide greater insights into frequency and severity, which are important considerations in any actuarial pricing model. Frequency and severity have implications not only for pricing, but also for how a PRI provider manages a large portfolio of country exposure. This management process is further complicated by single insurance policies that cover multiple investments in a number of countries.

A PRI provider can and likely will over time accumulate significant exposure in many countries. The generally low-frequency, high-severity potential of PRI might lead a casual observer to believe that the insurer is vulnerable to a catastrophic event or events with severe implications for its long-term viability. Such concern is generally greatly exaggerated, and the insurer's global aggregate exposure belies the much lower degree of "true" risk faced by the insurer. The challenge, then, is to portray the insurer's aggregate exposure in a way that more accurately reflects the true potential for losses across the portfolio. PRI providers could try to employ certain conventional insurance concepts in pursuit of this goal.

The concept of probable maximum loss (PML) is common in the insurance lexicon, and is most typically associated with property insurance. Reduced to its simplest definition, PML as used here is the maximum loss expected related to a set of insured assets as a result of defined events.[2] As the term suggests, probability is a key element in the determination of the PML for an insured risk or portfolio of risks. Probability could be very subjective, based on a firm's own experience and observations, or it could be based on an actuarial analysis using statistics and modeling usually more closely associated with automobile or natural catastrophe insurance.

Can a "scientific" approach to establishing PML be used to produce meaningful PML exposures for a book of PRI exposures? Most practitioners in the PRI business would argue that establishing an actuarial PML basis for evaluating (and for that matter, pricing) a portfolio of PRI risk is impracticable. We agree, and believe that even if such an effort were made, it would not produce results rigorous enough to draw meaningful conclusions that could be broadly applied.

First, the amount of publicly available information about loss history in the PRI market is limited, and much of what is available is short on details, making it difficult to draw definitive conclusions about the loss experience. Second, and related to the first reason, PRI, as a high-severity, low-frequency business, has not experienced enough losses over time to construct an actuarial pricing or PML model, even if all the necessary information were publicly available. Third, the PRI product is heterogeneous, covering a wide variety of exposures against a range of perils over potentially long periods using nonstandardized policy forms. Similarly, the circumstances surrounding PRI losses tend to be unique from one loss event to another. Moreover, the general nature of insured political risk events can change over long periods. So even if there were greater depth and detail to the loss history and that information was publicly available, it is still questionable whether any model attempting to price and determine the PML for a portfolio of political risk exposures would be useful. Fourth, recoveries are an important element in the long-term profitability of PRI, whereas generally no recoveries are made in the lines of insurance for which PML calculations are more commonly used. This adds another element of complexity to this exercise, since loss mitigation and recovery strategies can vary widely among PRI providers and produce dramatically different results.

If a more conventional approach to establishing PML figures for PRI is not likely to prove useful, is there another approach that could still achieve the goal of putting a PRI provider's exposures in a more realistic context and more accurately reflect its "true" exposure? As noted above, the lack of detailed public information about loss history, and the generally low-frequency, high-severity nature of the losses do not support an actuarial basis for pricing PRI or for establishing a reliable and transparent PML methodology. However, enough information is publicly available to support a probabilistic approach to measuring political risk exposures. MIGA has paid three claims over approximately 18 years. More significant is the experience of OPIC, which has published claims reports, annual reports, and other information about its experience over the 30-year period 1971–2000. This information yields highly relevant data about the principal perils that PRI covers (that is, expropriation, currency inconvertibility, political violence, and nonhonoring of sovereign debt obligations).

Although varying from year to year, OPIC's estimated "current exposure to claims"[3] averaged about $3.9 billion annually. Typically, such exposure under its expropriation coverage approximated this figure, exposure under currency inconvertibility coverage was somewhat less, and exposure under political violence coverage was substantially less. Claims settlements[4] and net losses after recoveries can be measured against these exposures, both for the entire period and on an annualized basis.

Expropriation. From 1971 through 2000, OPIC settled some $634 million in expropriation claims, of which $217 million was paid in 2000 in respect of infrastructure project expropriation claims in Indonesia. Until 2000, OPIC had attained 100 percent recovery on expropriation claims, and it negotiated a recovery arrangement with Indonesia for the claims in 2000 as well.

Thus, over the entire period, OPIC expropriation claims settlements totaled about 16 percent of its average current exposure to claims. This means that in an average year, OPIC's expropriation settlements were about one-half of 1 percent of its exposure, conservatively measured. Furthermore, even if OPIC had not made any recoveries on the Indonesia claims in 2000, its net losses would represent less than 6 percent of average exposure to expropriation claims over the entire period, and a trifling percentage on an annualized basis.

Currency inconvertibility. OPIC's inconvertibility claims experience over the period 1971–2000 yielded total settlements of $111 million, recoveries of $88 million (nearly 80 percent), and net losses of $23 million. Using the benchmark $3.9 billion mentioned above as a typical exposure level, gross settlements under this coverage would account for less than 3 percent of exposure for the entire period, and far less in any one year. A private insurer may not have access to the same channels of recovery that OPIC has had on such claims; nonetheless, some recovery is likely on any such claim, and some claims—for example, on loan payments where promissory notes rather than a depreciating currency can be used as salvage—can eventually yield 100 percent recovery. Where the insurer acquires blocked local currency in addition to the rights of the insured lender against the borrower, usually a variety of devices are available for disposing of the blocked currency in a way that yields some hard currency abroad. More likely, the blockage will come to an end, allowing the local currency to be exchanged for hard currency at a new and possibly less favorable exchange rate. While the insurer is at risk that a deep depreciation of the value of the currency could occur in the meantime, this is not necessarily the case, and the new exchange rate is certain to produce some recovery.

Political violence. OPIC's experience with political violence coverage reflects a pattern of small losses accumulating to extremely modest amounts overall, with little recovery. Political violence coverage has always accounted for a much smaller portion of OPIC's outstanding liabilities than either expropriation or inconvertibility, but even if each of those accounted for only one-third of the benchmark $3.9 billion figure, OPIC's aggregate political violence settlements of $30 million (from which there have been virtually no recoveries) would constitute less than 3 percent of corresponding exposure over the entire 30-year period, and an extremely small percentage on an annualized basis.

Nonhonoring of sovereign debt. OPIC does not provide coverage for straightforward nonhonoring of direct cross-border sovereign credits as a separate and discrete peril in the fashion provided by private insurers. That and the lack of detailed public information about the loss experience of the private PRI market with this product make it more difficult to draw the kinds of conclusions identified above. (This product is relatively new in the private PRI market compared with the more traditional perils already discussed). Nonetheless, some parallels could be drawn between inconvertibility coverage and nonhonoring coverage, the most important of which is the high like-lihood of significant recoveries. Certain anecdotal information supports this conclusion. Zurich Surety, Credit and Political Risk has published details regarding 19 nonhonoring claims it paid in 2004 and 2005 related to a sovereign default in the Dominican Republic. In this case, full recoveries are anticipated under the government of the Dominican Republic's formal rescheduling of this debt. The principal factor that could undermine the application of a probabilistic approach to evaluating nonhonoring exposures are reschedulings that entail a haircut on principal or interest or both. The history of Paris Club reschedulings confirms that such haircuts can take place. A more thorough analysis of the experience of sovereign debt reschedulings, including haircuts, would be a valuable step in a process for establishing a probabilistic approach to nonhonoring exposures in the private PRI market.

Of course a great deal of public information is available about the history of sovereign defaults that could be used as the basis for determining something closer to a PML analysis of a portfolio of nonhonoring exposures. But some of the same factors cited earlier related to the unique nature of PRI insurance and PRI policies would still have to be taken into account.

Single-country catastrophic events. Notwithstanding the extraordinary results attained by OPIC and MIGA, and indications that private insurers have also fared well, the possibility of a disastrous situation arising in a single country still must be considered. The historical record might be instructive if such single-country disasters could be investigated. But instances approaching that standard in the last 50 years are not easily found. In fact, it is difficult to identify a case, following Cuba's fall to Castro, where insurable events have resulted in devastating consequences, unredeemed by significant recoveries, to most existing foreign investment. The ascendancy of leftist regimes in the República Bolivariana de Venezuela and Bolivia and concerns about the Russian Federation government's designs on strategically sensitive sectors of the economy have revived the notion that classical expropriations of the type that were common in the 1960s and 1970s could occur again. But even in the three countries mentioned, expropriations have been limited, selective, and targeted, and in República Bolivariana de Venezuela, they have been largely compensated for by the government.

OPIC's results averaged across all countries might, in theory, mask less favorable results for individual countries, but this seems not to have been the case. In situations in which a country produced major problems of one kind or another for investors, OPIC settlements before recoveries following the onset of the problems in the country fell short, and often very far short, of OPIC's outstanding exposures at the outset of the problems. This suggests that severe events with the potential for causing losses did not persist in the country.

Following the government's expropriations after its revolution in 1979, the Islamic Republic of Iran came to a settlement of most of its disputes with investors, probably as a result of international economic and political pressure, and to some extent simply to restore vital international economic ties. Of interest is the fact that not all OPIC-insured U.S. investors pursued claims, which suggests that either they had other ways of offsetting their losses, or they came to satisfactory terms with the Iranian government without involving their insurer. OPIC's expropriation claims payments (excluding recoveries) in Islamic Republic of Iran totaled approximately 30 percent of its maximum expropriation exposure at the onset of the revolution.

Most countries that receive significant foreign direct investment, but that fall into exchange difficulties resulting in currency inconvertibility, endeavor to work themselves out of those situations out of economic self-interest, rather than accepting the constraints that the marketplace imposes on countries that do not. As with expropriation exposures, claims settlements for currency inconvertibility were significantly less than exposure at the outset. Available data on OPIC's inconvertibility claims and exposures per country suggest that episodes of currency blockage generally produced claims payments of less than 10 percent of exposure levels prevailing at the onset of the events, except in a few cases where one or a handful of policies accounted for the bulk of the exposure.

Insufficient data on OPIC per county political violence exposure levels, and too few aggregate claims in relation to exposures overall, prevent firm conclusions from being drawn about the likelihood of large losses in relation to exposure. The bulk of such claims payments arose in three Sub-Saharan African countries afflicted with persistent armed conflict. Experience suggests that, absent any catastrophic events of the kind normally excluded from PRI policies (nuclear events, for instance), and absent prolonged, organized warfare, where exposures are reasonably dispersed and unrelated, political violence losses are unlikely to be sustained universally.

The question still arises of whether OPIC's or MIGA's claims and loss experience could be used as the basis for a reliable probabilistic analysis of a private PRI provider's portfolio. Put another way, can a private insurer's loss experience be expected to produce results

similar to those of two government-owned agencies with public sector mandates and the ability to harness the potentially significant
influence of the U.S. government and any special intergovernment
agreements in the case of OPIC, or the powers of persuasion that are
available to the World Bank Group (of which MIGA is a part) over
a member country?

It is true that because they are governmental agencies OPIC and
MIGA represent a different segment of the PRI market than private
PRI providers, and that their involvement in a project can carry a
certain deterrent effect against actions by a host government that
could otherwise lead to a loss under a PRI policy. On this basis it
could be argued that their claims history should not be used as a
proxy for a private insurer's effort to construct a probabilistic
approach to analyzing its portfolio. However, this argument over-
looks a number of factors that justify a closer alignment of a private
insurer's loss experience with that of OPIC and MIGA.

First, deterrence does not necessarily play a significant role in the
settlement of all investment disputes. And when necessary, private
PRI providers can themselves harness significant resources to mitigate a potential loss before it occurs, and to recover a loss after paying a claim. A major multinational insurance company that provides
PRI and trade credit insurance (for example, Zurich Financial Services) with a significant economic presence in many markets can be
a deterrent to malfeasance by a host government and play a significant role in the recovery of a claim. Many companies and banks will
make investments and loans only if they can procure PRI. By mis-
treating the insurer's customer and facilitating a claim against the
insurer, that government could make it more expensive if not
impractical for the insurer to continue insuring trade and investment
in that country. This is no small penalty for a poor country that is
dependent on external trade and foreign investment. In addition,
the insurer may be able and willing to put its own resources to work
to support customers encountering difficulties, and in the event it
has to pay a claim, to recover the loss. Zurich already has a successful track record in intervening on behalf of its customers to resolve
problems and recover losses. When appropriate and potentially
effective, the insurer can also call upon the U.S. government to assist
the insurer in its efforts to manage challenging situations.

Second, the advent of close cooperation between the public and
private PRI market, as explained in Joanne Palmer's work (chapter
8 in this volume), and the expansion of the Berne Union to include
private PRI providers, have further enhanced the credibility and

influence of private PRI providers while making the Berne Union an even more dynamic and influential organization.

Third, governments and multilateral organizations have only limited influence on certain kinds of political risk events (for example, political violence).

In sum, while the role of ECAs and organizations like OPIC and MIGA can add an element of deterrence in a project, major players in the private PRI market, too, can bring to bear significant capabilities in dealing with the same kinds of problem situations that entities like OPIC and MIGA are believed to deter.

Enter Global PRI Policies

An issue raised at the Fifth Biennial MIGA-Georgetown Symposium in November 2006 was an expectation that multicountry or global policies would become more prevalent.[5] Zurich's experience is that this has indeed been the case, and it is attributed to several factors. First, the overall heightened perception of risk and uncertainty in the global environment has raised the profile and value of PRI among risk managers and other users of the product. Some companies that may have not used PRI at all or used it only selectively in certain countries are now more inclined to use it on a broader basis. Second, concerns about the potential for risks in one country or market to have ancillary or spillover impacts in other countries or markets in which the company also has exposures makes trying to pick and choose where to insure a much more difficult and riskier proposition. Third, companies are inclined to view buying global policies as more cost effective than purchasing coverage for individual projects or countries. Whether this is the case, however, is a function of many factors that can vary depending on the insured's specific exposure profile.

From an insurer's perspective, global policies pose their own challenges, the most significant of which relates to the accumulation of country exposure. Most global policies provide an overall policy limit significantly lower than the sum of all of the insured's global exposures. The obvious reason for this is that the insured does not expect to suffer catastrophic losses in all the insured countries. The insured may, for example, select a policy limit equivalent to the highest single country exposure in the portfolio. A loss of something less than that would still leave the insured with coverage left over to cover other losses in that country or elsewhere in the portfolio. A more risk-averse customer may elect a policy limit that covers its maximum exposures in more than one country. In some cases, the insured's guiding principle may be as much a function of its premium budget as its actual exposures or best estimate of likely losses.

A prudent insurer will have maximum country limits up to which it can underwrite exposures in those countries. When issuing a global policy in which the sum of the underlying exposures is substantially higher than the policy limit, the question for the underwriter becomes how to allocate the policy limit to its country limits without knowing where the losses will occur. The most conservative approach would be to allocate to each country the actual exposure in each country as reported by the insured. For example, with a policy limit of $100 million and underlying exposures of $50 million in each of five countries, the underwriter would block $50 million in each of the five countries in its portfolio. In other words, the underwriter has used up $250 million of country limit across five countries even though the most it could pay out over the life of the policy is $100 million. This creates a significant amount of redundancy in the insurer's portfolio and is clearly not as efficient a use of country capacity as insuring each underlying project individually. Unless the insurer chooses not to insure global policies and instead reserve capacity only for individual projects, the insurer would be well advised to explore ways to reduce or eliminate the redundancy associated with global policies without compromising the integrity of its portfolio management methods.

Conclusion

Public and private PRI providers function in very different operating environments. Public insurers must fulfill certain public policy goals while charging a reasonable price for their products. Those prices must be sufficiently attractive to draw enough business to demonstrate that the insurer is adequately addressing its mandate. The Organisation for Economic Co-operation and Development (OECD) Consensus establishes some boundaries to ensure that pricing by public insurers is not "a race to the bottom." The OECD Consensus can also shield public insurers from the suggestion that they compete unfairly with the private market. Like public insurers, private insurers have a public face and view being a good corporate citizen as an important to their success. But private insurers also have as one of their driving forces the maximization of shareholder value.

This cannot help but make pricing a key factor in their business models. The private market is also highly regulated, especially in the United States; thus, having a structured and disciplined approach to pricing takes on added significance. Furthermore, the generally cyclical nature of the insurance business, and to a much lesser extent of the PRI market, makes it necessary for private insurers to be able to adapt their pricing to changing market conditions.

The obstacles to creating a purely actuarial pricing model for PRI create the room for the "art" in the "art versus science" debate about how to price PRI. For the success of a product like PRI, there is no substitute for experience and access to information. While invaluable, these factors alone cannot sustain the long-term profitability of PRI without a sound approach to pricing the product. While public PRI providers must take into account the political environment in which they operate, private PRI providers must take into account the corporate environment in which they operate, which means having a structured approach to pricing that will ensure they are contributing to the financial success of the company of which they are a part.

Some of the factors that go into pricing PRI are also relevant to how PRI providers manage their country accumulations. Frequency and severity are important building blocks in attempting to build any insurance pricing model. But while it is a daunting task to apply those concepts in building a PRI pricing model that can reliably predict losses, these concepts as they apply to PRI are useful in evaluating the magnitude of risk on a PRI provider's books. OPIC's and MIGA's loss and claims experience may be helpful in this process. The limited number of claims paid by MIGA could be interpreted as establishing a case that its participation in a transaction adds a meaningful degree of deterrence in an insured project. OPIC's more extensive claims history and its superior record on recoveries also suggests that it too can bring measurable value to a transaction.

However, it would be going too far to conclude that simply being government-owned entities explains their historical performance. Political risk insurance is a heterogeneous product subject to the effects of a myriad of variables on a long-term basis in the dynamic arena of emerging markets. It is a common refrain in the PRI industry that no two transactions are alike. A product like this requires that a serious and successful PRI provider devote the resources and expertise necessary to write long-term PRI successfully. Those private insurers that are able to harness those capabilities can achieve results good enough to allow them to use the loss experience of public insurers like OPIC and MIGA as a reasonable basis for measuring and evaluating their country exposures.

Notes

1. The author wishes to acknowledge the work of Felton McL. Johnston in analyzing OPIC's claims history, which is discussed in this section.

2. Probable expected loss is another term used to refer to this concept.

3. This number represents OPIC's entire exposure to claims arising in each year, rather than its total exposure to claims under all policies outstanding in each year. The latter figure would include committed coverage amounts that could only be used in future years.

4. A substantial portion of OPIC's claims have been settled by issuing OPIC guaranties of payment in lieu of cash. The term "claim settlements" includes both cash payments and the amounts of such guaranties.

5. The term "global polices" could mean single policies covering a very large number of investments in many countries, or a relatively small number of investments in a small number of countries. But in all cases it refers to single policies covering more than one investment in more than one country.

Public Sector Pricing:
How to Balance a Public Mandate with
Adequate Returns for Political Risk

Joanne Palmer

The world is currently experiencing the most serious credit crisis in a century, and adequately pricing political risks has become considerably more difficult. Even without this new volatility, the world of political risk insurance (PRI) has unique pricing challenges. Moreover, public sector insurers have a range of mandate perspectives, which can result in distinctive pressures on pricing practices. Most public sector insurers operate alone, but increasing cooperation with private insurers can affect their pricing. These partnerships can affect pricing in both directions This chapter assesses the way in which a public sector mandate affects the pricing practices of public insurers, describes some of the technical challenges that all insurers face as they try to properly price complex political risks, shows how some public insurers have approached these issues, and finally examines the effects of increased public sector cooperation with private insurers.

Joanne Palmer is Director, Political Risk Insurance, for Export Development Canada.

Public Sector Drivers

Without exception, public sector providers of PRI are mandated to foster international investment and trade. In many cases, this is an evolving role, especially in this troubled financial market, but the principal focus on supporting investors and exporters by providing specialized insurance remains the same. This is true whether describing export credit agencies, the U.S. Overseas Private Investment Corporation (OPIC), or multilateral agencies. Within this sphere are a number of differences with respect to mandate focus, use of commercial principles, and perspectives on the role of public agencies as compared with that of private sector providers. These factors do result in different pricing outcomes, though in the end, not to as dramatic a degree as might be expected. Nor does there appear to be a huge difference in pricing outcomes between public and private providers.

The public sector's mandate distinguishes it from the private sector primarily in that it is much more important for public institutions to support the growth of cross-border investment and exports than to maximize revenue from the insurance provided. In theory, this would be expected to result in extremely low premiums and a complete disregard for balancing revenue against future claims. Although such an approach might be popular with the exporters and investors the agencies want to support, contrasting pressure is exerted by the agencies' other stakeholders. Most taxpayers and government owners, or member countries for a multilateral, want to ensure that the agency is pricing adequately for the risk undertaken and not burdening government coffers. While profit is not the driving force and excessive profits are not seen to be within a public service mandate, public insurers are expected to develop sound principles for adequately pricing the political risks they insure. As a result, public agencies are as interested as the private sector in getting it right: charging low enough rates that the insurance is affordable while earning enough to cover losses covered by their policies.

Other underlying objectives of a public sector entity can be reflected in pricing. The most common one is support for small business, with a number of agencies offering preferential rates. The usual approach is to take the normal premium range and slash it across the board by a set proportion (such as the 30 percent discount offered by Export Development Canada [EDC]). These practices are intended to grow this mandate-rich segment of international trade and investment while still maintaining adequate pricing for risk on smaller exposures.

A number of public sector agencies pride themselves on operating with commercial principles and make an attempt to be more responsive to commercial market factors in pricing insurance risk. They try to include economic factors such as government bond spreads and also try to incorporate what is known of private market pricing. EDC and the Export and Finance Insurance Corporation (EFIC) of Australia are vocal examples of agencies that believe it important to adopt a commercially sound approach to pricing risk. Nonetheless, both agencies are tempered by their public mandates and try not to disadvantage their own exporters and investors against competition supported by other official agencies with different approaches.

A potentially important differentiator among public sector providers is the insurer of last resort perspective. At one end of the spectrum are agencies like OPIC for which this is a significant requirement, such that the applicant for coverage must prove the insurance requested is not available from the private sector. Other agencies see themselves more in a gap-filling role, providing stable capacity, but assuming that sustainability of that capacity is predicated upon a more favorable mix of business than just last resort insurance. These agencies will quote prices to brokers and customers potentially in direct competition against private sector providers. In these circumstances, public sector providers must have defensible commercial principles backing up the pricing quoted. Otherwise, the public insurer is vulnerable to claims that it is using its resources as a public sector entity to displace private sector insurers, an allegation not welcomed by most public sector entities.

So in the end, an agency's public sector mandate adds a layer of complexity to the somewhat daunting prospect of trying to properly price political risks. The public insurer must not charge too much or it will not be successful in promoting international investment and trade, and will be criticized for making excessive profits. At the same time, it must not charge too little or it will be a burden on governments and may be seen to be crowding out the private sector.

Technical Challenges of Pricing Political Risk Insurance

Contributing greatly to the challenge of establishing the right premium is the complexity of the PRI product. Much classic PRI covers risk events (expropriation, political violence, and currency inconvertibility) that fit poorly into the mainstream actuarial models of the insurance world, leading to the allegations that pricing political risk is more art than science. In truth, however, most insurers, both public and private, have adequate models from which they derive risk-related premiums that, in turn, more than cover the claims that they pay.

While the risk covered is more straightforward in the case of sovereign and subsovereign nonpayment risk than it is with classic PRI, and there is greater confidence in assessing the probability of default, finding appropriate benchmarks for pricing this type of insurance can be challenging, too.

Many types of actuarial models do not work easily for classic PRI because it is difficult to model events that are catastrophic and happen infrequently; that is, the limited history of covered events lessens predictability. Even in the last few years, with almost weekly occurrences of political violence, government leaders threatening expropriations, or other political events potentially covered by PRI, no single insurer has paid a significant body of claims. This makes it challenging for an individual insurer to derive the basis of an actuarial model of risk. OPIC, as the only insurer with an extensive history of published claims experience, is an important source of data. OPIC's data have been incorporated by a number of other insurers, such as the Multilateral Investment Guarantee Agency (MIGA) and Zurich, into their own in-house models.

Adding to the lack of frequency of risk events, the fact that PRI policies commonly have durations as long as 15 years makes the prediction of future events that much more challenging. In addition, the risks covered under a single policy have varying, often unrelated, causes adding again to the complexity of assigning the right probability of occurrence. Within the same policy the insurer can be covering various acts by the government and different parties, and losses can range from fractional to total. A common tendency is to price the worst scenario and add to that a discounted portion of premium for the other risks.

Notwithstanding the difficulties in correctly predicting loss, most public and private insurers base their premium quotes on an assessment of the probabilities of the various political risk events occurring, many derived from in-house models that incorporate various country, sector, and transaction-related parameters.

Another factor making pricing difficult is the lack of adequate benchmarks for PRI premiums, beyond the logic that they should be less than a bank would charge for full commercial and political risk if lending to the foreign entity. Benchmarks for the sovereign nonpayment cover are more readily available. Many private sector insurers use bond spreads or other evidence of previous borrowings by the government and charge a portion of that spread. The credit default swap market has been used in the past, but those rates tend to be volatile and often shorter in tenor than the tenor of proposed coverage. As noted below, most public sector insurers refer to the Organisation for Economic Co-operation and Development (OECD) minimum premiums, a readily available benchmark, but one that is not updated frequently enough to reflect prevailing economic conditions.

The recent rise in global or multicountry policies has resulted in clients requiring a substantial discount factor over what would have been charged when separately pricing and charging for coverage of each investment. Under current practice, a portfolio of investments in various countries is placed under one policy limit to which the premium is applied. Various approaches to weighting and addressing the variable risks of each country are applied by insurers. At best, the insurer tries to be compensated for the worst risk in the portfolio and tries not to add in too much additional risk for the minimal additional premium policyholders are willing to pay.

For private sector insurers, country capacity superimposes itself heavily over straight risk-based calculations of premiums, and adds significant volatility to pricing. It is common for insurers to experience high demand in the same markets, making capacity for future business tight and causing premiums to skyrocket in those markets. In addition, rates for classic PRI will rise in a market where banks have required sovereign nonpayment cover from PRI providers. Sovereign nonpayment cover often requires significantly higher rates than those normally charged for classic PRI, and in such cases, a private sector insurer will tend to price classic PRI higher than it would normally on a risk-alone basis. Government insurers usually have more expansive country capacity and, even when they do not, tend not to demand higher prices for tight country constraints. This is the single biggest differentiator in pricing practices between public and private sector PRI providers.

The competitive lending environment affects both private and public insurers in their insurance of loans. All insurers have had to accommodate the tightening spreads of the bank clients they cover. Very simply, if the banks are charging X for comprehensive risk, then no matter what their risk models indicate, political risk insurers must charge less than X for covering only a portion of the associated risk. Furthermore, the increasingly soft PRI industry, with its rapid growth in capacity, has put significant downward pressure on premiums charged by private sector insurers, which can also affect some public sector insurers' views of the right price to charge.

In addition to a potential claim payment, the policyholder's premium is also paying for the partnership in loss mitigation. Both public and private sector insurers can play an important role in preclaim advocacy on the policyholder's behalf. To the detriment of insurers, this type of potential help is rarely incorporated into the price.

Overall, there are a number of risk factors that are difficult to assess but form the basis of premium quotes, and then a number of other factors, such as the structure of policies, the competitive environment, and country capacity, that can play a substantial role. All together these add an element of truth to the assessment that a certain amount of "art" is required in the pricing of these complex risks by insurers.

Public Sector Approaches to Pricing PRI

Methods of pricing classic PRI by public sector insurers vary greatly, with one common factor. All agencies make an attempt to base their pricing on perceptions of the associated risk. Even PWC of Germany's one standard price for expropriation risk is based on an assumption that the presence of a bilateral investment treaty between the host government and Germany makes the risk uniform. What are not the same among the agencies are which differentials are considered most important and the benchmarks used.

A summary of the pricing methodologies of a wide range of export credit agencies and MIGA and OPIC is presented in the annex 8A to this chapter.

Public insurers' approaches to coming up with the actual premiums for the classic risks of expropriation, political violence, and inconvertibility vary widely. Most public insurers use country differentials, commonly basing the price on the OECD country classification minimum premiums, with some adjustments. Examples of agencies using this approach include OKB (Österreichische Kontrollbank Aktiengesellschaft, Austria), EKN (Exportkreditnämnden, Sweden), Atradius, COFACE, and EGAP (the Czech Export Finance and Insurance Corporation). Some have developed their own in-house risk models and some use benchmarks like the credit default swap market (for example, SACE Group, Italy).

OPIC takes the sector route, with different basic rates for each risk in sectors such as oil and gas, infrastructure, and manufacturing, then taking into account the country factor. SID has a similar approach.

In addition to sector and country considerations, many public insurers then adjust the pricing further by factors specific to the transaction. For example, Compania Espanola de Seguros de Credito a la Exportación (CESCE) differentiates between investments based on government concessions and other private investments, and looks at the experience of the investor and other project-level risks. Atradius charges more for projects in excess of €50 million. Compagnie Française d'Assurance (COFACE), Companhia de Seguro de Créditos, SA (COSEC), and Export Credit Guarantee Corporation of India Ltd. (ECGC), are a few of the many agencies that take project-level considerations into account when finalizing their pricing.

In addition to these varied approaches to pricing for risk, public insurers also differ greatly in the extent to which they want to apply commercial principles to their pricing. The Export Finance and Insurance Corporation (EFIC), Garanti-Instituttet for Eksportkreditt (GIEK), Exim Bank of Malaysia BHD (MEXIM), and Export Development Canada (EDC) all take private sector pricing—to the extent to which it is known—into account in their pricing of political risk.

Many export credit agencies do not allow selection of risks covered. Public insurers such as OPIC and EDC, which do allow for selection of risks, may offer a multiple risk discount. In EDC's case, for example, this discount is as much as 30 percent for three risks and 10–20 percent for two risks. Such discounts definitely accrue to the benefit of the customer; there is certainly no risk basis for charging less in return for adding more risk.

Public insurers may also vary in their approaches to minimum premium revenue. Rather than being risk related, this is a fee charged in return for the trouble of putting the policy in place. Many public insurers do not charge one, or charge one only on an exceptional basis, or charge a nominal application fee instead. Those that do tend to limit it to a portion of the premium that would have been charged over the first three years or fewer of a policy (for example, MIGA charges 50 percent of three years of premium and CESCE charges 15 percent).

All these practices result in divergent pricing ranges for coverage of classic political risks. For example, OPIC's published pricing range, depending on sector, for expropriation alone is 40 to 85 basis points and CESCE's is 15 to 50 basis points. Atradius's range for investments up to €50 million is 65 to 110 basis points for all three risks, whereas PWC charges 50 basis points. While there is some variance, in the end, the average premiums charged by ECAs are not substantially different from one another.

Far more uniform are the practices associated with pricing of sovereign and subsovereign nonpayment risk. Save for OPIC, most of this cover offered by the public sector supports exports rather than investments. Most export credit agencies use the OECD framework of minimum premiums, not only as a guideline for minimum pricing, but for actual pricing as well. The agencies will price at the minimum rates for sovereign risk and might add an increment if the obligor is not fully sovereign. Some, such as EDC and EFIC, will attempt to substitute pricing that is more reflective of market factors such as current government bond spreads, and of private sector pricing trends but will match OECD pricing if more commercially based pricing will put their exporters at a disadvantage.

Though they do charge more as risk increases, public sector insurers generally do not significantly increase the price of their insurance as they reach country limits or other capacity constraints. Instead, they may be more selective of the business they accept. This is a notable difference from private sector practices and stems from the public sector mandate, which takes precedence over maximization of revenue. Thus, much more stable pricing tends to be available from the public sector in markets where the private sector has been very active.

Public-Private Sector Cooperation

The increase over the last decade in public sector cooperation with private sector political risk insurers has likely had an effect on pricing, especially when a public sector insurer is reinsuring in the private sector.

MIGA, for example, often reinsures on a facultative basis. MIGA usually sets a premium rate for a transaction, and then offers the opportunity to the private sector to reinsure at that rate. If the rate is lower than that normally charged by a private sector insurer, the insurer must decide if the proposed rate is acceptable, either because having MIGA front the policy potentially helps lessen the risk or the business is desirable for other reasons and warrants a drop in the rate. EDC also reinsures in the private sector and has had similar experiences. EDC sometimes faces circumstances that require rein-surance but find that such support is only available at a higher rate than EDC wants to charge. In those cases, one option is to structure the policy with a policy premium rate of two different premium rates, combined so that the policyholder gets the benefit of the EDC rate for part of the liability. This would especially be done in situations in which EDC needs the reinsurance and is supporting an investor or exporter who is facing competition. At other times, EDC may reconsider the basis of its pricing if it seems to be consistently pricing lower than the private market, especially if associated risks have risen, because it is not EDC's objective to displace private market insurers on the basis of price.

As noted, the most common reason for a dramatic discrepancy between public sector and private sector insurers' premium rates is country capacity constraints. In these circumstances public-private sector cooperation would have little effect on pricing. A private sector insurer with limited capacity will find it more important to preserve the earning power of scarce country liability and will decline the opportunity to reinsure at a lower price; nor in such circumstances are public sector insurers likely to significantly raise their premiums.

Though hard to quantify, given that pricing is so often held in confidence, public-private sector cooperation does appear to be playing at least a minor role in lowering prices available to policyholders.

Conclusion

Public sector insurers have distinct mandates from those of private insurers, yet in the end they are both pricing to risk, and no huge differences appear to arise in pricing outcomes. In fact, increased cooperation between private and public insurers may be resulting in more closely aligned premiums—to the benefit of the policyholder—through its contribution to a downward trend on both sides. The exception occurs when country capacity is scarce; then public insurers may play an important role in providing more stable and predictable pricing.

What is common to all political risk insurers, public or private, is that adequately pricing this complex product is a major challenge—and this challenge is not going to get easier in these turbulent times.

ANNEX 8A   CLASSIC PRI PRICING APPROACHES BY PUBLIC SECTOR INVESTMENT INSURANCE PROVIDERS

Insurer	Country Differentials	Sector Differentials	Other Factors	Selection of Risks	Minimum Premium Revenue
Atradius	OECD country classification system is used as a basis for transfer risk. The political risk service group provides ratings for expropriation and war risk.		Charges more for projects in excess of €50 million.		Minimum premiums of three years for equity and four years for debt.
CESCE	OECD country classification system is used as a basis for transfer risk for debt cover. Transfer risk for equity is on an annual percentage rate.	Analyzes expropriation, political violence, and breach of contract on a project basis, and assigns one of three risk categories. Process is then to use a matrix of premiums reflecting these categories.	Differentiates between investments based on government concessions and the other private investments and looks at the experience of the investor and other project-level risks.	Yes	Charges 15 percent.
COFACE	OECD country classification system is used as a basis with seven categories for nontransfer risk and five categories for expropriation and political violence risk.	Yes	Characteristics of the project: the rating of the project established by an internal model, the sector, geographical location of the project, and ability of the		No

Insurer	Country Differentials	Sector Differentials	Other Factors	Selection of Risks	Minimum Premium Revenue
COSEC	Developed in-house risk analysis on the basis of the risks covered and country risk classification (five categories of country risks).		Consideration also given to the sustainability of the project and its importance to the development of the host country together with the experience of the investors with such investments.	Yes	No
ECGC	Country risk is considered together with transactional considerations.		Factors considered include: country risk perception, investment size, investment policies in the country, status of the investor, techno-economic feasibility study of the project, period and terms of repatriation, past experience, and BU experience.		No

ANNEX 8A CONTINUED

Insurer	Country Differentials	Sector Differentials	Other Factors	Selection of Risks	Minimum Premium Revenue
ECGD			Develop in-house risk assessments on all markets. Assessment base on own market and claim experience combined to calculate an expected loss, which is in turn translated into a price that covers risks and costs.		No
ECIC SA	Based on internal sovereign ratings and term of cover.				No
EDC	Developed in-house model that uses a number of external indicators. Each risk (expropriation, political violence, transfer, and conversion) is separately rated in each country for the premium quote.	Sector differences taken into consideration at transaction level. Preferential pricing for small equity or asset coverage.	Country-level pricing modified with consideration for sector, geographical location of the project, ability of the investor, and tenor. Market pricing also considered.	Yes, allows for selection of risk (10 to 30% discount for fewer than three risks).	Minimum fee equivalent to one to three years' premium.

Insurer	Country Differentials	Sector Differentials	Other Factors	Selection of Risks	Minimum Premium Revenue
EFIC	Considers CDS as one of a few proxy benchmarks, not the sole instrument.		Benchmarks to private sector pricing (Lloyd's market) and other partner insurers.		Incorporates a "Policy Fee," which is difference between mutually agreed-on cancellation fees and the premium and stand-by fees already received.
EGAP	Published rates, uses the OECD risk categorization of countries, and then aligns category with a specific premium rate.	No	For simplicity and transparency, no adjustments are made for sector, size of transaction, or any specific political factors. Specific surcharge is only for a BoC risk.	Allows for selection of risk.	Minimum fee equivalent to three years' premium. If not paid, a charge fee for the reservation of insurance funds for a max. amount of €1,200.
EKF	Developed in-house model based on a number of external benchmarks.	Yes	Adjustments for transaction-specific factors.		Minimum premiums of three years.
EKN	OECD country classification premium used.				No

ANNEX 8A CONTINUED

Insurer	Country Differentials	Sector Differentials	Other Factors	Selection of Risks	Minimum Premium Revenue
FINNVERA			Limited exposure to political risk insurance; therefore pricing on a case by case risk assessment.		Minimum premiums of three years.
GIEK			Approach is based on own experience and knowledge combined with market pricing.		Case-by-case basis if canceled before minimum three-year policy period.
KEIC	OECD country classification premium used.				No
MEXIM			Standard rates in combination with market rates as benchmarks.		Yes if canceled before minimum three-year policy period.

Insurer	Country Differentials	Sector Differentials	Other Factors	Selection of Risks	Minimum Premium Revenue
MIGA	Developed in-house model based on a number of external benchmarks.		Pricing is based on a "cost plus" approach whereby the premium model allocates administrative expense and risk cost to the project under consideration. The premium rates are determined by the model output together with estimates of market rates which can further pricing.		If canceled before three years, a penalty equal to 50% of the premium for the three years is charged.
NEXI	Claim history basis.		CDS as a general reference but not directly reflected because the scope of political risk covered by CDS is substantially different from that covered by investment insurance.		Do not accept cancellation other than in case of extinction of covered rights or interest.

ANNEX 8A CONTINUED

Insurer	Country Differentials	Sector Differentials	Other Factors	Selection of Risks	Minimum Premium Revenue
OEKB	OECD country classification system is used as a basis for pricing; however, note that premium rates are lower than the OECD benchmarks.				No with exception of case by case with a minimum policy retention premium of two–three years.
ONDD	Premium rates are based on an in-house model which uses seven risk categories for the three standard political risks in addition to various other factors.				Minimum premiums of three years.
PWC	50 basis points across all countries. Case-by-case for high-risk countries. One rate pricing structure possible because of a wide network of bilateral investment treaties enabling different country risks to become comparable treaty risks.	No	No		A one-year minimum premium.

Insurer	Country Differentials	Sector Differentials	Other Factors	Selection of Risks	Minimum Premium Revenue
SACE	Premium is based on CDS markets. For each country and tenor, a sovereign CDS is taken and adjustments are applied in order to take into account sector, size, and specific political risk factors.			Yes	
SID		Premium rates are based on sectors. For each sector and for each risk covered, there are premium rates for current and for the standby amount of cover.		Yes	Minimum premiums of three years.
SINOSURE	Developed in-house premium table, which is divided by country category and covered risks.	Yes	Consideration of sector, local partners, and experience of investor could adjust base rates.		A minimum premium of three years, which is defined as the initial policy period.

Sources: Direct and published information.
Note: CDS = Credit default swap. Information is accurate to the extent of the author's knowledge of pricing practices at the time of publication.

Expropriation and the Share Pledge Dilemma: An Assessment of Individual Rights and Compensation Claims

Srilal M. Perera

A continuing dilemma in project finance concerns the retention of a pledge on shares by lenders to a project company in a host country. Problems arise when the equity investors in the project company seek to make a claim under political risk insurance (PRI) coverage against a host government's expropriation of the project company. Investors, lenders, and political risk insurers alike have been affected by the lack of effective solutions to the consequent issues. The pledge itself is a legitimate form of security, which lenders take in many routine commercial financings involving lending. However, what seems to be commonplace, routine, and legally acceptable from a commercial perspective takes on an entirely different dimension in the face of an act of expropriation by a host government of the equity investor's ownership rights in the project company.

The problem can be described in the following manner: Owners of a project company incorporated in a host country seek to finance the project with equity and debt. The normal financial structure of a

Srilal M. Perera is Chief Counsel/Advisor of MIGA. The opinions and conclusions expressed here are entirely his own and are not those of the Multilateral Investment Guarantee Agency.

project involves equity provided by shareholders of the project company and debt financing (loans) provided by commercial lenders. In such a structure, the lenders providing debt financing have no recourse to the assets of the equity owner or "sponsor"[1] (or parent company) except for the sponsor's shares in the project company. As collateral security in the event of a default by the project company, the lenders take a pledge on the shares owned by the sponsor and other assets of the project company. For investment projects in many host countries, placing liens on shares[2] and other assets of the project company is a standard business practice, especially in large-scale, highly leveraged infrastructure projects.

If a host government expropriates the project company, the title to the pledged shares and the party who thereafter can claim direct, indirect, or beneficial ownership of the shares may become unclear.[3] The problem is exacerbated for a sponsor whose equity is covered by PRI against expropriation. Attempts by the sponsor to secure PRI to cover expropriation are intended mainly to circumvent the complex issues arising from ownership of the shares. Political risk insurers, however, are reluctant to cover an equity investment that has pledged shares;[4] they are unwilling to assume rights to pledged shares because the shares may be deemed to constitute evidence of ownership of the project company, and circumstances that preclude their automatic access to title of shares free and clear of encumbrances may jeopardize recovery from the host country Therefore, political risk insurers have normally required the insured party that has experienced an expropriation to assign and transfer to them, free and clear of any encumbrances or liens, the shares of the project company before paying compensation.[5] Lenders have been equally intransigent in agreeing to release the pledge in an expropriation situation, regardless of whether political risk insurers are involved.

This chapter explores the issues sponsors, lenders, and political risk insurers might face when a pledge on shares exists and a government act of expropriation occurs. It seeks, through analysis of various salient factors, to recommend the most viable avenues for recovery from the expropriating government that becomes the sole obligor for the payment of compensation. The objective is for the reader to gain a better understanding of those elements that may offer practical solutions to the impasse affecting investment decisions and provision of insurance cover against political risks. The effects of expropriation on each of the actors and the understanding of the relevant issues beforehand should help investment decisions and ultimately the successful resolution of those issues should the parties encounter an expropriation.

The Rationale

In "nonrecourse" or "limited recourse" project financing, lenders look to the project company's assets and the sponsor's shares in the project company as sources of collateral security.[6] Lenders may require security in the sponsor's shares and the assets of the project company to accomplish three objectives: (i) to adhere to the commercial principle that following a default, all debt obligations need to be satisfied before equity is compensated; (ii) to use the shares and assets as collateral security, which could be sold to redeem debt; and (iii) to gain control of the project company—by virtue of the lien on shares (and consequent transfer of title to lenders upon a default)—in the event of default.

It stands to reason that lenders need to be able to rely on these principles if the default by the borrower is a commercial default. In a commercial default, the responsibility is entirely that of the borrower who is unable to service the debt, either because of default by ultimate borrowers from onlending, through bad business practices, or as a result of any other event, such as commercial bankruptcy. As a consequence of the default, lenders can insist that the defaulted debt be cured before distributions to equity are addressed. The lenders can take control of the project company by foreclosing and transfering title to themselves or to a third party, thus allowing the lenders to sell the project company to recover the outstanding debt.

Expropriation: The Interceding Event

A common problem among the various actors, primarily the lenders, in the share pledge issue is their unwillingness to recognize that the commercial principles underlying the rationale cited above may not remain valid in the face of an extraordinary or exceptional political situation, such as an expropriation. The intervening act of expropriation[7] by a host government results in the sponsors being denied their ownership rights in the project company and may render certain underlying commercial principles devoid of any practical significance. Some fundamental issues emerge in the face of an act of expropriation.

Upon occurrence of an act of expropriation, it can be presumed that the project company is now under the control of the host government or one of its agents. Therefore, the sponsor will have lost control of the project company. If, after the expropriation, the now government-controlled project company defaults on the loan, it could be argued that the cause of such default can no longer rest with the project company because its control or ownership has, de jure or de facto, changed hands. The government or government-owned and -controlled entity may be deemed a successor company and thus be responsible for the assets and the liabilities of the succeeding entity. An expropriation could, therefore, be characterized as a forced acquisition whereby the host government assumes ownership of the project company, its assets, and its liabilities. In such circumstances, the challenge is to determine how individual rights of lenders, sponsors, and political risk insurers should be assessed and how their expectations for payment of compensation from the host government, as the only obligor, can be managed.

The Lenders: Is There Continuing Primacy of the Debt?

Lenders in a project finance context generally seek to secure the debt with the assets of the project company and the sponsor's shares of the project company. The more highly leveraged the project financing is, the more sources of security the lenders tend to seek. In negotiating the security documents with the project company, the lenders will seek to ensure that all project assets and income generated from such assets will first benefit the lenders. No one will argue against the rationale for such action. In a commercial context, these are completely valid measures.

However, an act of expropriation by a host government that fundamentally deprives the sponsor of its ownership rights can have the impact of negating the above rationale used by lenders to secure a pledge on the shares. Here, the project company may be replaced by the expropriating state (or one of its agents); and the project company would have also lost management control.

Moreover, the lenders may find it difficult to sell the shares to redeem the debt. In an expropriation situation, the shares are likely to have little or no salvage value in a market context. Therefore, the lenders will have only the expropriating state to turn to to recover the outstanding debt. From the lenders' standpoint, it could be argued that, because the expropriating government now owns or controls the project company, the government can be deemed to have succeeded to the company's assets and liabilities as if there had been an acquisition. The debt being a company liability, it can be argued that the government[8] has now assumed the project company's debt obligation to the lenders, particularly if the default on the loan occurred after the act of expropriation.

Secured creditors will probably have better leverage under law to press rights for recovery than unsecured creditors based on the standing (*jus standi*) they would have before an applicable judicial forum, including arbitration if this is the mode for dispute resolution under a bilateral investment treaty or the project agreements, even in a situation of expropriation. Early arbitrations, while not confirming the principle that debt has primacy over equity, nonetheless deemed that a secured creditor, like an equity holder, had standing to pursue an international claim.[9] In the case of Compagnie Générale des Eaux de Caracas (*Belgium v. Venezuela*) the government of República Bolivariana de Venezuela was held responsible for the secured debts of the project company the government expropriated.[10] The logic for this inference rests on the fact that a secured lender, by virtue of its collateral security over the assets, can be damaged by a governmental action and therefore can have direct right to recovery of the debt under international law. It was not concluded in this award, however, at any point that debt could replace equity or that it would be given preferential treatment vis-à-vis claims against the expropriating government.[11]

David Bederman explains that unsecured lenders, however, confront a higher threshold of risk in obtaining standing before a court to recover the debt (Bederman 2000). The rationale is that damage to an unsecured lender by governmental actions is not proximate enough to the alleged action of the host government.[12] Consequently, any assertion of the rights of recovery of the debt remain with the party having jus standi, which is the project company. Nonetheless, several developments in the law point to an emerging legal principle under international law that unsecured lenders would also have their rights recognized if the expropriatory actions taken by a government directly affected their rights (Bederman 2000).

The available case law appears to confirm the above view. The *Banco Nacional de Cuba v. Chemical Bank New York Trust Company*[13] case is illustrative of the legal principles involved. The National Bank of Cuba argued that, in a situation in which a state nationalized property, it nationalized the project company or enterprise and not the creditors of the enterprise. It was argued, therefore, that under international law, there was no obligation to recognize creditors' claims. The U.S. 2nd Circuit Court, before which the case was argued, rejected this argument and stated that under international law creditors rights were deemed to be rights that could be expropriated, particularly in circumstances where the creditors' assets (the loans) to the project company were directly affected by the expropriation of the debtor's assets.[14] In summary, debt was deemed to be a property right that could be subject to an expropriation (Bederman 2000). In this case, the creditors were unsecured.

Similarly, in the Iran–U.S. Claims Tribunal, the Claims Settlement Declaration that governs the disposition of claims by U.S. nationals against the government of the Islamic Republic of Iran, specified that outstanding debts of creditors were property rights that came within the jurisdiction of the tribunal.[15] In the Sedco case[16] following the Iranian revolution, the project company was effectively nationalized by the Iranian government. The nationalized entity then defaulted on the loans extended to the project company before its nationalization. It must be noted, once again, that the Claims Settlement Declaration did not pronounce that debt took preference over equity in consideration of outstanding claims. Nor did the tribunal apply such a principle in the cases before it. The tribunal also did not consider whether a creditor was secured. In fact, the principle can be drawn from the above case law that equity and debt are pari passu or have equal status as claims against the expropriating state.

In fact, to secure standing for the lenders, debt obligations of the project company are now worked into key project documents such as power purchase agreements, project agreements, and concession agreements. Many of the standard termination payment obligation clauses include a requirement to compensate outstanding debt, in addition to the equity. Such agreements have often been concluded between the host government[17] and the project company;[18] thus, the host government explicitly recognizes the existence of debt. Whether a government will negotiate with the lenders independent of the sponsor of the project company when considering a termination payment (or, in the absence of any contractual documents, the issue of compensation) is entirely at the discretion of the host government. Given the lenders' control over the shares, the lenders could initiate procedures against the government for compensation, although the sponsors would have, based on the earlier discussion, an equal right to pursue remedies.

Lenders have tended to fortify their rights recently through the conclusion of "step-in rights" or "direct" agreements with host governments. These agreements recognize the lenders' right to step in under the project agreements, such as when a concession agreement or power purchase agreement is breached and the loans are in default. Thus, as a matter of standing, the lenders would have a direct right to pursue remedies for recovery against the host government, to the exclusion of rights under equity. As mentioned earlier, another element in the project finance structure relates to termination payments under the key project agreements when material breaches of the agreement result in its termination. The termination payment obligations often require payment of the outstanding debt by the host government. This obligation is particularly applicable in the event of "political *force majeure*" events or "government events of default." Together, the above factors should give lenders adequate legal and contractual privity as well as ensure their right to directly pursue remedies against the host government to redeem the debt obligation, without the need to use the pledged shares.

The Sponsors: Overcompromising Ownership Rights

The dilemma of the share pledge issue is created by the sponsors of the project company—in a highly leveraged financing structure, it is usual for the sponsor to pledge the shares in favor of the lenders. Indeed, it is rational for them to offer collateral in a purely commercial context. The sponsor's willingness to compromise their ownership rights, even in an exceptional or extraordinary political event such as an expropriation, is at the heart of the problem. But the sponsor's expectation that a political risk insurer could resolve the dilemma by providing PRI cover for the very shares that have been pledged to the lenders appears to be misguided.

Some practical considerations need to be emphasized. Regardless of whether the sponsor procures PRI, in some instances, finance documents, including the security documents, will require that insurance proceeds be remitted to an escrow account in favor of the lenders.[19] In some cases, compensation paid as the result of an expropriation is allocated to an expropriation compensation account that is a part of the debt service account held in favor of the lenders. Thus, procuring PRI for expropriation would not accrue to the benefit of the sponsor if any claims payment under an insurance policy automatically reverts to an escrow account in favor of the lenders. The inclusion of escrow accounts to facilitate receipts such as insurance payments normally reflects commercial considerations rather than the situation created by a political event such as expropriation. However, current wording seen in a review of security documents would not preclude the placement into escrow of insurance payments resulting from expropriation. In a commercial case, the cause for the default would rest squarely with the project company, whereas in an expropriation, attribution of the default to the project company may not be readily assumed. The clear omission then, on the part of the sponsor, is to argue persuasively with the lenders that, in an expropriation situation, the project company as originally structured ceases to be the borrower, and the lenders would fail to reap the benefits of retaining the pledge on the shares for the reasons cited above. Thus, the nature of an expropriation as described above should be a core reason for the sponsors to propose to the lenders a practical alternative for a release of liens on the shares of the project company unless, irrespective of causality, the sponsors are contractually obligated to surrender title to the shares.[20] This latter premise of contractually surrendering shares regardless of causality is precisely what sponsors should attempt to avoid, perhaps in the pledge agreement with the lenders. Instead, the sponsors should attempt to differentiate between an expropriatory event and other commercial events in a pledge agreement that conditions an automatic surrender of shares to the lenders only for commercial defaults.

Finally, and separately, to the extent that title to the shares remains with the sponsors, they have an equal and independent right to proceed against the host government to seek compensation for the loss. In practical terms, however, because of the lien on the shares, the lenders could either prevent the sponsor from receiving compensation or take legal action to secure any compensation that is received.[21] Furthermore, the host government may also require the shares to be transferred to it free and clear of any liens before the government pays any compensation, to avoid multiple claims on the basis of ownership.

The Host Government: Avoiding Multiple Claims

In an expropriation, the sole entity responsible for any compensation will be the host government. Some forms of direct expropriation not only vest ownership of a project company in the host government or a government agency, but sometimes also nullify the shares of the existing project company.[22] Under international law, however, the obligation to pay compensation continues to rest with the host government.[23]

From the standpoint of the host government that has expropriated a project company, any discussion the host government would have about rights to compensation will be with whoever claims to be the owners of the project company. At a fundamental level, the host government could question the standing of the lenders to pursue independent rights as owners of the expropriated project company, but the host government would most surely seek to avoid multiple claims based on ownership. Multiple claims based on ownership can emerge, at least in theory. The sponsor can claim that it has de jure title to the shares. However, based on the liens, the lenders can argue that they are de facto owners of the shares with the possibility of converting title of the shares to themselves.[24] Of course, political risk insurers, who are subrogated to the rights of the sponsor on payment of a claim based on expropriation, could also argue that they are the owners of the shares by virtue of potential subrogation rights.[25]

In reality, however, in accordance with the applicable project documentation, either (i) negotiated settlement will occur between the host government and all parties having a beneficial interest in the project company (ensuring that no further claims would be mounted against the host government), or (ii) dispute resolution will occur through arbitration. A review of the relevant and standard project documentation leads one to believe that arbitration is often the right course to resolve the matters. An expropriation by the host government may be deemed either a political *force majeure* event or a government event of default (for example, in a typical concession agreement). A government event of default would lead to a suspension of the obligations and responsibilities of the contract parties. If the default or the event is not finally cured or remedied, the party affected—in a situation of expropriation, usually the project company—can declare a termination of the agreement. A termination of the agreement would require the other party, in this case the host government, to make a termination payment. Nonpayment of the termination payment by the host government would constitute another breach and consequently lead to dispute resolution under the terms of the agreement.

The rights to and processes and procedures of recovery by the sponsor of the project company against the expropriating government are not in any way diminished by a lack of contractual arrangements that specify a termination payment. A proposal or claim for compensation will require that the accounts of the project company be presented to either the host government or an arbitration forum. Such accounts would clearly and automatically delineate, among other line items, the value of assets and liabilities (and, therefore, any debts owed by the company as seen in chapter 13 of this volume).

Political Risk Insurers: Insuring a Void?

The dilemma for political risk insurers in dealing with the share pledge problem is equivalent to that of the sponsor. The reason insurers insist on having shares free and clear of liens relates directly to the insurer's subrogation rights. When an expropriation occurs and the host government does not pay compensation, the sponsor turns to the insurer for compensation. As a precondition for paying that compensation, the insurer will require validation of ownership of the expropriated property. The shares provide that validation. The insurer is placed in the same position in relation to the host government as the sponsor would have been in asserting the rights to compensation originally owed by the host government to the sponsor of the project company. An uninsured sponsor would have faced the same issue of validating ownership with the host government before the government would agree to pay compensation. By permitting liens to be placed on its shares, the sponsor has effectively limited not only its own rights to compensation but also the insurer's rights of recovery from the host government. This is precisely the situation that the insurer will be in when it subrogates to the rights of the sponsor upon payment of an insurance claim. Thus, by insisting on the transfer of title to the shares free and clear of encumbrances, the insurer is ultimately preserving the clear evidence of ownership that could be required by the host government for purposes of compensation. This requirement is so fundamental that sponsors should not expect insurers to remedy the problem without having the possibility from the outset of transferring clear title of shares.

One other relevant matter needs to be addressed. If, indeed, the shares, which are the insurable interest, are placed under lien in favor of the lenders and, in turn, in a situation of default the title to the shares immediately reverts to the lenders, the insurable interest in the policy would have passed to an uninsured third party.[26] This would render the insurance policy with the sponsor to be subject to immediate termination, because the holder of the policy ceases to have an insurable interest. Consequently, the insurers would not be under any legal obligation to pay compensation under the policy.

If the shares are pledged, and a political risk insurer still proceeds to provide an insurance policy covering expropriation, the insurer runs the serious risk of having any recoveries from the host government be subject to the lenders' rights to such funds. Thus, from the standpoint of the political risk insurer, no meaningful cover can be provided for a sponsor who has already pledged its shares unconditionally to lenders. But to the extent that the sponsors, the lenders, and the political risk insurers agree to uphold and recognize individual legal rights of recovery in an expropriation, based on clear and uncompromised rights at the time of the expropriation, there is no reason why political risk insurers should not agree to cover the equity component, even while the shares are pledged to the lenders. This would, of course, be based on an understanding that the shares are being secured only for commercial events of default by the borrower. On the occurrence of an expropriation, the lenders should be prepared to release any liens on the shares they hold.

Maximizing Recovery: Forging a United Front

A disturbing element in discussions of this issue is the propensity for each actor to insist on preserving its prerogative to pursue individual rights without regard to the legitimate interests of the other actors. It is natural that lenders would do so, given the large amount of money they have committed in the first instance. While this mode of recovery is perfectly legitimate in commercial circumstances, in an extraordinary situation such as expropriation, it could become impractical and disadvantageous to all parties.

In an expropriation situation, it should be in the interest of all concerned parties to do what is required by law to seek compensation. Thus, the concerned parties should act jointly, both preemptively and after an act of expropriation, if one occurs, to maximize recovery.

Working jointly to maximize recovery requires recognition of the underlying basic principle that an expropriation is an extraordinary, exceptional situation beyond the control of either the sponsors or the lenders. Neither is it a situation that can be cured by merely having procured PRI if the shares have already been pledged, given the reasons advanced above. Finally, it must be noted that the principal applicant for compensation in an arbitration proceeding may be the project company[27] represented through its sponsor. The lenders, by virtue of direct agreements, can also become active and direct co-applicants in an arbitration proceeding. On this basis, the lenders and the owners of the project company can agree at the outset to the following:

- The lenders can conclude a direct agreement with the government recognizing their step-in rights to directly negotiate with the government in situations of a default on the loan caused by an expropriation by the host government.[28]
- The lenders should ensure that the sponsor includes outstanding debt as a component of the termination payment in the relevant provisions of the project agreement with the host government. This would require lenders to be involved in negotiating the fundamental project documents, such as an implementation agreement, a concession agreement, or a power purchase agreement, together with the sponsor of the project company. (Many such agreements currently do have these provisions.)
- The lenders can secure the shares as collateral, but will agree to use the shares as collateral only for commercial purposes and not when default is caused by political action such as an expropriation. In the latter situation, the lenders can continue to hold a lien without transferring title, only to the extent that the lenders are to be allowed to control and direct the project company in all postexpropriation actions for recovery. The lenders should undertake that they will not in any way jeopardize any rights to compensation of the sponsor by claiming title to the shares or by selling shares to third parties without the consent of the sponsor or, as the case may be, of the political risk insurer.
- The sponsor and the lenders agree to be adequately represented in all recovery actions with the preparation and presentation of a comprehensive set of accounts that clearly delineate the outstanding debt and value of shares of the project company that has been expropriated. Separate line items in such accounts must clearly represent the equity and debt. These accounts can then be presented to the host government.[29] (Faisal Quraishi in chapter 13 of this volume presents examples of the preparation and presentation of the accounts of a project company.) If there is a negotiated settlement with the government, all concerned parties should agree on the amount of the debt and the amount of equity owed and share the compensation proportionally. If the matter proceeds to arbitration, similar financial accounts for the project company must be presented in the pleadings and the arbitrators must be compelled to make specific pronouncements, based on the pleadings, as to the amount of debt owed and the value of the

equity in the compensation package, if awarded. This course leaves no doubt about the expropriating government's obligations to pay compensation and what is owed to the lenders and what is owed to the sponsor.

- A political risk insurer should require that all of the above conditions be in place if the insurer is to agree to insure the sponsor despite the lien placed on the shares by the lenders. Then, upon payment of compensation under a PRI policy, the political risk insurer will replace the sponsor upon transfer of title to the shares to the political risk insurer, and all recovery efforts must proceed on the same basis as stated in (a) through (d) above.

- Irrespective of the above, if the lenders or the sponsor (and the political risk insurer if it replaces the sponsor) wish to independently assert their claims against the government, they should be permitted to do so without compromising the legal rights of any party and should be permitted to retain their rights to shares of any recoveries, unless otherwise agreed to by all parties.

The conditions above should be adequately addressed in the project documents or a claims-cooperation agreement between and among the appropriate parties.

An alternate course of action that could avoid the issues outlined above would be for the lenders to procure political risk cover for the loans. Although premiums would have to be funded and would therefore interfere with the margins, this course of action would be one of the clearest ways to avoid the confusion and overconcentration on individual rights for purposes of recovery from the government.

Conclusion

With the prospect that a host government will have to pay compensation if it breaks a contract, the various debt and equity components that make up an investment should be spelled out from the beginning in project agreements. Not only should a prospective host government be made aware of these investment components, but it should also be contractually bound to recognize them and the individual owners of those components in the event of an expropriation. The conclusion of a project agreement and similar contractual agreements between sponsors and lenders with a host government should allay concerns, particularly on the part of lenders, that one party will attempt to jeopardize the rights of others in such a situation. Furthermore, the case law cited above indicates that both secured and unsecured lenders have independent legal rights to assert claims against a host government that has expropriated a project company with financing from lenders.

Recognizing that an act of expropriation is a unique political event beyond the control of the lenders and sponsors, (or political risk insurers as their subrogees), all affected parties must recognize that they can no longer adhere to the principles that normally apply to commercial situations. In such circumstances, it would be prudent for the parties to recognize that the most favorable outcome will be attained if the parties jointly press recovery efforts against the host government obligor. To achieve a successful outcome it is equally imperative that lenders conclude agreements with host government authorities to secure independent legal rights against the host government should there be a default on a loan to the project company resulting from governmental actions.

The execution of a pre-agreement among all parties (including political risk insurers) to an investment, as suggested above, can clarify and give the assurance needed to all parties that their interests will be adequately preserved and protected should an expropriation occur and compensation be sought. More important, such an agreement will in no small measure contribute toward enabling investment projects to go forward in areas critical to the economic progress of developing-country host states.

Notes

1. The "sponsor" is an equity owner of the project company. The sponsor receives profit through equity ownership (dividend streams).

2. "Shares" means the capital invested by the sponsor in the project company in the host country, and it is the context in which the term is used in this chapter.

3. The underlying assumption here is that the government expropriating the property will require the party asserting ownership to the project company that has been expropriated to show evidence of ownership. The problem would also be complicated if the government follows its own corporate formalities and forcibly transfers the shares to itself or cancels the shares, replacing them with new shares.

4. The question arises as to whether the sponsor would be able, on the basis of the insurance policy, to transfer title to the pledged shares to the political risk insurers upon payment of compensation.

5. See, for example, Section 4.7 of the Contract of Guarantee for Equity Investments of the Multilateral Investment Guarantee Agency. The reason for this requirement rests with the insurers' need to prove ownership of the project company that has been expropriated. Ownership can be demonstrated only by producing clear and uncontested title to the shares of the company. The insurers obtain such title upon subrogating to the rights of their insured party upon payment of compensation for a valid claim. Recovery from the expropriating government can be seriously jeopardized if evidence of clear title to the shares cannot be obtained.

6. This is in contrast to "full recourse lending" where the lenders also have recourse to the assets of the parent company of the project enterprise.

7. This discussion is restricted mainly to direct forms of expropriation in which there is little doubt that intervention by the host government has denied the sponsor of its ownership rights in the project company. Indirect forms of expropriation, such as regulatory expropriation or creeping expropriation, can make the fundamental premises of this discussion even more complex.

8. Certain complications of state responsibility can arise out of the characterization of the succeeding state entity, particularly if it is a state-owned public authority or enterprise. For the purposes of this chapter , however, the expropriating government is assumed to be the succeeding obligor.

9. For example, P.S.R. Hugo Farrington's case (U.S. v. El Salvador) in Whiteman (1937) , pp. 1371–2.

10. Reported in 9 R.I.A.A. pp. 329–46 (1903).

11. See, in this regard, an excellent article by Bederman (2000).

12. Dickson Car Wheel Co, case (United States v. Republic of Mexico, Mexican American General Claims Commission (1931), 4 R.I.A.A. 669.

13. *Banco Nacional de Cuba v. Chemical Bank New York Trust Company,* 822 F.2d 230 (2nd Cir.1987).

14. *Banco Nacional de Cuba v. Chemical Bank New York Trust Company,* 822 F.2d 230 (2nd Cir.1987) at p. 239

15. 1 C.T.R. Article II, Paragraph 1.

16. *Sedco, Inc. et al. v. Iran Marine Industrial Company et al.,* Award No. 419-128/129-2.

17. In a recently concluded implementation agreement, the "buy-out" clause, which is similar to a termination payment, states that in the event of a government event of default (which also includes expropriation) the buy-out amount that the government agrees to pay "shall be equal to the sum of the outstanding debt obligations of the project

company plus the sum of equity/share capital as per the accounting books...".

18. The same issues as presented in note 8 may arise if the government counterparty to the contract is a state-owned enterprise. To reiterate, for the purposes of this chapter it is assumed that the counterparty will engage the state's full responsibility.

19. Normally, these remittances will be held by an independent escrow agent who is instructed to hold the account until such time as the debt is paid in full. If a default is declared on the loan, the lenders do have the right to the funds in the escrow account. Again, this chapter is predicated on the existence of project documentation or contracts.

20. Arguably, in a legal context, if causality is disregarded and the lenders enforce the collateral security to cure part of the debt, then the sponsor ought to have an equally valid legal right to claim, in exchange, part of the loan equivalent to the amount realized by lenders and still owed by the host government.

21. In such circumstances, the lenders can only be prevented from pursuing a legal course of action contractually.

22. The Barcelona Traction case before the International Court of Justice (Barcelona Traction, Light and Power Co. (*Belgium v. Spain* [1970] I.C.J. Reports)) is one such example, where the Spanish courts nullified the shares of one of the project companies. The shares were held in trust offshore for the benefit of some of the bondholders. The nullification of shares was deemed to be a constructive taking.

23. While the act of expropriation by a sovereign state is considered legal, it is also an established principle under international law that such expropriation should be accompanied by "prompt, adequate and effective compensation." See Restatement of the Law Third, Foreign Relations Law of the United States, Section 712.

24. In reality, the lenders may be able to convert title to the shares to the lenders' name. One other complication can arise for such a conversion. The ability to do so may depend on the laws of the host country, because the shares are those of the project company, which is registered in the host country. The lenders could also claim that once the shares are foreclosed and title has passed to them, they are de jure and de facto owners and could equally assert that the host government need only encounter a single party (the lenders) having multiple claims.

25. Political risk insurers generally cover only a portion of the equity interests (normally up to 90 percent) with the remaining portion self-insured by the sponsor.

26. Some very abstract situations can be anticipated for passage of title. The insured party can transfer title to the shares to the insurer while still under lien upon payment of compensation. The insurer in turn may be required to pass legal title of the shares to the host government in exchange for compensation, in which case the lenders will find themselves holding shares whose title is with the host government!

27. The lenders could have independent rights to assert a claim under a bilateral investment treaty.

28. The problem of pledged shares is relevant only in an expropriation situation. The same set of issues can also arise for coverage of breach of contract where any future proceeds from an award in favor of the project company is pledged to the lenders. The fundamental issues, however, are not dissimilar.

29. The legitimacy of the loan to the project company can be further established because most financial regulations in host countries require the registration of foreign loans with the central bank or similar institution.

References

Bederman, D. J. 2000. "Creditor's Claims in International Law." *The International Lawyer* 34 (1): 235–54.

Whiteman, Marjorie. 1937. *Damages in International Law,* 2 vol. Washington, DC: Government Printing Office.

Emerging Issues in the Enforcement of Foreign Arbitral Awards

Joseph R. Profaizer

The enforcement of foreign arbitral awards is key to the international legal system. Simply put, parties will not participate in a voluntary system if they cannot predict and rely upon the outcome. As a practical matter, this means that parties that agree to resolve their differences by international arbitration must have the confidence that any award that is properly issued by an arbitral tribunal will be paid or performed, either voluntarily or involuntarily, through the enforcement mechanisms that exist worldwide.

Political risk insurers and insureds rely upon international arbitration agreements—and any awards ultimately issued as a result of disputes arising out of those agreements—in their private contracts and those contained in bilateral or multilateral investor-state investment treaties. Moreover, the enforcement of international arbitral awards is crucial to the issuance of arbitration award default insurance. Hence, the enforcement of international arbitral awards is vitally important to the political risk insurance community.

As arbitration has rapidly and increasingly become the most used dispute resolution mechanism in both international commercial disputes and among parties conducting business with sovereign

Joseph Profaizer is an attorney at Paul, Hastings, Janofsky & Walker, LLP (Washington, DC).

states, the enforceability of awards has become correspondingly important. As a threshold matter, this increasing popularity is not surprising. Pursuant to the United Nations Convention on the Recognition and Enforcement of Foreign Arbitral Awards (the "New York Convention"), arbitral tribunals issue awards enforceable nearly everywhere in the world. Arbitration provides the only international dispute resolution mechanism whose awards are not only "portable," but also that its users can tailor to their individual needs and that promises neutrality of the decision makers to the dispute. If arbitral awards cannot be relied upon, however, the well-deserved foundation for the reliability and growth of international arbitration is at risk. There are, however, effective legal mechanisms to address a party that refuses to pay an adverse award.

Ideally, enforcement of arbitral awards does not need as much focus as other issues in international litigation or arbitration. This is as it should be—and usually is—because in the vast majority of cases, an arbitral award that is issued against a party is voluntarily complied with and followed by prompt payment or by negotiation among parties as to the mode of payment. However, a number of high-profile disputes, including over a billion dollars in outstanding awards against Argentina that have yet to be paid, have brought this issue into greater focus. Although parties in the past two decades have increasingly turned to international arbitration as an efficient and effective mechanism to resolve disputes, the system may be facing a new test, because these Argentine awards and several other significant awards have yet to be successfully enforced. For all of its benefits, arbitration, like any dispute resolution mechanism, is an effective tool only if, at the end of the day, the prevailing party can collect its award and rely upon the rule of law to enforce the award. The international legal system has developed mechanisms to enforce awards when they are not voluntarily paid or performed to effectuate these principles.

The Key to the System's Success: Voluntary Compliance

Although estimates vary slightly, experts conclude that approximately 95 percent of international commercial and investor-state arbitrations are satisfied without recourse to enforcement mechanisms (Dugan and others 2008). Parties' compliance with awards is essential to the arbitral system, which, after all, is voluntary and lacks compulsory power. Arbitrator-sanctioned seizure of assets, for example, would constitute vigilante justice in most countries. What, then, is the incentive for countries and companies to comply with awards? In an increasingly global marketplace, companies and countries alike have a political and economic interest in honoring contracts and adhering to the rule of law, because there is no international legal police body.

From a sovereign country's perspective, so far, cooperation with foreign investors and participation in the global market have served as strong incentives for most countries to comply with awards issued against them in investor-state arbitration, even when the amounts involved are not insignificant. For example, the Czech Republic paid a $269 million award, plus interest and arbitrators' fees, that was issued against it in 2003 in *CME Czech Republic B.V. (The Netherlands) v. Czech Republic*.[1] The Czech Republic voluntarily paid the award notwithstanding a parallel arbitral tribunal that came to the opposite conclusion regarding the Czech Republic's liability.[2] At the time it was issued, the award was the largest international arbitration award against a state that was known publicly, though larger awards have since been issued. More recently, in October 2008, Chile paid voluntarily (after completing its appeals) an award of $5.9 million and $2.9 million in interest in an International Center for Settlement of Investment Disputes (ICSID) arbitration, *MTD Equity Sdn. Bhd & MTD Chile S.A. v. Chile*.[3]

Theoretically, companies, unlike sovereign countries, may not have the same political and economic incentives to comply with arbitral awards, may find it easier to "hide" from awards, and, consequently, may be less apt to comply with them. However, that this has not been the case in practice is owing to the fact that most national courts are supportive of attempts to enforce international arbitral awards, consistent with their support of international arbitration pursuant to the New York Convention, the United Nations Commission on International Trade Law (UNCITRAL) Model Law on International Commercial Arbitration, and corresponding domestic legal regimes, as discussed below. Even when the international principles behind the enforcement of arbitral awards are not followed by a party receiving an adverse award, there are global and local mechanisms for enforcement of the award, because countries and companies know that their assets can be attached wherever they might exist. This creates a strong political and economic incentive to voluntarily comply with arbitral awards. Therefore, companies and countries generally have little incentive to resist awards when they know that eventually those awards will be enforced.

A Presumption of Enforceability:
Evolving Enforcement Mechanisms

An essential incentive for compliance—for countries, but especially for companies, which might otherwise have an easier time ducking and dodging—are the enforcement mechanisms enacted in most national legal systems and the New York Convention.

One of the most widely ratified treaties in the world, the New York Convention was enacted in 1958 and currently has 144 signatories. The New York Convention was a watershed event in the international arbitral system and a principal reason for its rapid expansion, because it essentially makes arbitral awards portable; that is, an arbitral award that is issued in one signatory country will be presumptively enforceable in another. The New York Convention opened up an entire world that allowed political risk insurers and insureds, and anyone doing business abroad, to take that arbitration award, to take that arbitration clause in a contract or treaty, to arbitrate a dispute, to receive an award, and then enforce it wherever the money might be.

Before the ratification of the New York Convention, a winning party in an arbitration would be forced to confirm the award (that is, render it binding by force of law) both at the place of the arbitration, *and* in any jurisdiction in which it sought to enforce the award — which often meant in the jurisdiction in which the assets that the winning party sought to execute upon were located. This requirement of a second confirmation subjected an arbitral award to the courts of any jurisdiction in which a party sought to enforce an award, creating extra obstacles and potential years of litigation.

The New York Convention creates a presumption of enforceability by eliminating the requirement of a second confirmation (subject to limited exceptions). Under the New York Convention, after an award is confirmed at the place of the arbitration, the award takes on the effect of a local court judgment in most countries around the world, allowing a beneficiary of a valid arbitral award to execute on the loser's assets in the jurisdiction in which they can be located. The New York Convention has been successfully implemented and applied for the last 50 years, creating the ability for political risk insurers and other international businesses to resolve disputes through arbitration and then enforce the award wherever the losing party's assets may be located. Likewise, the Inter-American Convention on International Commercial Arbitration creates a presumption of enforceability and shifts the burden of establishing an exception to the party resisting enforcement.

In addition, national arbitral legislation and other international arbitration conventions have followed suit, providing for an award's presumptive enforcement, subject only to narrow, enumerated exceptions. Many countries, for example, have adopted the UNCITRAL Model Law on International Commercial Arbitration, which provides that an international arbitral award shall be recognized as binding irrespective of the country in which it is made.

Awards issued by the ICSID under the Washington Convention (which applies only to investor-state disputes) involve even fewer barriers to enforcement than awards subject to the New York Convention. ICSID awards are, at least in theory, self-executing, and do not require even an initial recognition of the award at the place of the arbitration, as required under the New York Convention. Thus, ICSID awards in some respect take on the juridical character of a national court judgment, and a beneficiary can bypass any confirmation process and attempt to enforce the award directly in any country that is a signatory to the Washington Convention. The self-executing nature of awards under the Washington Convention is often a crucial factor for investor-claimants in deciding whether to bring arbitration under ICSID or other available rules, such as the UNCITRAL Arbitration Rules. To illustrate the point, of the at least 46 known investment arbitrations brought against Argentina since 2001, 43 have been brought under ICSID and only 3 have been brought outside the Washington Convention. This is due, in large part, to the benefits of the enforcement in ICSID arbitrations.

Enforcement in Practice: What Happens When a Party Refuses to Pay?

Although almost all parties voluntarily comply with their obligations to abide by international arbitral awards, there have been an increasing number of instances when, for economic, political, or other reasons, parties have not complied with arbitral awards. In this respect, international arbitration is not unlike national legal systems—that is, sometimes debtors simply do not pay.

Perhaps the most famous example is *Karaha Bodas Co. v. Pertamina*, a case involving an aborted investment in Indonesia by Karaha Bodas Co. (KBC), owned by a group of foreign investors. The contract dispute began when the Indonesian government forced KBC to abandon development of a geothermal power facility in the wake of the Asian financial crisis. An award for $261 million was rendered against Indonesia in 2000 by a Geneva-based arbitral panel convened under the UNCITRAL arbitration rules. Thereafter, Swiss and Indonesian courts denied Pertamina's vacatur petitions, and KBC began enforcement proceedings under the New York Convention in courts in Canada, Hong Kong (China), Singapore, and the United States. After Indonesia refused to pay voluntarily or to comply with parallel enforcement orders in each of the countries in which they were pursued, KBC executed against Pertamina's assets in Hong Kong, China and New York. Ultimately, after numerous hearings, appeals, and interventions by Indonesia to contest payment of the award, KBC collected in 2006 the entire award plus postjudgment interest, totaling almost $320 million.

Significantly, KBC's dispute with Pertamina did not arise under an investment treaty, though in many ways it was similar. Had KBC had access to ICSID arbitration and the Washington Convention (an option available in most international investment treaties), enforcement might have been expedited, because KBC could have bypassed the unusually painstaking review of the New York Convention undertaken by the national courts in assessing their discretion to enforce the arbitral award. However, given Indonesia's recalcitrance, this cannot be definitively stated.

The process of enforcing the award in *Karaha Bodas Co. v. Pertamina* illustrates both the key benefit and a remaining obstacle of the New York Convention. Crucial to KBC's ultimate success in enforcing the award was its ability under the New York Convention to follow Indonesia's assets and execute the award in a jurisdiction in which Indonesia had assets that could be seized, a clear benefit of the New York Convention. However, the process also illustrates that, even under the New York Convention, prevailing parties still can face a lengthy process in enforcing an international arbitral award. Nonetheless, when a losing party refuses to comply, there are effective mechanisms that the prevailing party can use to enforce its award.

Looking Ahead: Will Argentina Set a Precedent?

Although *Karaha Bodas Co. v. Pertamina* was the first and most prominent example of a recalcitrant losing party, it is not the only example. Argentina, among other countries, is poised currently to test the arbitral system. At the time of the writing of this chapter, Argentina has yet to pay nine awards, consisting of over a billion dollars, outstanding against it, as table 10.1 illustrates.

Table 10.1 Unpaid Awards Issued Against Argentina as of May 1, 2009

Case	Award date	Award amount ($ millions)	Status
CMS Gas Transmission Co. v. Argentine Republic, ICSID Case No. ARB/01/8	May 12, 2005	133.2	Annulment application denied
LG&E Energy Corp. v. Argentine Republic, ICSID Case No. ARB/02/1	July 25, 2007	57.4	Request for annulment pending
Enron Corp. and Ponderosa Assets, L.P. v. Argentine Republic, ICSID Case No. ARB/01/3	May 22, 2007	106.2	Request for annulment pending
Compañía de Aguas del Aconquija S.A. and Vivendi Universal S.A. v. Argentine Republic, ICSID Case No. ARB/97/3	August 20, 2007	105.0	Request for annulment pending
Sempra Energy International v. Argentine Republic, ICSID Case No. ARB/02/16	September 28, 2007	128.2	Request for annulment pending
Azurix Corp. v. Argentine Republic, ICSID Case No. ARB/01/12	July 14, 2006	165.2	Request for annulment pending
Continental Casualty Co. v. Argentine Republic, ICSID Case No. ARB/03/9	September 5, 2008	2.8	Request for annulment pending
BG Group Plc. v. Argentine Republic, UNCITRAL	December 24, 2007	185.2	Challenge of award pending before Washington, DC, court
National Grid Plc. v. Argentine Republic, UNCITRAL	November 3, 2008	54.0	Unpaid
Siemens A.G. v. Argentine Republic, ICSID Case No. ARB/02/8	February 6, 2007	237.8	Request for annulment pending

Source: Author.

Since the Argentine financial crisis of 2001–02, during which time Argentina allegedly breached or abrogated an enormous number of agreements with foreign investors, Argentina has faced a barrage of arbitration claims under international investment treaties. Consequently, as of early 2009, Argentina faced 46 known international treaty cases. Damage awards were issued in nine of those cases and 18 were still pending. (A number of others were denied at jurisdiction, discontinued, or suspended.) According to public reports, Argentina has yet to pay any of the more than a billion dollars in awards issued against it.

Perhaps most notably, Argentina has refused to pay an award of $133.2 million issued against it in *CMS Gas Transmission Company v. The Argentine Republic*,[4] even after its application for annulment of the award was rejected. As table 10.1 indicates, Argentina has annulment applications pending in nine other disputes, seeking to avoid payment of awards ranging from $2.8 million to $237 million.

In the past, Argentina has stated that it will pay the awards issued against it if it is allowed to take advantage of the ICSID procedures permitting it to seek to annul the award. Because of the significant number of cases that are pending against Argentina that it might seek to annul, this seemed to be a significant incentive for Argentina. Nevertheless, as noted above, Argentina did not pay the CMS award. Subsequently, ICSID ad hoc annulment committees have begun to take action to prevent Argentina from continuing to refuse to pay its awards. One significant decision came in *Compañía de Aguas del Aconquija S.A. and Vivendi Universal S.A. v. Argentine Republic*, in which the ICSID ad hoc committee offered Argentina the opportunity "to provide the Committee with a more elaborate official letter to be issued by Dr. Guglielmino in his capacity as the *Procurador del Tesoro de la Nación Argentina* and as Agent of Argentina in the present annulment proceeding" within a time period of 30 days from notification of the decision.[5] As of the writing of this chapter, Argentina had not provided any bank guarantee or security as a result of these decisions. Another ICSID ad hoc annulment committee has taken further action to require Argentina to provide security pending the annulment process. On March 5, 2009, an ICSID annulment committee conditioned the continued stay of enforcement of the US$128 million award upon Argentina's placing $75 million into escrow.[6] As of this writing, Argentina had not complied with this order.

The resolution of these cases could prove pivotal for the international arbitral system. Whether Argentina voluntarily complies with the enormous number and amount of awards against it—or whether it manages to avoid them—will have significant consequences for the credibility of the system. If Argentina refuses payment of the awards, it could set a precedent for other sovereign states to follow suit. In the short and medium term, other sovereigns will face similar tests, and will likely look to the Argentine cases as precedent. In the short to medium term, for example, the Russian Federation may face arbitral awards against it, and in the medium to longer term, Bolivia, Ecuador, and República Bolivariana deVenezuela may face awards as well.

The manner in which the enforcement of awards plays out in the Argentine and other pending cases will influence the potential conduct of sovereign states and commercial actors, should they find themselves in similar circumstances. If a party that has received an adverse award does not voluntarily comply, the current international legal system provides mechanisms, both global and local, for finding and executing on the right assets. This balance of legal and economic incentives underpins the issuance of, and recovery based on, political risk insurance policies. Political risk insurers and their insureds should, therefore, closely follow these developments.

Notes

1. See *CME Czech Republic B.V. (The Netherlands) v. Czech Republic,* UNCITRAL, Final Award of March 14, 2003.

2. See *Ronald Lauder v. Czech Republic,* UNCITRAL Arbitration, Final Award of September 3, 2001.

3. See *MTD Equity Sdn. Bhd & MTD Chile S.A. v. Chile,* ICSID Case No. ARB/01/7, Award of May 25, 2004.

4. See *CMS Gas Transmission Company v. Argentine Republic,* ICSID Case No. ARB/01/8, Award of May 12, 2005.

5. See *Compañía de Aguas del Aconquija S.A. and Vivendi Universal S.A. v. Argentine Republic,* ICSID Case No. ARB/97/3, Decision on the Argentine Republic's Request for a Continued Stay of Enforcement of the Award rendered on August 20, 2007 (November 4, 2008) (hereinafter the *Vivendi Decision*).

6. See Decision on the Argentine Republic's Request for a Continued Stay of Enforcement of the Award, *Sempra Energy International v. Argentine Republic,* ICSID Case No. ARB/02/16 (US/Argentina BIT) (March 5, 2009).

References

Dugan, Christopher, F., Noah D. Rubins, Don Wallace, and Borzu Sabahi. 2008. "Enforcement of Awards." In *Investor-State Arbitration*, ed. C. Dugan, N. Rubins, D. Wallace, and B. Sabahi. New York: Oxford University Press.

To Risk or Not to Risk? The State's Perspective of Investor-State Dispute Resolution at the 20th Anniversary of MIGA

Ignacio Torterola and Ronan McHugh

The world is currently witnessing significant changes in investor-state relations arising from the ongoing financial credit crisis and global recessionary pressures. The recent and continuing seismic shifts in the regulation of financial capital herald a new era of global governmental activism in capital markets that, alongside stimulus plans and bailouts, may yet culminate in significant nationalizations of corporate assets, public-private ring fencing of so-called toxic assets, further governmental decisions to support (or not) certain

Ignacio Torterola is an attorney for the Argentine government in cases against Argentina before ICSID tribunals and other international tribunals with jurisdiction over investment matters. He is currently based in Washington, DC, representing the Argentine Treasury Attorney General's Office before ICSID. Mr. Torterola is the former Deputy Coordinator of the Argentine Republic's defense before international tribunals. Ronan McHugh is an attorney with Pillsbury Winthrop Shaw Pittman LLP in Washington, DC. His practice focuses on counseling clients in international disputes, including investor-state matters. The opinions expressed herein belong to the authors and do not reflect in any way whatsoever the position of the Argentine government or any other government or institution.

companies, and fundamental changes in financial and other business regulation.[1] The decisions that will be made in these areas by governments throughout the world may ultimately affect us all, and the international law of investor-state dispute resolution will likely be picking up the pieces of this activism and regulation for many years to come. Given this situation, it is fitting on this 20th anniversary of MIGA to consider the current state of investor-state dispute resolution and its recent developments—this system is the bedrock upon which disputes spawned in today's environment will be decided.

Many new developments in the area of investor-state dispute resolution have occurred in the last several years, especially with respect to arbitration. The Argentine financial crisis of 2001 created many investment disputes—some of which have been resolved while others linger on. These disputes resulted in significant new themes and approaches within investment arbitration and public international law. While there has been much discussion about these disputes and the issues they have produced from the perspective of the investor, less has been written from the state perspective. Seeking to redress this imbalance, this chapter intends to offer the state perspective, in the hope that it may be relevant in the current economic conditions. This will include not only an Argentine perspective, but also that of other countries—even some investment-exporting states that occasionally (and which may more frequently) appear as defendants in investor-state arbitrations. In setting forth this state perspective, this chapter also provides systemic conclusions that may allow for improvement of the investor-state arbitration system so that it may offer greater reliability to investors and help in the development of host states.

The State's Perspective on Investor-State Arbitration: The Argentine Experience

The Argentine investor-state dispute experience has been traumatic, to say the least, because of the following circumstances: (i) the dramatic economic and social crisis that gave rise to the disputes[2]; (ii) the problems associated with the anomalies detected in the investment model; and (iii) the defects detected in the investor-state arbitration system,[3] which are similar to those experienced by other countries.[4] The number of cases against Argentina—at least from the point of view of those of us who have defended it—has caused these problems to be more evident.[5]

In *Harnessing Foreign Direct Investment for Development*, Theodore Moran (2006) questions the participation of foreign investments in the extractive and infrastructure sectors. He clearly states that while foreign investment provides development and advanced technology, investments in the extractive and infrastructure sectors face the highest number of accusations of corruption and other practices contrary to the very idea of development and, indeed, may retard development.

The case of Argentina is a clear example of many of the statements made in Moran's work. Argentina's privatization policy in the 1990s brought about conspicuous progress in the country, especially in cutting-edge industries and in the commercial sector of the economy, but it also brought with it many associated inefficiencies, especially in the regulated sectors, that were uncovered when the social and economic crisis erupted.[6]

The water sector provides a classic example of the inefficiencies of the foreign investment model when applied to extractive industries and infrastructure in Argentina. The privatized companies in the sector obtained the right to provide water services through extremely aggressive offers that rendered the business of water provision effectively unviable economically. Immediately after having been granted the concessions, the privatized companies rapidly renegotiated the terms of their agreements, in violation of Argentine administrative law and with damage to the Argentine taxpayer. Furthermore, (and this may be our only disagreement with Moran) the state effectively became hostage to the concessionaire, because all competition had been eliminated, enabling the concessionaires to take advantage of their dominant position to force the state to renegotiate terms more favorable to the companies.[7] In many cases, the recklessness of the offers made by the investors was coupled with the investors' failure to properly analyze the feasibility of the concession agreements.[8] In addition to these factors, investors frequently failed to comply with their agreed-on obligations to provide service improvement investments pursuant to their concession agreements. And, even when promised works were performed, other companies within the same enterprise executed them, and were paid above-market internal transfer prices. In economic terms, the supposed public benefits of the privatization process—the source for these investments—was eviscerated by, in effect, subsidies to the investors at the expense of the Argentine taxpayer. Finally, in a number of the Argentine water privatization cases, collusive activities by Argentine regulators seemed to condone or even promote investors' breach of obligations, raising suspicious anomalies concerning compliance with the concession contracts.[9]

In conclusion, the arbitrators in the Argentine cases have faced not only the complicated enough problem of the consequences of the economic and social crisis of 2001 in Argentina but also the multidimensional matrix and larger scenario of the question of the entire Argentine privatization experience and process. The truth is that out of nine decisions rendered so far against Argentina, the record is balanced. Four arbitral tribunals determined that Argentina wrongfully impaired the concession contracts and rejected the necessity defense (CMS, Enron, Sempra, and BG). Two tribunals agreed that the contracts were wrongfully affected but the consequences were mitigated because of the exceptional circumstances at the time of the measures (LG&E and Nat. Grid, partially accepted the necessity defense). In one case the necessity defense was accepted *in totum* (Continental); in another case the claim was rejected because of a lack of damage as a consequence of the measures (Metalpar); and finally, in two cases the claims were put to rest because of jurisdictional problems. As it has been recently pointed out—by Luke Peterson (2009) in "Argentine Crisis Arbitration Awards Pile Up, but Investors Still Wait for a Payout" and Joseph Stiglitz (2007) at the Ninth Annual Grotius Lecture Series—the record in favor of Argentina might even grow to the extent the developed world takes necessity measures in the face of the current international economic crisis. (Peterson [2009] exemplifies the kind of measures citing the discontent of Lehman Brothers' foreign investors or the Chinese shareholders in the Belgian Bank Fortis SA/NV).

Third Countries' Experiences in Investor-State Arbitration: Current Issues and Trends

During the last two years as Procuración del Tesoro de la Nación/International Centre for Settlement of Investment Disputes (PTN/ICSID) Liaison[10] I had the opportunity to discuss academically the advantages and pitfalls of investor-state arbitration with many practitioners and state lawyers. This section reflects the opinions collected from practitioners with different interests in this type of arbitration.[11] It also reflects the discussions and conclusions of the February 2009 UNCTAD Multi-Year Expert Meeting on Investment for Development,[12] which confirms third countries'—developed or developing—positions on the issues discussed below.

Investor-state arbitration trends[13] are briefly summarized in the following.[14]

Treaty Interpretation Issues

Two particular issues can be highlighted to illustrate states' perceptions of a troubling trend in international investor-state relations: (i) the failure of arbitral tribunals to apply treaties consistently, and (ii) tribunals' application of treaties in a manner that expands the treaties beyond their intended or anticipated scope.

When interpreting bilateral investment treaties (BITs), tribunals have consistently—in one way or another—applied the rules of the Vienna Convention on the Law of Treaties (the "Vienna Convention").[15] However, in doing so, tribunals have reached different and sometimes contradictory results, even when analyzing and applying the same rule to the same facts. Suffice it to mention, as examples, the emergency proceedings brought against Argentina or the well-known precedents in the Lauder and CME cases.[16] Inconsistent application of rules creates instability for investor-state relations because neither party knows precisely the ground upon which it stands. The UNCTAD Multi-Year Expert Meeting on Investment for Development noted this exact issue in its "key points" on the development dimension of international investment agreements, stating:

> The challenges arising out of this situation also manifest themselves prominently in the current system of investor-State dispute settlement, including through the continuing divergence in arbital interpretations of core treaty provisions. Governments and firms [i.e., investors] alike need to find better Solutions for dealing with this aspect of International investment relations. Preventive measures, including better treaty language and effective means of dispute avoidance, are important in this regard. (UNCTAD 2009, 2)

In addition to this inconsistency issue, despite tribunals' frequent formal statements that they are abiding by the Vienna Convention, they have many times clearly departed from the text of the convention, and from the context in which the treaties were duly negotiated, to expand the rights and obligations in treaties.

The fair and equitable treatment standard. Until recently, the fair and equitable treatment standard was related to ideas of equal treatment, due process, and national treatment.[17] This (now minority) line of thought is still supported by the doctrine.[18] With regard to the concept of fair and equitable treatment, the tribunal in *Alex Genin v. Estonia* held that

> Article II(3) of the BIT requires the signatory governments to treat foreign investment in a "fair and equitable way." Under international law, this requirement is generally understood to "provide a basic and general standard which is detached from the host State's domestic law." While the exact content of this standard is not clear, the Tribunal understands it to require an "international minimum standard" that is separate from domestic law, but that is, indeed, a minimum standard. Acts that would violate this minimum standard would include acts showing a wilful neglect of duty, an insufficiency of action falling far below international standards, or even subjective bad faith. Under the present circumstances—where ample ground existed for the action taken by the Bank of Estonia – Respondent cannot be held to have violated Article II(3)(a) of the BIT.
>
> Article II(3)(b) of the BIT further requires the signatory governments not to impair investment by acting in an arbitrary and discriminatory way. In this regard, the Tribunal notes that international law generally requires that a state should refrain from "discriminatory" treatment of aliens and alien property. Customary international law does not, however, require that a state treat aliens (and alien property) equally, or that it treat aliens as favourably as nationals. Indeed "even unjustifiable differentiation may not be actionable." In the present case, of course, any such discriminatory treatment would not be permitted by Article II(1) of the BIT, which requires treatment of foreign investment on a basis no less favourable than treatment of nationals.[19] [emphasis in original]

Nevertheless, beginning in the late 1990s, especially with the wave of cases initiated around 2000, which changed the practice landscape,[20] this standard grew into a much broader concept that covers, in some cases, the so-called investor's legitimate expectations.[21] These cases include the decisions in *OEPC v. Ecuador* [22] and *MTD v. Chile*,[23] as well as the decision in *Tecmed v. Mexico*.[24] It would also be repeatedly used in proceedings brought against Argentina in the aftermath of the economic and social crisis of 2001.[25]

There is a third category of cases, however, involving the *reasonable expectations of the investor*, which takes into consideration the importance, in certain narrower circumstances, of the investor's legitimate expectations but, at the same time, establishes a higher threshold for accepting the violation of the fair and equitable treatment standard.[26] The decision of the tribunal in *Waste Management v. Mexico* helps understand this third category of cases:

> ... that the minimum standard of treatment of fair and equitable treatment is infringed by conduct attributable to the State and harmful to the claimant if the conduct is arbitrary, grossly unfair, unjust, idiosyncratic, is discriminatory and exposes the claimant to sectional or racial prejudice, or involves a lack of due process leading to an outcome which offends judicial propriety—as might be the case with a manifest failure of natural justice in judicial proceedings or a complete lack of transparency and candour in an administrative process. In applying this standard it is relevant that the treatment is in breach of representations made by the host State which were reasonably relied on by the claimant. ...Evidently the standard is to some extent a flexible one which must be adapted to the circumstances of each case.[27]

The overreaching interpretation of the fair and equitable treatment standard is frequently the first issue that comes up in conversations with seasoned practitioners, whether public officials or not. This broad interpretation encompasses obligations that go beyond the international minimum standard of treatment originally contemplated. North American Free Trade Agreement (NAFTA) member representatives have often expressed concerns about the broad interpretation of the standard, even when the NAFTA Free Trade Commission's interpretation was promulgated to dispel such concerns. The Free Trade Commission's interpretation of the fair and equitable treatment standard establishes the following:

1. Article 1105(1) prescribes the customary international law minimum standard of treatment of aliens as the minimum standard of treatment to be afforded to investments of investors of another Party.

2. The concepts of "fair and equitable treatment" and "full protection and security" do not require treatment in addition to or beyond that which is required by the customary international law minimum standard of treatment of aliens.

3. A determination that there has been a breach of another provision of the NAFTA, or of a separate international agreement, does not establish that there has been a breach of Article 1105(1).[28]

The broad interpretation of the fair and equitable treatment standard, combined with a compensatory practice such as that applied by the tribunals in the Enron and Sempra cases, undermines, and causes a departure from, the compensation standards applicable to the fair and equitable treatment standard. The compensation granted as a result of a transient violation of the fair and equitable treatment standard compensates the investor for the entire life of the investment contract, effectively treating the issue as if the investment had been expropriated permanently. However, the fact that these decisions leave the shares of the investment company in the hands of the claimant, and able to continue to trade, causes an inappropriate windfall.

Moreover, the tribunals that have supported the idea of the legitimate expectations of the investor have not sufficiently explained how these expectations can be read as part and parcel of the fair and equitable treatment standard. In BIT arbitration, the primary source of law is the treaty, and the principles of law and customary international law are secondary sources. None of these sources have been cited as the origin of the broader concept of the "legitimate expectations" fair and equitable treatment standard in investor-state arbitration. This does not mean to deny investors the right to be properly compensated for the totality of the damages suffered and subject to compensation by the terms of a BIT. It only questions the grounds upon which such damages may be awarded.

The expropriation standard. The expropriation standard has not changed much in the last 50 years, except as it relates to the conceptual transition between expropriations in their traditional sense expressed in the Hull formula[29] and the existence of other actions that may have an impact on private property tantamount to expropriation (this latter case is usually referred to as indirect expropriation).

Controversy remains, however, with the criteria used to distinguish between a legitimate exercise of the state's regulatory powers and the concept of indirect expropriation.[30] Because of the public interests involved, the discussion of the expropriating effect of certain regulatory measures has been closely followed by civil society organizations, to the extent that such organizations could have an impact on the regulatory power of the state.

Arbitral tribunals have used different tests to determine at what point a regulatory measure adopted by a government constitutes an act of expropriation as opposed to the legitimate exercise of regulatory power. Some of the criteria used include: (i) the test of the effect of the measures,[31] (ii) the test of the purpose or intention of the measures, (iii) the proportionality test,[32] and (iv) the test of the substantial deprivation of property.[33] Different tribunals have varied in using these rationales jointly or separately; as a result, there is currently no uniform set of criteria.

Even though expropriation has consistently been argued in investor-state arbitrations, only in a few decisions has compensation been granted as a consequence of the expropriation standard. In most recent cases, arbitral tribunals have been more inclined to mandate compensation based on a breach of the fair and equitable treatment standard.

Corruption in the Legal Transaction That Gives Rise to the Dispute

Modern times and democratic values demand a high degree of transparency—which has led to a number of recent cases challenging the jurisdiction of tribunals based on the existence of corruption or *false representations*[34] made by the investor in the procurement of the investment.

Despite the fact that several cases follow this line of interpretation, the ruling in *World Duty Free v. Kenya* stands out. After carefully analyzing the facts of the case, the tribunal thoroughly addressed the acknowledgment by international law that acts of corruption are acts contrary to international public order.

The tribunal in *World Duty Free v. Kenya* followed the rationale of the award issued by arbitrator Lagergren in the celebrated ICC decision No. 1110,[35] as well as other international precedents,[36] conventions, and other international agreements.[37] The tribunal concluded:

> In light of domestic laws and international conventions
> relating to corruption, and in light of the decisions taken
> in this matter by courts and arbitral tribunals, this Tribu-
> nal is convinced that bribery is contrary to the interna-
> tional public policy of most, if not all, States or, to use
> another formula, to transnational public policy. Thus,
> claims based on contracts of corruption or contracts
> obtained by corruption cannot be upheld by this Arbitral
> Tribunal.[38]

The tribunal even recognized a principle that has been largely acknowledged by domestic courts: "the courts of justice cannot be used in order to pursue the payment of credits obtained through unlawful means."[39] Furthermore, it acknowledged that corruption has an impact on international morals as well as on the development of nations:

> ... [W]hether one is taking the point of view of good gov-
> ernment or that of commercial ethics it is impossible to
> close one's eye to the probable destination of amounts of
> its magnitude, and to the destructive effect thereof on the
> business pattern with consequent impairment of indus-
> trial progress. Such corruption is an international evil, it
> is contrary to good morals and to an international public
> policy common to the community of nations.[40]

While this decision is to be applauded, yet another issue that must be considered is the test for corruption, that is, the evidentiary threshold required to substantiate a corruption claim. In *World Duty Free*, the evidentiary activity was not one of an insurmountable nature—or at least so it would seem based on the tribunal's account—since claimant itself advanced the existence of such act.[41] However, in some cases this kind of evidence may be very difficult to produce because of the time elapsed between the investment and the events giving rise to the dispute, and then the time between the origination of the dispute and the debate before the arbitration tri-bunal. Other challenges to collecting the evidence may also exist.

The tribunal in *Methanex* suggested a five-step test to reach a determination on the existence of acts of corruption, even if corruption could not be conclusively proven. Nevertheless, there is no unanimous trend in arbitration practice with regard to this issue.[42] Yet, the issue is in serious need of a consistent approach, a consistent application of that approach, and an approach that recognizes the challenges of assembling the materials to prove and support such a claim, taking into account the seriousness of such an accusation.

Again, this is a significant issue from a state's perspective. An investor who obtains an investment through improper means, even with the connivance of elements within a state (those elements obviously acting beyond, and without, authority), and then has the audacity to bring that investment to a tribunal alleging violation of a BIT by the state, should be treated accordingly. This is not just necessary from the state's perspective and for the protection of its taxpayers, but is also necessary from the perspective of other transnational investors, who themselves have been cheated as a consequence of the improper procurement.

Increasing Transparency Requirements

The desire for a higher degree of transparency from the state perspective has also been included in civil society's claims for access to the information in investor-state arbitration, as a consequence of the significant public interests involved. The NAFTA countries have been pioneers with regard to transparency in investor-state arbitration.

This claim for participation and information has been at times accepted and at times denied by tribunals, as explained below. It should be mentioned, however, that the amendment to the ICSID Arbitration Rules in force since 2006 have greatly benefited transparency and the participation of third parties in ICSID arbitrations.[43]

The tribunal in *Aguas del Tunari v. Bolivia*[44] expressed its willingness to accept rules of transparency and the participation of third parties in the arbitration. It determined, nonetheless, that these rights belonged to the parties and the tribunal could not render a decision in relation thereto when parties opposed. As a result, it strictly interpreted the arbitration rules and denied the *amicus curiae* participation.

The tribunal in *Aguas Argentinas SA v. Argentine Republic*,[45] on the contrary, established certain criteria that would make it possible for *amicus curiae* to participate in the proceedings, even allowing the presentation of pleadings by such *amicus* (even though it denied a request for access to the documents of the case).[46] The same arbitrators in a related proceeding made a more detailed analysis of the participation of *amicus*. However, in this latter case, they rejected the participation of the *amicus* because it failed to meet the necessary requirements.[47] In both cases, the investor opposed the participation of third parties in the arbitration, whereas the Argentine government gave its consent and supported the participation request.

Furthermore, within the context of the UNCITRAL, Canada (and Argentina) promoted transparency requirements for investor-state arbitrations. In February 2008, the UNCITRAL Working Group on Arbitration Rules discussed transparency in investor-state arbitration cases. Unfortunately, it became necessary to take the issue to the UNCITRAL Commission because the working group could not reconcile the conflicting positions of the negotiators, which led to a temporary postponement of a more thorough discussion of the possibility of including transparency obligations in the UNCITRAL Arbitration Rules, when applied specifically to investor-state arbitration.[48]

Closely associated with increased transparency, but also related to all of the issues raised in this chapter, is the continued discussion about and possibility of the creation of an appellate mechanism. Argentina has supported the need for such a mechanism and its position on this issue was strengthened when the first awards in relation to the emergency cases were notified to the parties. Even though the facts of the cases were identical, the rendered decisions were at times contradictory, not only in relation to the outcome of the cases but also with respect to the positions of the arbitrators.[49] Argentina's stance in support of an appellate process was also taken up by the United States in the Trade Act 2002 and when proposing amendments to the ICSID Arbitration Rules.[50] The Trade Act 2002 specifically sets forth the following:

> (G) seek to improve mechanisms used to resolve disputes between an investor and a government through ...

> (iv) providing for an appellate body or similar mechanism to <u>provide coherence</u> to the interpretations of investment provisions in trade agreements...[51] [emphasis added]

This issue will continue to be discussed for some time, but from the state perspective it is important and ought to be an addition to the process.

Arbitrator Conflicts of Interests

Real or suspected arbitrator conflicts of interests have been repeatedly alleged in investor-state disputes. This matter is in urgent need of regulation.[52] The U.S. Department of State has adamantly asserted the need to ensure the independence and impartiality, whether real or apparent, of arbitrators. In the *Grand River* case (under ICSID additional facilities), the Canadian investor appointed James Anaya, a professor at the University of Arizona, as an arbitrator. The attorneys for the Department of State challenged Mr. Anaya because of his involvement in the defense of and advice on issues related to human rights and indigenous peoples, which, in the opinion of the United States, affected his impartiality to act as an arbitrator in the case.[53]

ICSID rejected the challenge raised by the United States, pointing out that Mr. Anaya resigned from his position as attorney in the aforementioned human rights cases (he kept providing advice on this subject at the University of Arizona, however).[54] The officials of the Department of State expressed their dissatisfaction with the decision.[55]

These issues indicate that the creation of specific arbitrator conflict rules for investor-state arbitration is necessary, given that the nature of these disputes differs from international commercial arbitration. One area of difference is that numerous investor-state disputes may arise from the same or similar common facts, that is, a sovereign's political decisions. Therefore, many investor-state cases present very similar features, which can create a conflicts matrix typically unknown in commercial arbitrations.[56]

In addition, of course, more typical conflict issues can also arise. Based on the apparent nature of the conflict, its existence could be assessed through the usual conflict rules. Current arbitral tribunals and institutions sometimes have proven insufficiently responsive to the issues raised in such challenges.[57] From a state's perspective, better explanations of challenge decisions by arbitral institutions are required than those that have often been provided. Indeed, given the matters with which investor-state disputes deal, these institutions may even consider greater monitoring of where arbitrators come from; by whom, why, and how they are chosen; how often they are selected; and with what results.

Conclusion

From the above, number of conclusions can be made. First, many of the current issues affecting investor-state arbitration originate in its close relationship to and identification with international commercial arbitration. Although it is true that they are almost identical procedurally, they are not the same with respect to substance. Because of the public values at stake in investor-state disputes, it is necessary to consider the consequences of regulatory cases that go far beyond business considerations.

Second, increased appearance of transparency and impartiality would significantly improve investor-state arbitration as an adjudicative dispute resolution system. In this regard, an appellate mechanism—or another significant substitute—would greatly assist in improving the legitimacy of the system, especially if the members of any such mechanism are chosen on the basis of merit and proportionally represent developed and developing countries.

Third, this chapter does not propose deferential treatment to states (a kind of *in dubio pro state*) as other practitioners emphasize, but it is necessary, nevertheless, to take into consideration states' needs to regulate matters that encompass significant public interests. This need is becoming increasingly self-evident in today's global economic climate, as governments seek to pro-actively remedy issues arising from the credit crunch and recession.

Finally, arbitral decisions have to be reasonable, well founded, and delivered through a fair and transparent adjudicative system. Where this is not so, the resulting award can become unpalatable for civil society and compliance with the award becomes painful and burdensome.

Notes

1. See James P. Bond's "Opening Remarks: MIGA at Twenty: Learning from the Past, Looking to the Future," MIGA-Georgetown Symposium on International Political Risk Management: Navigating in a New World, Georgetown University, Washington, DC, December 4, 2008. See also UNCTAD (2009, 3), which noted: "In light of the current economic and financial crisis, the changing dynamics of international investment relations and the emerging trend towards a review of liberal FDI policies, the role of IIAs [international investment agreements] as becoming more and more important for ensuring stability and predictability was discussed....In the midst of the global food, fuel and financial crises, it is pertinent to underline the need to adequately

reflect a proper balance between predictability and stability on the one hand, and flexibility to regulate investment on the other hand."

2. "In the last weeks of 2001, Argentina experienced a financial collapse of catastrophic proportions. In one day alone, the Argentine peso lost 40% of its value. As the peso collapsed, a run on the banks ensued. According to *The Economist*, throughout the collapse, 'income per person in dollar terms ... shrunk from around $7,000 to just $3,500' and 'unemployment rose to perhaps 25%.' This economic chaos meant that, by late 2002, over half of the Argentine population was living below the poverty line. The crisis soon spread from the economic to the political sphere. In December 2001, one day of riots left 30 civilians dead and led to the resignation of President Fernando de la Rua and the collapse of the government. A tragicomic spectacle of the succession of five presidents taking office over a mere ten days followed.

"In response to the crisis, which has been likened to the Great Depression of the 1930s in the United States, Argentina adopted a number of measures to try to stabilize the economy and restore political confidence. Among these efforts was a significant devaluation of the peso through the termination of the currency board which had pegged the peso to the U.S. dollar, the pesification of all financial obligations and the effective freezing of all bank accounts through a series of measures known collectively as the *Corralito*" (Burke-White and von Staden 2007, 309–10). Despite Argentina having experienced previous economic crises, the crisis of the 2000s was unprecedented as to the levels of unemployment and political dissatisfaction and the catastrophic consequences that left half of the Argentine population living below the poverty line. In addition, the crisis modified the social map in Argentina and heavily impacted the large middle class that once characterized Argentina.

3. Among others, these defects in the dispute resolution process— actual or apparent—include conflicts of interests of arbitrators, transparency of proceedings, compliance with customary principles of international law, problems arising from the realities versus the characterizations of the transactions that gave rise to the arbitrations, including corruption in the procurement of the agreement and collusion between the regulating body and the company subject to control. In addition, in the Argentine case, the vast number of cases added associated complications.

4. In this regard see the section of this chapter titled "Third Countries' Experiences in Investor-State Arbitration: Current Issues and Trends."

5. A 2008 study by UNCTAD reports the increase in the number of state-investor arbitrations since 2000. Most of these cases have taken place since 2003, when there was a massive initiation of emergency

proceedings against Argentina. The survey clearly shows that 70 percent of the proceedings were brought in the four years preceding publication of the paper, and that they total 259 cases. These statistics only refer to cases heard by ICSID, which is the only organization that keeps a publicly available source of data. The number of cases may in fact be much higher.

6. During the 1990s, Argentina received several billions of dollars in foreign direct investment. Most of those investments were for participation in Argentine companies doing commercial business in Argentina. Few ICSID cases were brought against Argentina from companies operating in the commercial sector (for example, Metalpar, CIT, Daimler Chrysler) despite the fact that the bulk of the foreign investment occurred in this sector. On the contrary, almost all the companies doing business directly with the state brought cases or claims against Argentina because of the emergency measures.

7. The state as "hostage" analogy arises on many infrastructure projects and concessions. For example, once a large infrastructure project is started it is of no use until finished and, absent a termination, which carries with it its own attendant costs and difficulties, the contractor–concession holder is frequently in the negotiation driver's seat.

8. See the decision of the tribunal in *National Grid v. Argentine Republic*, ¶103, acknowledging claimants' lack of performance of proper due diligence before investing and stating: "In any case, the thoroughness of the due diligence carried out by the Claimant prior to the decision to invest in Transener should not be considered in isolation from the overall due diligence carried out by the consortium, which was shared among consortium members."

9. It takes two to tango.

10. Dr. Torterola's current position at the Embassy of the Argentine Republic before the United States of America, representing Argentina before the ICSID and other international tribunals.

11. Because of the sensitivity of the issues discussed, the names of the officials with whom the author has talked will be kept confidential, except for those cases for which their opinions are public because they were addressed in specific publications. However, the opinions contained herein, including those of the author, shall not be attributed to the states mentioned.

12. The Multi-Year Expert Meeting on Investment for Development, titled in 2009 "The Development Dimensions of International Investment Agreements," took place at the Palais des Nations, United Nations (Geneva), February 10–11. While the meeting took place after the MIGA–Georgetown Symposium "On International Political Risk Management," the conclusions gathered in Geneva only give further

support to remarks during the Georgetown Symposium reflected herewith. Ignacio Torterola, one author of this chapter, was Argentina's delegate to the aforementioned UNCTAD conference. The outcome of the conference as well as many of the discussion papers are publicly available at http://www.unctad.org.

13. This section is not intended to provide a determinative review of the myriad themes and subthemes within investor-state arbitration today, but instead is devoted to briefly describing some key issues in the area that help to put states' positions in perspective.

14. As has been repeatedly mentioned in the decisions of tribunals, in investor-state arbitration the precedent rule does not apply. Therefore, previous awards are not binding upon other tribunals. There is no doubt, however, that the decisions of former tribunals are discussed and briefed by parties and previous decisions have an influence on the decision of arbitrators. See, in this respect, *AES Corporation v. Argentine Republic*, ICSID case ARB/02/17 (Dupuy, Bockstiegel, Bello Janeiro), ¶24. See also *Enron Corporation and Ponderosa Assets v. Argentine Republic*, Decision on Jurisdiction (Ancillary Claim), (Orrego Vicuna, Gross Espiell, Tschanz), Decision of August 2, 2004, ¶8.

15. See Parkerings-Compagniet AS v. Republic of Lithuania, ICSID Case ARB/05/8 (Levy, Lew, Lalonde), Decision of September 11, 2007, ¶275. See also *CMS Gas Transmission Company v. Argentine Republic*, ICSID Case ARB/01/8 (Orrego Vicuña, Lalonde, Rezek), Decision of May 5, 2005, 290–5. See also *National Grid v. Argentine Republic*, UNCITRAL Case (Rigo Sureda, Kessler, Garro), Decision of November 3, 2008.

16. Dealing with exactly the same facts, the tribunal in Lauder decided, in contrast to the tribunal's decision in a parallel claim in CME, that the Czech Republic through its Media Council had committed no breach of treaty. See *Lauder v. Czech Republic*, UNCITRAL Case (Briner, Cutler, Klein) September 3, 2001. See also *CME Czech Republic v. Czech Republic*, UNCITRAL Case (Kuhn, Schwebel, Handl), Decision of April 9, 2001.

17. See American Journal of International Law (1929); Sohn and Baxter (1961).

18. See *Mondev International Ltd. v. The United States of America*, NAFTA Case (Stephen, Crawford, Schwebel), Decision of October 11, 2002, ¶¶ 119, 127. See also *Parkerings-Compagniet AS v. The Republic of Lithuania*, ICSID Case ARB/05/8 (Levy, Lalonde, Lew), Decision of September 7, 2007.

19. See *Alex Genin, Eastern Credit Limited, Inc. and A.S. Baltoil v. The Republic of Estonia*, ICSID Case No. ARB/99/2 (Fortier, Van den Berg, Heth), ¶¶367, 368.

20. See McLachlan and others (2007, ¶7.73).

21. Claimants in Parkerings defined the concept of legitimate expectations as "the basic expectations that were taken into account by the foreign investor in making its investments." The tribunal stated, "In order to determine whether an investor was deprived of its legitimate expectations, an arbitral tribunal should examine … the basic expectations that were taken into account by the foreign investor to make investment." See *Parkerings-Compaignet v. the Republic of Lithuania*, ¶330

22. *Occidental Exploration and Production Company v. The Republic of Ecuador*, London Court of International Arbitration Administered Case No. UN 3467 (Orrego Vicuña, Brower, Barrera Sweeney), Decision of July 1, 2004.

23. *MTD Equity Sdn. Bhd. and MTD Chile S.A. v. Republic of Chile*, ICSID Case No. ARB/01/7 (Rigo Sureda, Lalonde, Oreamuno Blanco), Decision of May 25, 2004.

24. Douglas disapproves of the fair and equitable treatment standard established in *Tecmed*, stating that "the Tecmed standard is actually not a standard at all; it is rather a description of perfect public regulation in a perfect world, to which all states should aspire but very few (if any) will ever attain" (Douglas 2006).

25. See, among others, *CMS Gas Transmission Company v. Argentine Republic*, ICSID Case No. ARB/01/8 (Orrego Vicuña, Lalonde, Rezek), Decision of May 12, 2005; *National Grid PLC v. Argentine Republic*, UNCITRAL Case (Rigo Sureda, Garro, Kessler), Decision of November 5, 2008; *BG Group PLC v. Argentine Republic* (Aguilar Alvarez, Garro, Van den Berg), Decision of December 24, 2007; *LG&E Energy Corp. LG&E Capital Corp. & LG&E International Inc. v. Argentine Republic*, ICSID Case ARB/02/1 (Maekelt, Rezek, Van den Berg), Decision on Liability of October 3, 2006.

26. In *Parkerings*, the tribunal, referring to the lacking disclosure of the Sorainen Memo, stated, "… However, such a conduct, while objectionable, does not, in itself, amount to a breach of international law. It would take unusual circumstances to decide otherwise." See *Parkerings-Compaignet AS v. The Republic of Lithuania*, ¶307.

27. See *Waste Management Inc. v. Mexico*, ICSID Case AF/00/3 (Crawford, Civiletti, Magallón Gómez), Decision of April 30, 2004. The decision in *Continental Casualty Co. v. Argentine Republic*, Case No. ARB/03/9 (Sacerdoti, Veeder, Nader), Decision of September 5, 2008, would also fall within this category.

28. "Free Trade Commission Clarifications Related to NAFTA Chapter 11, July 31, 2001." http://www.worldtradelaw.net/nafta/chap11interp.pdf.

29. According to the Hull formula and to the practice of tribunals, a measure must meet four requirements to avoid being considered illegal or expropriatory in nature: (i) the measure must pursue a public good, (ii) it must have been adopted in compliance with due process and the existing legal framework, (iii) it must not have been discriminatory, and (iv) any person deprived of their property must have been duly compensated. These four requirements have been recognized in most BITs.

30. See *Saluka Investments BV v. Czech Republic*, UNCITRAL Arbitration (Watts, Fortier, Behrens), Partial Award of March 17, 2006, ¶¶263, 264; Técnicas Medioambientales Tecmed SA v. United Mexican States, ICSID Case No. ARB (AF)/00/2 (Grigera Naón, Fernandez de Rosas, Bernal Berea), Decision of May 29, 2003, ¶121.

31. See *Ronald Lauder v. The Czech Republic*, UNCITRAL Arbitration (Briner, Cutler, and Klein), Final Award of September 3, 2001, ¶368; *Middle East Cement Shipping and Handling Co. SA v. Arab Republic of Egypt*, ICSID Case ARB/99/6 (Bockstiegel, Bernardini, Wallace), Award of April 12, 2002, ¶368; *Compañía de Desarrollo de Santa Elena v. Costa Rica*, ICSID Case ARB/96/1 (Fortier, Lauterpach, Weil), Award of February 17, 2000.

32. *Técnicas Medioambientales Tecmed SA v. United Mexican States*, ICSID Case No. ARB (AF)/00/2 (Grigera Naón, Fernandez de Rosas, Bernal Berea), Decision of May 29, 2003, ¶121.

33. *Pope and Talbot Inc. v. The Government of Canada*, Interim Award (Lord Dervaird, Greenberg, Belman), Decision of June 26, 2000, ¶102.

34. "False representations" here should be understood as express or implied statements made by an individual or a corporation for the purpose of making a certain legal transaction, which deceives or may deceive the interlocutor.

35. *World Duty Free Company Limited v. The Republic of Kenya*, ICSID Case ARB/00/7 (Guillaume, Rogers, Veeder), Decision of October 4, 2007, ¶¶ 148.

36. *World Duty Free Company Limited v. The Republic of Kenya*, ¶¶149–156.

37. *World Duty Free Company Limited v. The Republic of Kenya*, ¶107.

38. *World Duty Free Company Limited v. The Republic of Kenya*, ¶157.

39. *World Duty Free Company Limited v. The Republic of Kenya*, ¶148.

40. *World Duty Free Company Limited v. The Republic of Kenya*, ¶107.

41. *World Duty Free Company Limited v. The Republic of Kenya*, ¶157.

42. Even the very tribunal in the World Duty Free case established a high evidentiary threshold to prove the existence of corruption. See World Duty Free, ¶166. See also *Methanex Corp. v. United States of America*, NAFTA Case (Veeder, Rowley, Reisman), Decision of October 18, 2005.

43. ICSID's Rule 37(2) provides that in the face of a submission by *amicus curiae* the tribunal must consult with the parties (it no longer needs to request their consent). The participation of the third party will be allowed if the person requesting to participate can bring some perspective or knowledge to the proceedings that the parties are not in a position to provide; if the submission addresses a matter that is within the scope of the dispute; and if the third party has a legitimate interest in participating in the proceedings. The submission may not disrupt the parties' burdens in the dispute and both parties must be given the opportunity to present their observations on the content of the submissions of the *amicus curiae*.

44. *Aguas del Tunari SA v. Republic of Bolivia*, ICSID Case ARB/02/3 (Caron, Alvarez, Alberro-Semerena), Decision on the Participation of the *Amicus Curiae* of January 29, 2003.

45. *Aguas Argentinas SA, Suez, Aguas de Barcelona SA and Vivendi SA v. Argentine Republic*, ICSID Case No. ARB/03/19 (Salacuse, K. Köhler, Nikken), Order in Response to a Petition for Transparency and Participation as *Amicus Curiae*.

46. The criteria are those currently contained in Arbitration Rule 37(2), given that the order on the participation of the *amicus* is prior to the introduction of the amendments to the Arbitration Rules. See *Aguas Argentinas SA v. Argentine Republic*, Order, ¶¶ 17 et seq.

47. *Aguas Argentinas SA, Suez, Aguas de Barcelona SA and Vivendi SA v. Argentine Republic*, ICSID Case No. ARB/03/17 (Salacuse, K. Köhler, Nikken), Order in Response to a Petition for Transparency and Participation as *Amicus Curiae*.

48. See Meeting of the Working Group on the UNCITRAL Arbitration Rules, February 2008. The Working Group had decided that the General Rules would not contain specific rules for each type of arbitration. However, it has been argued that these issues that affect the public order cannot wait for future and hypothetical negotiations on a specific regulation for investor-state arbitration. It should be noted that the United Nations' Special Representative for Human Rights submitted a Declaration backing the incorporation of transparency principles into the UNCITRAL Arbitration Rules. The Organisation for Economic Co-operation and Development (OECD) has also recognized the need for transparency in investor-state arbitrations as a consequence of the significant public interests involved in this type of dispute (OECD 2005).

49. See, for example, Waibel (2007).

50. The possibility of an appellate mechanism is also included in the 2004 Model Bilateral Investment Treaty.

51. Trade Act 2002, 19 USC section 3802(b)(3)(G)(iv), quoted by B. Legum (2004, 289).

52. ICSID is allegedly working on the creation of investor-state disputes guidelines to solve or prevent these types of situations. The International Bar Association has adopted guidelines applicable in principle to commercial arbitrations ("IBA Guidelines on Conflicts of Interest in International Arbitration" 2004).

53. "However, upon learning of his involvement in various human rights matters, including proceedings before UN and regional human rights bodies, the US Government filed a challenge to Prof. Anaya, alleging that these facts raised justifiable doubts as to his independence or impartiality to preside as a tribunal member in the NAFTA case" (Vis-Dunbar and Peterson 2007).

54. In the opinion of the ICSID, for the purpose of rejecting the challenge, Anaya's position as attorney in issues of human rights involved a particular situation (from which he had resigned) very different from the advisory role he was still performing then. See Vis-Dunbar and Peterson (2007) who maintain that, "Ultimately, the ICSID would draw a distinction between Prof. Anaya's earlier human rights work and his current role of advising students: 'the former requires advocacy of a position; the latter involves instruction and mentoring.'" The ICSID decision can be found at http://www.naftaclaims .com/Disputes/USA/GrandRiver/GRE-USA-Anaya_Challenge -28-11-07.pdf .

55. A U.S. government source, speaking to *Investment Treaty News*, expressed disappointment with the ICSID, holding, "Allowing an arbitrator who is concurrently acting in other matters adverse to one of the parties to the arbitration to continue sitting as an arbitrator is improper and contrary to established practice regarding challenges to arbitrators." This source also expressed disagreement with the decision by the ICSID to permit the challenged individual to "cure" the alleged conflict by discontinuing certain outside activities, rather than ceasing to serve as arbitrator (Vis-Dunbar and Peterson 2007).

56. "According to Loretta Malintoppi, a Paris-based lawyer with Eversheds, who has undertaken research on arbitrator conflicts for the International Law Association, investment treaty arbitration is susceptible to this types of alleged conflicts in a way that international commercial arbitration is not.

"While stressing that she takes no position on any pending challenges to arbitrators which are currently ongoing, Malintoppi...notes that, in contrast to international commercial arbitration, where the legal issues are often grounded in unique contractual or legal instruments, investment treaty disputes may raise many of the same types of legal questions (e.g. jurisdictional requirements under treaties, definitions of standard BIT obligations such as Fair & Equitable Treatment or National Treatment, etc.) As a result, investment arbitration has witnessed challenges which are targeted at the dual-role adopted by arbitration practitioners (i.e., serving as arbitrator and counsel simultaneously, albeit in parallel cases)" (Peterson 2008, 4).

57. *Aguas Argentina SA, Suez, Vivendi & Aguas de Barcelona v. Argentine Republic,* ICSID Case ARB/03/19, Decision on the Second Proposal to Disqualify Prof. Gabrielle Kauffman-Köhler, May 12, 2008; *Aguas Argentina SA, Suez, Vivendi & Aguas de Barcelona v. Argentine Republic,* ICSID Case ARB/03/17, Decision on the Second Proposal to Disqualify Prof. Gabrielle Kauffman-Köhler, May 12, 2008; *AWG v. Argentine Republic,* UNCITRAL Case, Decision of May 12, 2008; *EDF International SA, SAUR International SA and Leon Participaciones Argentinas SA v. Argentine Republic,* ICSID Case ARB/03/23, Challenge decision regarding Prof. Gabrielle Kauffman-Köhler of June 25, 2008.

References

American Journal of International Law. 1929. "The Law of Responsibility of States for Damage Done in Their Territory to the Person or Property of Foreigners." *American Journal of International Law* 23 (133, Special Supplement).

Burke-White, William, and Andreas von Staden. 2007. "Investment Protection in Extraordinary Times: The Interpretation and Application of Non-Precluded Measures Provisions in Bilateral Investment Treaties." *Virginia Journal of International Law* 48 (2): 307–410.

Crawford, James. 2008. "Treaty and Contract in Investment Arbitration." *Arbitration International* 24 (3): 351–74.

Douglas, Z. 2006. "Nothing If Not Critical for Investment Treaty Arbitration: Occidental, Eureko and Methanex." *Arbitration International* 22 (1): 27–52.

Legum, B. 2004. "The Introduction of an Appellate Mechanism: The US Trade Act of 2002." In *IAI International Arbitration Series No. 1 Annulment of ICSID Awards,* ed. E. Gaillard and Y. Banifatemi. Paris: International Arbitration Institute.

McLachlan, C., L. Shore, M. Weiniger, and L. Mistelis. 2007. *International Investment Arbitration: Substantive Principles.* New York: Oxford University Press.

Moran, T. 2006. *Harnessing Foreign Direct Investment for Development: Policies for Developed and Developing Countries.* Washington, DC: Center for Global Development.

OECD (Organisation for Economic Co-operation and Development). 2005. "Transparency and Third Party Participation in Investor-State Dispute Settlement Procedures. Statement by the OECD Investment Committee." Working Paper on International Investment No. 2005/1, OECD, Paris. http://www.oecd.org/LongAbstract.html.

Peterson, Luke E. 2007. "Analysis: Arbitrator Challenges Raising Tough Questions as to Who Solves BIT Cases." *Investment Treaty News*, January 17. http://www.iisd.org/pdf/2007/itn_jan17_2007.pdf.

———. 2009. "Argentine Crisis Arbitration Awards Pile Up, but Investors Still Wait for a Payout." Law.com, accessed June 25, 2009. http://bilaterals.org/article.php3?id_article=15437.

Sohn, L., and R. Baxter. 1961. "Responsibility of States for Economic Injuries to Aliens." *American Journal of International Law* 55: 545–84.

Stiglitz, Joseph. 2007. "The Ninth Annual Grotius Lecture, Regulating Multinational Corporations: Towards Principles of Cross-Border Legal Frameworks in a Globalized World Balancing Rights with Responsibilities." 23 (3): 451–558.

UNCTAD (United Nations Conference on Trade and Development). 2008. *Investor-State Dispute Settlement and Impact on Investment Rulemaking*. New York: United Nations.

———. 2009. "Report of the Multi-year Expert Meeting on Investment for Development on Its First Session." TD/B/C.II/MEM.3/3, UNCTAD, Geneva.

Vis-Dunbar, D., and L. Peterson. 2007. "ICSID Rejects US Challenge to Arbitrator in Grand River NAFTA Case." *Investment Treaty News*, December 14.

Waibel, Michael. 2007. "Two Worlds of Necessity in ICSID Arbitration: *CMS* and *LGE*." *Leiden Journal of International Law* 20 (3): 637–48.

Calculating Damages: Arbitrators, Counsel, and Experts Can Do Better Than They Have in the Past

Andrea Saldarriaga and Mark Kantor

When an award is released, parties and their counsel behave very much like shareholders in a general shareholder meeting: they skip all the literature and rush to the last page to see the numbers. The legal theories wielded during the jurisdictional and merit debates somehow fade in the face of the amount awarded ... or denied.

When an investment treaty award grants monetary compensation to the investor, the losing state has to adopt the administrative and sometimes legislative measures to allocate funds from the public treasury to satisfy the award. In this way, compensation becomes the concrete part of the award of which the public becomes aware, far less than the reasoning underlying the award.

The earliest investor-state cases may have involved relatively small awards, but in recent years, a number of awards granting substantial sums to investors have been issued by the International

Andrea Saldarriaga is an arbitration consultant; Mark Kantor is an independent arbitrator.

Center for Settlement of Investment Disputes (ICSID) and bilateral investment treaty (BIT) tribunals. Moreover, investors now routinely ask for very large damage sums, amounts that are widely repeated in the media regardless of the sum ultimately awarded. It should be noted, however, that there is a significant difference between the amounts claimed and the amounts recovered in investment disputes. In the context of the North American Free Trade Agreement (NAFTA), for example, Bart Legum noted,

> [...] the total amount of damages asserted in the claims decided [prior to 2004] amount[ed] to a little over US$1.2 billion, yet the total recovery by claimants was US$23 million. The total recovery amounts to a little under two cents on the dollar. (Franck 2007, 57, quoting Legum 2004)

Also, according to Professor Susan Franck (2007), claims in investment treaty disputes averaged about $330 million for all known cases up to June 2006, but awards averaged about $10 million (Franck 2007, 60). Even if since 2006 some investors have been compensated with large sums,[1] it appears that the average recovery continues to be low.[2]

Yet the question of compensation often only receives a cursory analysis in investment arbitration awards. Although the prospect of awarding higher amounts has been accompanied by a tendency toward more ample disclosure of the tribunal's reasoning on the measure of compensation,[3] existing practice still displays a variety of insufficiencies and discrepancies. On the legal side (the section of this chapter titled Law of Damage Claims), there is (i) an enduring inconsistency in the application of standards and measures for compensation; (ii) a more stringent burden of proof than may be found in other type of disputes; and (iii) a propensity to grant protective treatment to states. On the valuation side (Valuation of Damage Claims section of this chapter), the methods of valuation and other valuation concepts are loosely applied.

Along with the analysis of the existing practice of tribunals in investment disputes, this chapter offers suggestions to overcome some of the concerns confronted when calculating compensation in investment arbitration.

Law of Damage Claims

This chapter turns first to a discussion of the law of damage claims.

Standards and Measures of Compensation

As rightly pointed out by the tribunal in *LG&E v. Argentina*, "[i]t is well established in international law that the most important consequence of the committing of a wrongful act is the obligation for the State to make reparation for the injury caused by that act."[4] This principle was acknowledged by the International Court of Justice (ICJ) in its landmark decision on the Factory at Chorzów[5] and included by the International Law Commission in Article 31 of its Draft Articles on Responsibility of States for Internationally Wrongful Acts (hereinafter ILC's Draft Articles).[6]

The complex task of awarding such reparation[7] requires, as a first step, determining the applicable standards and measures of compensation despite the as-yet unsettled state of the law (in particular concerning treaty violations other than expropriation).

The standard introduced by Chorzów. The decision in the Factory at Chórzow ICJ case enunciates the underlying standard to be applied when determining compensation for internationally wrongful acts:[8]

> The essential principle contained in the actual notion of an illegal act—a principle which seems to be established by international practice and in particular by decisions of arbitral tribunals—is that reparation must, so far as possible wipe out all the consequences of the illegal act and re-establish the situation that would, in all probability, have existed if that act had not been committed.[9]

This standard has been adopted by the ILC's Draft Articles. In practice, the standard is understood to require "full reparation."[10] The full reparation standard has been invoked by investors and states in equal measure to support differing claims for compensation. It has also been accepted by arbitrators as the starting point for the analysis of investment treaty damage claims.[11]

The standard introduced by Chorzów seems capable, in practice, of being interpreted in divergent fashions. For example, in four different cases against Argentina (Vivendi, Enron, LG&E, and BG) the standard was invoked as the starting point for the tribunals' analyses of compensation. However, when calculating compensation, Vivendi used a "sunk investment costs" approach,[12] Enron relied upon a "discounted cash flow" (DCF) valuation,[13] LG&E applied a "business interruption" model,[14] and BG relied on a "comparable transactions" valuation method.[15]

The Chorzów rule calls for compensation of the injured party's "expectancy interest," that is, compensation that seeks to return the investor to a position in which the investment has been made but the injury had not occurred. Therefore, the Chorzów formulation should only be invoked when compensation is intended to protect the injured party's expectancy interests (Kantor 2008, 52). The standard set out in Chorzów, therefore, does not support the award of compensation based solely on the "reliance interest" or compensation that seeks to return the investor to the position it would have been in if the investment had never been made.[16]

To conduct the calculation of the "full" compensation required by Chorzów, Professor Marboe points to the use of the "differential method," according to which,

> What has to be done is a comparison of the actual financial situation of the injured person with the financial situation that would have existed if the illegal act had not been committed. The adjudicating body must therefore make an assumption regarding the situation that 'would, in all probability, have existed' if the illegal act had not occurred and compare it to the actual situation after the breach. The difference is the damage that was caused by the illegal act. (Marboe 2006, 733.)

An additional question arises as to how to calculate the value of the injured enterprise before and after the illegal act. However, tribunals differ widely in the methods they employ for this purpose. The tribunals in both Enron and LG&E expressly stated that their intent was to put the investor in the situation as if the illegal act had never occurred, by comparing the company's situation before and after the measures adopted by Argentina.[17] To do so, though, the Enron tribunal used a DCF methodology to value the claimant's equity interest. LG&E, in contrast, rejected this approach and opted to calculate the difference between the amount of dividends actually received and the dividends that would have been received but for the adoption of the Argentine measures. This difference in the measure of compensation is explained by a different understanding of the application of the notion of fair market value (FMV) that is analyzed below.

Measure of damages for expropriation. There seems to be considerable agreement that the measure of damages for expropriation is the FMV of the investment. In fact, this approach has largely been incorporated into investment treaties. Moreover, tribunals in numerous awards have referred to FMV as the proper measure of compensation for expropriation.[18]

FMV has been defined by tribunals along the lines of the definition used by accountants, appraisers, and regulatory authorities, as

> [...] the price expressed in terms of cash equivalents, at which the property would change hands between a hypothetical willing and able buyer and a hypothetical willing and able seller, acting at arms length in an open and unrestricted market, when neither is under compulsion to buy or sell and when both have reasonable knowledge of the relevant facts.[19]

Investment treaties generally impose the FMV standard for so-called lawful expropriations. Those treaties are silent, however, regarding the proper compensation standard for so-called unlawful expropriations, for example, expropriations not effected for a public purpose, conducted in a discriminatory manner, or made pursuant to a process denying the injured investor due process or compensation.[20] Arbitrators have invoked this difference to introduce equitable considerations onto the compensation standard. Examples include moving the valuation date from the injury date to the award date to prevent unjust enrichment, protecting the amount awarded from foreign exchange fluctuations after the injury date, and granting restitution of property unlawfully seized.

For instance, the tribunal in *ADC v. Hungary* considered that, because Hungary's expropriation of the airport concession was unlawful, the claimants were entitled to the benefits of the significant increase in value of the concession that followed the expropriation. To reflect this conclusion, the tribunal departed from the "injury date" rule and used the date of the award as the valuation date.[21]

Measure of damages for breach of treatment obligations. Investors frequently contend that the FMV standard established in expropriation cases should also be applied for compensation decisions resulting from a state's breach of other international investment treaty obligations. Thus, investors argue that the full compensation required by the Chorzów standard, and the use of FMV to measure that compensation, is called for in cases involving such obligations as the fair and equitable treatment obligation.[22] States, however, consider that while FMV may be the proper measure for legal expropriations under many investment treaties, this measure is not applicable to damages following unlawful conduct, in particular the breach of other treaty standards such as no discrimination, fair and equitable treatment, or treatment contrary to most favored nation (MFN) or national treatment commitments.[23]

In cases involving the breach of such obligations, arbitrators have not been consistent in their approaches. Several recent awards against Argentina illustrate this point.

The CMS decision referred to the FMV measure, based on proximity of the circumstances of the case to expropriation. The tribunal was "persuaded that the cumulative nature of the breaches discussed here is best dealt with by resorting to the standard of fair market value."[24] The tribunal also indicated that "[...] it is not excluded that it [FMV] might also be appropriate for breaches different from expropriation if their effect results in important long-term losses." The tribunal proceeded to define FMV and to calculate the amount of compensation by comparing the estimated market values in the *"pesification scenario"* (the actual situation under the measures adopted by Argentina) and the *"non-pesification scenario"* (in the absence of such measures). The difference between the two scenarios was, for the CMS tribunal, the amount of damage caused by the adoption of the regulatory measures that resulted in violation of the treaty.[25] To avoid the problem of leaving CMS with continuing ownership of the shares when it was possible that those shares might in the future recover their value or drop further in value, the tribunal also granted Argentina an option for one year to purchase CMS's shares for $2.1 million (their postinjury reduced value). In that way, if Argentina later chose to rescind its unlawful acts and, as a result, the share value rose, Argentina would have made a choice by exercising (or not exercising) the share option as to whether CMS or Argentina would capture that future change in value. That share option is an often overlooked, but crucial, component of the CMS compensation decision.

In departing from the approach in CMS, the tribunal in *LG&E v. Argentina* concluded that the expropriation standard applied in the treaty to lawful expropriations was not suitable for determining the consequences of unlawful acts such as breach of the treaty's fair and equitable treatment commitment. The LG&E tribunal also argued that FMV is not the appropriate measure for compensation when the investor retains title to its investment and when the state's unlawful interference with property rights does not result in a loss equivalent to the total loss of the investment.[26] The tribunal decided that the proper measure in this case

> [...] is that of the identification of the "actual loss" suffered by the investor "as a result" of Argentina's conduct. The question is one of "causation": what did the investor lose by reason of the unlawful acts?[27]

The tribunal determined that "the actual damage inflicted by the measures is the amount of dividends that could have been received but for the adoption of the measures" and proceeded to calculate the amount of dividends that the claimant would have received but for the measures and subtracted from that amount the amount of dividends actually received to obtain the value of compensation.[28]

By limiting compensation solely to forgone dividends, the LG&E tribunal effectively declined to compensate the investor for any capital gains in the investment. Said another way, if a portion of the company's earnings is reinvested in the company to grow the enterprise, rather than being paid to the shareholders as dividends, that value is ignored in a "dividends forgone" calculation. The dividends forgone calculation would also result in zero compensation if the company was in a negative cash flow situation because it was in the midst of development or construction, even if the company was nevertheless acknowledged to be very valuable.

The subsequent *BG v. Argentina and National Grid v. Argentina* decisions, in contrast, refer to the FMV measure of compensation as "being made available by reference to customary international law."[29] Those tribunals cite the ILC's Draft Articles as support for that conclusion. In particular, the tribunal in BG noted that

> [...] principles of treaty hermeneutics militate for the conclusion that one should not read into Article 2.2 of the BIT [containing the standard of fair and equitable treatment] a standard that Argentina and the U.K. expressly confined to Article 5 of the BIT [provision on expropriation]. For other reasons, however, "fair market value" can be relied upon as a standard to measure damages for breach of the obligation to accord investors treatment in accordance with Article 2.2 of the BIT. While the Tribunal is disinclined to automatically

import such standard from Article 5 of the BIT, this standard of compensation is nonetheless available by reference to customary international law.[30]

In their calculations of the FMV of the affected investment, the tribunals in the BG and National Grid cases were guided by the values used in actual transactions relating to the companies affected by the measures adopted by Argentina—a "comparable transactions" method of measuring FMV.

Finally, the tribunal in *Sempra v. Argentina* followed closely the CMS approach and stated that

> In [...] cases [where] it might be very difficult to distinguish the breach of fair and equitable treatment from indirect expropriation or other forms of taking [...] it is [...] reasonable that the standard of reparation might be the same.[31]

Three comments may be made in connection with the above. First, FMV is particularly useful when the purpose of compensation is to compensate for the total loss or destruction of an asset or the permanent diminution in value of that asset. In this case it would serve as the basis for calculating damages and as a minimum value for compensation. As noted, the majority of BITs expressly require the use of FMV to calculate compensation for a *lawful* expropriation. Given the use of FMV as the standard for compensation with respect to *lawful* expropriations, it is essentially impossible to argue persuasively that the amount of compensation for an *unlawful* expropriation should be less than FMV.

Second, alternative measures of compensation may also be considered depending on the particular factual circumstances surrounding the dispute. When the investment is very recent or is in the process of being made, sunk investments appear to be a useful measure of compensation. As noted, this is a measure of the reliance interest and seeks to provide for the recovery of invested sums plus a reasonable rate of return on those sums up until the date of recovery.[32] If, however, there are significant intervening events between the date of investment and the date of the injury, the amount of invested capital will not reflect the FMV (up or down) of the investment on the injury date.

When the loss or destruction of the asset is not permanent, but rather is temporary, business interruption appears to be a useful measure of compensation. This method seeks to compensate the injured party for the diminution in value of the business for the period of time necessary for the business to restore itself. The business interruption computation calculates the amount of the temporary loss resulting from interruption of or interference with the injured business; in effect, the normal outcome is compared with the actual outcome. The UN Compensation Commission regularly used business interruption analyses to compensate injured businesses for the consequences of the Iraqi invasion of Kuwait.[33]

Finally, general legal principles may also find application in the process of determining compensation and assessing FMV. These principles include causation, foreseeability, a requirement in many legal systems that lost profits be proven with reasonable certainty and not be speculative, mitigation, and equitable considerations, including unjust enrichment.

Locus of the Burden of Evidence

State parties point out the uncertainty of forward-looking compensation. Accordingly, states regularly argue in investment treaty cases that such compensation should be awarded only upon proof satisfying a high threshold of evidence (that is, proof with "reasonable certainty"—not "speculative" amounts). Investors retort that the reason the evidence of future revenues is subject to uncertainty is the conduct of the host state, which prevented that future from crystallizing. Therefore, the claimant-investor should not be held to an unusually high standard of evidence.[34]

In recent practice, arbitrators have tended to impose a high evidentiary burden on the claimant (a high threshold for reasonable certainty) and to grant the benefit of the doubt to states. Unlike the situation in many national courts,[35] no difference is drawn between the standard of evidence (reasonable certainty) required to prove the existence in those awards of future-looking damages and the standard of evidence required to prove the amount of those damages (again, reasonable certainty).

The concern over the certainty of damages lies at the core of the decision of the tribunal in *LG&E v. Argentina*.[36] Despite having evidence of prior dividends from 1993 through 2005 at hand, the tribunal rejected the investor's claim for future dividends because "future loss to the Claimants is uncertain and any attempt to calculate it is speculative." The tribunal also noted that

[t]he uncertainty concerning lost future profits in the form of lost dividends results from the fact, noted above, that Claimants have retained title to their investments and are therefore entitled to any profit that the investment generates and could generate in the future. Any attempt to calculate the amount of the lost dividends in both the actual and "but for" scenarios is a highly speculative exercise. If the Tribunal were to compensate LG&E for lost future dividends while it continues to receive dividends distributed by the Licensees at a hypothetical low amount, a situation of double recovery would arise, unduly enriching the Claimants.[37]

Finally, the tribunal in LG&E determined that respect for due process obliged it to consider only the evidence that both parties were able to contest. Therefore, the panel set February 2005—the date indicated at the hearing as the final date for submitting evidence—as the date for calculating accrued losses.[38] The panel rejected the investor's efforts to submit further valuation evidence after that date. Notably, the LG&E tribunal did not discuss the share option tool employed in CMS to address the potential for double recovery. Moreover, the tribunal did not discuss the impact on the investor of continuing injuries after the award period despite Argentina's stated intention to continue the conduct the tribunal had already ruled was unlawful.

When considering matters of evidence, it should be noted that the ordinary burden of proof for factual matters is "preponderance of the evidence." By requiring proof of future-looking damages (such as lost profits) to a reasonable certainty, arbitrators impose a higher evidentiary standard on the claimant investor. The purpose behind the higher evidentiary standard is to avoid compensation for a future that is inherently uncertain. The uncertainty about that future has been created, however, by the state's conduct preventing that future from crystallizing, an obvious equitable consideration. Investment treaty awards often impose the reasonable certainty test on both the fact of future-looking damages and the amount of those damages. Some national courts (for example, U.S. and UK courts) take account of the equitable considerations involved by requiring the higher reasonable certainty evidentiary burden for the fact of forward-looking damages, but a lower evidentiary burden for the proof of the amount of those damages (Kantor 2008, 72–3). No investment treaty award has yet followed that approach.

Treatment of a State Party

It appears that in arbitration proceedings, states claim differential treatment based solely on their being states and having to respond to political demands,[39] while investors reject this claim. A review of arbitral decisions suggests that some investor-state tribunals grant states a form of protective treatment. This is done by applying a stricter test of reasonable certainty, as noted above. In addition, tribunals may employ "equitable considerations" to limit compensation. Also, arbitral panels may give the benefit of the doubt to states (the party causing the injury) rather than claimants (the injured party).[40] In many awards, this position is neither fully explained nor is any justification set out.

In the case of *AMT v. Zaire*, the tribunal expressly stated that it based its decision on "equitable principles." The tribunal asserted that in the calculation of damages it would consider the particular circumstances and risks taken when investing in a country like Zaire. It then criticized AMT's proposed valuation method for encompassing "interests practicable in the normal circumstances prevailing in an ideal country where the climate of investments is very stable [...]." Accordingly, the *AMT v. Zaire* tribunal rejected in large part AMT's claim for *lucrum cessans* (lost profits). In spite of this approach, the tribunal exercised its "discretionary and sovereign power to determine the quantum of compensation" and awarded the claimant an "all-inclusive" total sum that doubled the value of destroyed goods and property as calculated by the expert appointed by the tribunal. Presumably, the excess over the value of the tangible assets reflected the tribunal's attempt to value the investment's goodwill as a going concern. However, the tribunal provided no explanation for how this sum was calculated.[41]

Unlike the award in *AMT v. Zaire*, arbitrators should fully explain their reasons for deciding to treat states the same as, or different from, private respondents for compensation purposes and for applying "equitable considerations" that would favor one of the parties.

With regard to advocacy, counsel for investor claimants will wish to argue that a state respondent has the burden of persuading the tribunal that states should be treated more favorably than private respondents in calculating compensation. Conversely, counsel for state respondents will wish to argue that international investment law derives from different sources of law than commercial law. States are only bound by international customary rules and general principles of law evidenced by longstanding state conduct and by treaties specifically agreed to by the state. Therefore, the concept of state consent lies at the heart of international investment law. Thus, according to state respondents, differential treatment of states is justified.

Valuation of Damage Claims

Once an arbitral tribunal has determined the applicable legal standards, it may proceed to a corresponding valuation of the claim. Existing arbitral practice, however, displays a variety of insufficiencies.

Valuation Practice

First, arbitrators have a tendency to depart from widely accepted business concepts and valuation principles (such as the common meaning of the phrase "going concern"). The following cases are illustrative of this situation. In the *Sola Tiles* award, the Iran-U.S. Tribunal concluded that, although the enterprise (SIMAT) had been operating for almost three years before the expropriation date, it was not a going concern because, among other factors, "Simat has the briefest past record of profitability having shown a loss in 1976, its first year of trading, and a small profit the next year." Because the enterprise was not a going concern, the tribunal rejected claimant's request for goodwill and lost profits.[42]

Citing with approval the *Sola v. Iran* award, the NAFTA tribunal in *Metalclad* asserted that a minimum period of two or three years of continuing market presence was required before an enterprise would be treated as a "going concern." The tribunal noted,

> [h]owever, where the enterprise has not operated for a sufficiently long time to establish a performance record or where it has failed to make a profit, future profits cannot be used to determine going concern or fair market value.[43]

Accountants, valuation professionals, regulators, and the business community use the expression "going concern" to refer to operating business enterprises, in contrast with "liquidation value."[44] Thus, outside the hermetically sealed world of public international law, there is no requirement that a business entity have a continuous record of profitability to be treated as a going concern.[45]

Second, many existing awards exhibit a degree of inconsistency when trying to reconcile the standard of compensation with the measure and method to calculate such compensation, in particular when it comes to the calculation of market value.

The *Vivendi v. Argentina* award illustrates this point. In this case, the tribunal first ruled that the standard of FMV was applicable to treaty breaches other than expropriation.[46] In particular, the tribunal observed that "it is appropriate to assess compensation, at least in part, based on the fair market value of the concession."[47] The tribunal then proceeded to calculate such value and noted that "[a]t international law, depending on the circumstances arising in a particular case, there are a number of ways of approximating fair market value."[48]

The tribunal rejected a DCF "lost profits" valuation for lack of certainty. Then, after considering the application of alternative approaches to calculating FMV, the tribunal concluded that "investment value," understood as "the amount actually invested prior to the injurious acts," offered the "[...] closest proxy, if only partial, for compensation sufficient to eliminate the consequences of the Province's actions."[49] Historical investment costs, however, are not a measure of the current market value of an asset. Consequently, the tribunal applied a non-market measure of compensation despite its initial ruling that FMV was the appropriate standard of compensation.[50]

It is therefore necessary to define the purposes of the different methods of valuation and whether they are suitable for the determination of market value. In addition, the methods of valuation chosen by arbitrators must correspond to the decision about whether the investor should be compensated on the basis of the expectancy interest or the reliance interest, that is, whether compensation entails the assessment of market value.

Methods to Calculate Compensation

Accordingly, a careful consideration of the available methods is fundamental. An overview of these methods is provided below.[51]

Methods that do not establish market value. Among the valuation methods that do not establish market value is the "net book value" (NBV) computation. NBV calculates the difference between the enterprise's assets and its liabilities as recorded in its financial statements in accordance with Generally Accepted Accounting Principles (GAAP) or International Accounting Principles (IAP). An NBV calculation does not take account of changes in value of recorded on a company's financial statements at historical costs, rather than using the fair value (for example, NBV does not take into account changes in tangible assets that appreciate in value, such as the value of seedlings planted by a forest products company). Nor does NBV take account of assets expensed (for example, internally developed intellectual property such as "Windows" or drugs rights) or changes in goodwill (Kantor 2008, 8–17).

Another approach not establishing market value is "sunk investment costs" (or invested capital), which calculates the amount of capital invested in a project, plus a rate of return (usually an interest rate) from the date of investment to the award date. In certain cases, the amount is reduced for dividends received and the return of capital. Unless the capital was invested at a recent date in an arm's length transaction, this method does not take account of the impact of supervening events on market value.[52]

Methods that establish market value. Among the approaches that do establish market value is the "income-based approach." Methods employing the income-based approach convert future-looking anticipated economic benefits into a single present value amount; they can accommodate uncertainties by "risk-adjusting" the discount rate used to calculate the present value of the future stream of projected earnings or by "risk-adjusting" growth rates or revenue and expense assumptions (Kantor 2008, 8–17). For example, the DCF method measures the present value of the future net cash flows available to the company.[53] The adjusted present value method (APV) is a variant of DCF that measures the company's enterprise value as the value of the company without debt (the "unlevered enterprise") plus the present value of tax savings from the company's debt, then adjusts the resulting sum to introduce both the debt (the "leveraged enterprise") and the incremental bankruptcy risk created by adding that debt (Kantor 2008, 209–14). Each of these components may be discounted at different rates representing different risks. The "capitalized cash flow" (CCF) method, another popular income-based calculation, relies on a company's historical income levels. The reliability of the CCF method depends on the reliability of these historical figures. The CCF method is often preferred by valuation professionals in cases of companies with significant intangible assets and few fixed assets (Kantor 2008, 215–29).

The "market-based approach" relies on a market value estimated by comparing the business under review with similar businesses, business ownership interests, and securities that have been sold in the market, or to transactions involving similar companies. A comparability

analysis seeks to attribute to the company being valued the characteristics of a comparable company. Often, however, the extent of comparability is subject to question. Once the identity of the comparable
companies is agreed upon, the comparison may be made by using the
comparable's CCF value as a proxy for the subject company's value
(Kantor 2008, 119–30).

Finally, the "asset-based approach" estimates value by using
methods based on the current market value of assets net of liabilities. The adjusted book value (ABV) is a calculation of the difference
between a business's total assets (net of depreciation, depletion, and
amortization) and its total liabilities (including material assets and
liabilities not found in accounting balance sheets, such as depreciated assets, internally developed intellectual property, and goodwill). Unlike an NBV calculation that relies on GAAP or IAP
financial statements, however, all of the assets and liabilities in an
ABV calculation are adjusted to their fair market values, not the historical book amounts found on balance sheets prepared in accordance with accounting principles (Kantor 2008, 231–52).

Additional Remarks

In addition to the careful assessment of valuation methods, three
further comments appear useful. First, there is a greater need for
both cooperation with experts and communication with arbitrators.

Counsel and experts should focus on the need to simplify and
communicate their positions to the tribunal. Too often, arbitrators
are left confused by highly complicated damages presentations.
Counsel should also work with the experts and the other party to
determine points of agreement. Experts can be asked to exchange
drafts of their reports with the opposing party and then confer
regarding differences. Following that process, which may create
pressure for experts to retreat from exaggerated positions, the
experts may revise their reports and submit final reports to the tribunal. Those reports can be accompanied by a schedule of material
disagreements, thereby enabling the tribunal to focus its attention
on the material issues in dispute.

Second, arbitrators need to come to grips with compensation calculations and provide sufficient and clear reasoning for their findings. To focus the issues, arbitrators may, as recommended above,
request that experts submit a list of agreed-on matters and of material differences. Arbitrators could then decide if supplemental

reports seeking the use of more comparable methodologies and assumptions are required. In appropriate cases, arbitrators may also employ their own experts. In this event, arbitrators must pay attention to the expert's background and to giving the parties full and fair opportunity to be heard. Arbitrators should be mindful of the risk that the tribunal-appointed expert may improperly become the "fourth arbitrator." To avoid this risk, all interactions between the tribunal and their tribunal-appointed expert should be transparent to the parties and subject to examination and comment by the parties. Arbitrators should be especially mindful of the costs involved in asking for additional reports and in appointing their own expert. Those steps may be appropriate only in disputes sufficiently large to justify the significant additional expense.

Third, a more thorough grasp of business concepts by all parties involved seems warranted. A clear example of the divergence between a common understanding of valuation concepts among state regulatory and tax authorities, accountants, valuation experts, and the business community, on the one hand, and the investment arbitration community, on the other hand, is the use of the expression "going concern" in international investment law cases. As noted above, some investment treaty tribunals have employed the expression to require a business to have enjoyed several previous years of profitability.[54] These tribunals appear, in fact, to be concerned about the uncertainty of future earnings estimations, not whether the business is a going concern. By treating the concept of going concern as a rule of international law, rather than a question of whether the evidence in the case is sufficiently persuasive to support forward-looking damages, some arbitrators treat a question of the weight of evidence as, instead, a matter of legal principle. This contravenes accepted usage and creates confusion for participants in the compensation process.

Finally, looking first at the facts surrounding a compensation dispute may enable arbitrators and counsel to narrow the range of possible compensation theories available for application in the dispute. For example, if the date the capital was invested in a business was some time ago, and a number of intervening events have subsequently occurred, an arbitrator is unlikely to rely on the amount of invested capital to determine FMV. The impact of those subsequent events will have caused FMV to diverge from the amount of capital originally invested.

Conclusion

Dealing with compensation requires not only development of legal principles and standards, but also attention to areas such as business valuation and accounting that are neighbors to the law. This duality should be understood by all participants in the arbitral process—parties, counsel, arbitrators, and, in investment treaty arbitration, the public—to encourage a higher degree of consistency and predictability in the field of international investment law.

Doing better requires that arbitrators and counsel in investment cases fully understand valuation concepts and the purpose and functioning of the different valuation methods. Doing better also requires that arbitrators and counsel do not disregard principles and standards of compensation and the need to make them consistent with the valuation methods chosen to calculate compensation. Additionally, arbitrators and counsel need to acknowledge that focusing on the facts and considering the particular circumstances of each case is paramount, not only in choosing the most appropriate valuation method but also in identifying the parameters by which to adjust compensation, including equitable considerations.

Much attention has been devoted lately to the issue of compensation. Participants in the international arbitration community have seen their agendas filled with conferences and debates on compensation. Their inboxes and libraries have been inundated with articles, books, and research projects offering streams of legal and practical analysis of this issue. The hope is that the intensity of this debate and the quality of the discussion will bring into existence a new generation of investment treaty awards in which we all do better. And we hope the thoughts presented in this chapter will also contribute to this end.

Notes

1. For example, Azurix was awarded $165 million, Siemens $214 million, Enron $106 million, LG&E $57 million, Sempra $128, BG $185 million, National Grid $53 million, and Rumeli Telekom $125 million. These figures exclude interest, which in the majority of those cases, was compounded annually or semi-annually. See Azurix *v. Argentine Republic*, ICSID Case No. ARB/01/12, Award of July 14, 2006 (hereinafter *Azurix v. Argentina*), at ¶442; *Siemens v. Argentine Republic*, ICSID Case No. ARB/02/08, Award of February 6, 2007, at ¶403; *Enron Corporation and Ponderosa Assets, L.P v. Argentine Republic*, ICSID Case No. ARB/01/3, Award of May 22, 2007 (hereinafter *Enron v.*

Argentina), at ¶¶450, 452; *LG&E v. Argentine Republic*, ICSID Case No. ARB/02/01, Award of July 25, 2007 (hereinafter *LG&E v. Argentina*), at ¶115; *Sempra Energy International v. Argentine Republic*, ICSID Case No. ARB/02/16, Award of September 28, 2007 (hereinafter *Sempra v. Argentina*), at ¶¶482; *BG Group plc v. The Republic of Argentina*, arbitration pursuant to the UNCITRAL Arbitration Rules, Award of December 24, 2007 (hereinafter *BG v. Argentina*), at ¶467; *National Grid plc v. Argentine Republic*, arbitration pursuant to the UNCITRAL Arbitration Rules, Award of November 3, 2008 (hereinafter *National Grid v. Argentina*), at ¶296; and *Rumeli Telekom A.S. and Telsim Mobil Telekomikasyon Hizmetleri A.S. v. Republic of Kazakhstan*, ICSID Case No. ARB/05/16, Award of July 29, 2008 (hereinafter *Rumeli Telekom v. Kazakhstan*), at ¶¶814, 818.

2. The 2008 update in investment arbitration published by Linda A. Ahee and Richard E. Walck from Global Financial Analytics notes that by the end of 2007 the historical average recovery of successful claimants was about one-third of the amount claimed (Ahee and Walck 2009). The report also noted that the quantum of recovery during 2008 was "considerably less than in prior years" and "claimant's recoveries drop to 18.6% of the amounts claimed in 2008" when compared with recoveries during 2007. Yet, as Ahee and Walck point out, the report only includes ICSID awards and does not take account of two unpublished awards issued against Gabon and Georgia. It appears that the Gabon award is one of the year's largest. According to divergent reports, the amount awarded ranges between $100 million and $230 million.

3. The paucity of adduced reasons in the adjudication of damages was most noticeable in a number of earlier cases. For example, in the case *AMT v. Zaire*, in which it was established that Zaire had breached its obligations under the U.S.-Zaire BIT to provide protection and security and compensation for losses sustained resulting from an act of violence, the tribunal decided to award the claimant an amount that doubled the value calculated by the expert appointed by the tribunal without providing any explanation as to how the sum was conceived. In calculating the compensation that Costa Rica owed claimant for the expropriation of its property, the tribunal in the *Compañía del Desarrollo de Santa Elena v. Costa Rica* dispute established the value of the property by "approximating" two alternative assessments carried out by the parties at the time the expropriation was conducted. The tribunal provided no explanation as to how the final figure,. which corresponded to the midpoint of the two assessments, was obtained. See *American Manufacturing & Trading, Inc v. Republic of Zaire*, ICSID Case No.ARB/93/1, Award of February 21, 1997 (hereinafter *AMT v. Zaire*) at ¶¶7.16-7.21s; and *Compañía del Desarrollo de Santa Elena, S.A. v. The Republic of Costa Rica*, ICSID Case No. ARB 96/1, Award of February,

17, 2000, at ¶¶93–95. However, recent cases, in particular those mentioned at note 1, provide a more detailed analysis for their adjudication of damages.

4. See *LG&E v. Argentina*, at ¶29.

5. The Court noted in its decision, "It is a principle of international law that the breach of an engagement involves an obligation to make reparation in an adequate form. Reparation therefore is the indispensable complement of a failure to apply a convention and there is no necessity for this to be stated in the convention itself. Differences relating to reparations, which may be due by reason of failure to apply a convention, are consequently differences relating to its application." *Case concerning the Factory at Chorzów (Germany v. Polish Republic)*, Jurisdiction, Judgment No. 8, 1927, P.C.I.J., Series A, No. 9.

6. ILC's Draft Articles, Article 31 – Reparation: "(1) The responsible State is under an obligation to make full reparation for the injury caused by the internationally wrongful act."

7. According to Article 34 of the ILC's Draft Articles, full reparation may take the form of restitution, compensation, and satisfaction. For the purpose of this chapter, reference is made only to compensation.

8. A large number of recent awards have invoked this standard as the starting point of their assessment of damages claims: *S.D. Myers, Inc. v. Canada*, arbitration pursuant to the NAFTA and the UNCITRAL Arbitration Rules, Partial Award of November 13, 2000, at ¶¶311–315; *Metalclad Corp. v. United Mexican States*, ICSID Case No. ARB(AF)/97/1, August 30, 2000 (hereinafter *Metalclad v. Mexico*), at ¶120; *MTD Equity Sdn. Bhd. & MTD Chile S.A. v. Chile*, ICSID Case No. ARB/01/7, Award of May 25, 2004, at ¶238; *Enron v. Argentina*, at ¶359; *LG&E v. Argentina*, at ¶31; *Compañía de Aguas del Aconquija S.A. and Vivendi Universal v. Argentine Republic*, ICSID Case No. ARB/97/3, Award of August 20, 2007 (hereinafter *Vivendi v. Argentina*), at ¶8.2.4; *Rumeli Telekom v. Kazakhstan*, at ¶792.

9. See *Case concerning the Factory at Chorzów (Germany v. Polish Republic)*, PCIJ Proceeding, Merits 1928, P.C.I.J. Series A,. No. 17, p. 21.

10. The standard is reflected in articles 31 and 36 of the ILC's Draft Articles. As noted by Professor Crawford in his commentary to article 31 "[t]he obligation placed on the responsible State by article 31 is to make 'full reparation' in the Factory at Chorzów sense. In other words, the responsible State must endeavour to 'wipe out all the consequences of the illegal act and reestablish the situation which would, in all probability, have existed if that act had not been committed.'" See ILC's Draft Articles, commentary to article 31, at (3) (emphasis added).

11. See note 8.

12. See "Valuation Practices" and "Methods to Calculate Compensation" sections of this chapter.

13. See "Methods to Calculate Compensation" section of this chapter.

14. The business interruption measure of compensation seeks "to calculate the amount of the temporary loss resulting from interruption of or interference with the injured business – the normal outcome is compared with the actual outcome for the affected period of time." This approach measures current value and seeks to compensate the affected party for the diminution in value of the enterprise for the period of time necessary for the injured enterprise to recover. See Kantor (2008, 42–3) and "Methods to Calculate Compensation" section of this chapter.

15. See "Methods to Calculate Compensation" section of this chapter.

16. See note 52. This second case corresponds to the valuation approach recommended by Professor Brownlie in his dissenting opinion in *CME v. Czech Republic*. He argued that the proper standard for compensation in the case of expropriation of the investor's interest was "appropriate compensation" rather than "full compensation." Professor Brownlie based his position on UN General Assembly Resolutions and on the different wording of the Czech-Netherlands (just compensation) and the Czech-US (fair market value) BITs. In this manner, Professor Brownlie argued for the recovery solely of the reliance interest, by permitting the investor to recover *damnum emergens* (that is, sunk investment costs; invested capital minus capital already recovered, together with a return on the sunk costs). See Kantor (2008, 50).

17. See *Enron v. Argentina*, at ¶380; *LG&E v. Argentina*, at ¶¶49, 60.

18. See, for example, *Azurix v. Argentina*, at ¶424; *Enron v. Argentina*, at ¶362.

19. See, for example, *CMS Gas Transmissions Company v. Argentine Republic*, ICSID Case No. ARB/01/8, Award of May 12, 2005 (hereinafter *CMS v. Argentina*), at ¶402. See also *Azurix v. Argentina*, at ¶424, and *Sempra v. Argentina*, at ¶405. These awards use a definition of FMV from the International Glossary of Business Valuation Terms, American Society of Appraisers, ASA Web site, June 6, 2001, p. 4.

20. In *Vivendi v. Argentina*, the tribunal expressly indicated that "[t]he Treaty thus mandates that compensation for lawful expropriation be based on the *actual* value of the investment, and that interest shall be paid from the date of dispossession. However, it does not purport to establish a *lex specialis* governing the standards of compensation for wrongful expropriations. As to the appropriate measure of compensation for the breaches other than expropriation, the Treaty is silent." (footnotes omitted). See *Vivendi v. Argentina*, at ¶8.2.3.

21. *ADC Affiliate Limited and ADC & ADMC Management Limited v. The Republic of Hungary*, ICSID Case No. ARB/03/16, Award of October 2, 2006.

22. See *AMT v. Zaire*, at ¶7.03; *CMS v. Argentina*, at ¶395; *LG&E v. Argentina*, at ¶¶12, 33; and *BG v. Argentina*, at ¶420. Investors tend to invoke the treaty provision on expropriation and the standard of FMV contained therein in claims to compensate the breaches of other treaty standards such as fair and equitable treatment. Marboe notes that it is "hardly possible" to find a treaty that would contain the standard of full compensation; instead, the standard contained in a large number of BITs and model treaties is that of "adequate, prompt, and effective" compensation. Many treaties refer this standard to the FMV. Using the definition of FMV cited in *CMS v. Argentina* and stated above, Marboe concludes that fair market value does not mean the investor will receive full compensation: "[t]he expropriated individual will not necessarily receive all the financial loss he or she has suffered as a consequence of the expropriation. Rather the calculation shall be based on the opinion of a hypothetical third person on the value of the affected property" (Marboe 2006, 730–1). Thus, the FMV standard is an "objective" standard, not a "subjective" standard measuring the loss in value from the perspective of that particular investor and with that particular investor's characteristics.

23. See, for example, *Archer Daniels Midland Co. & Tate & Lyle Ingredients Americas Inc. v. The United Mexican States*, arbitration pursuant to the NAFTA, ICSID Case No. ARB(AF)/04/05, Award of November 21, 2007 (hereinafter *ADM & TLIA v. Mexico*), at ¶261. It should be noted, however, that a number of states do not point to this difference. These states tend to agree with FMV as the proper measure for compensation for violations other than expropriation and generally contend only the methods used by investors to calculate such FMV. See, for example *Vivendi v. Argentina*, at ¶8.2.9 and *LG&E v. Argentina*, at ¶33.

24. See *CMS v. Argentina*, at ¶410.

25. See *CMS v. Argentina*, at ¶¶399 ss.

26. See *LG&E v. Argentina*, at ¶¶33–40. Similarly, the tribunal in *BG v. Argentina* considered that the measure of compensation for breach of treatment obligations cannot be "automatically imported" from a treaty provision governing expropriation. Rather, as stated in *ADM & TLIA v. Mexico*, compensation will depend on the "the specific circumstances of the case (citing SD Myers ¶ 69) [...] 'leaving considerable discretion in establishing the methodology to determine damages'." See *BG v. Argentina*, at ¶ 422 and *ADM & TLIA v. Mexico*, at ¶ 278. See also note 31.

27. See *LG&E v. Argentina*, at ¶45.

28. See *LG&E v. Argentina*, at ¶¶48, 60.

29. See *BG v. Argentina*, at ¶ 422 and *National Grid v. Argentina*, at ¶¶269, 275.

30. See *BG v. Argentina*, at ¶¶421–422.

31. See *Sempra v. Argentina*, at ¶403. See also *Vivendi v. Argentina*, at ¶8.2.10, offering a similar argument. In awards pursuant to the NAFTA, tribunals have noted that Chapter XI (on investment) only contains guidance on compensation with regard to expropriation (the FMV standard). The silence of NAFTA with respect to the measure of compensation for breaches of other obligations contained in Chapter XI has been interpreted by a number of tribunals as limiting application of FMV as the measure of compensation for breaches of obligations other than expropriation. For instance, the tribunal in *Feldman v. Mexico* observed that "[...] the only detailed measure of damages specifically provided in Chapter 11 is in Article 1110(2-3), 'fair market value,' which necessarily applies only to situations that fall within Article 1110." The tribunal in *SD Myers v. Canada* further noted that "[...] by not identifying any particular methodology for the assessment of compensation in cases not involving expropriation, the Tribunal considers that the drafters of the NAFTA intended to leave it open to tribunals to determine a measure of the case, taking into account the principles of both international law and the provisions of the NAFTA." The recent tribunal in the *ADM & TLIA v. Mexico* case, citing the decisions in *Feldman v. Mexico* and SD *Myers v. Canada*, confirmed this approach. See *Marvin Roy Feldman v. United Mexican States*, ICSID Case No. ARB(AF)/99/1, Award of December 16, 2002, at ¶¶195–197; *S.D. Myers, Inc v. Government of Canada*, arbitration pursuant to NAFTA and the UNCITRAL Arbitration Rules, Second Partial Award of October 21, 2002, ¶309; and *ADM & TLIA v. Mexico*, at ¶¶277–279.

32. See notes 16 and 52.

33. See note 14 and "Methods to Calculate Compensation" section of this chapter.

34. See, in general, the analysis in *LG&E v. Argentina*.

35. For treatment in U.S. cases, see commentary by Dunn (2005) cited by Kantor (2008, 72–3). A similar distinction is drawn in many English cases.

36. The *Vivendi v. Argentina* case also illustrates how some investment treaty arbitral tribunals have set the "reasonable certainty" threshold very high. In this case, the claimant alleged that the company to be valued was a revenue-generating enterprise with 65 percent recovery rate on its first invoices. In addition, claimants offered evidence of high invoice recovery rates for other utilities in the same region. The tribunal considered that this evidence was insufficient to demonstrate a history of profitability. The tribunal stated that, in the absence of a record of profits, the claimant must provide "convincing evidence of its ability to produce profits in the particular circumstances

it faced." The tribunal noted: "A claimant which cannot rely on a record of demonstrated profitability requires to present a thoroughly prepared record of its (or others) successes, based on first-hand experience (its own or that of qualified experts) or corporate records which establish on the balance of the probabilities it would have produced profits from the concession in question in the face of the particular risks involved, other than those of Treaty violation." The tribunal concluded that the claimants had failed to establish with a "sufficient degree of certainty" that the concession would have been profitable. Therefore, the arbitrators rejected the application of the DCF method to measure compensation and proceeded to calculate compensation based on the "actual investment" method. See *Vivendi v. Argentina*, at ¶¶8.3.8 – 8.3.10. See also "Valuation Practices" section of this chapter.

37. See *LG&E v. Argentina*, at ¶90.

38. See *LG&E v. Argentina*, at ¶¶90–95.

39. In *AMT v. Zaire*, the respondent state pleaded as an argument to deny or reduce compensation for the investor the fact of being a state going through difficult circumstances. According to Zaire, this situation "[...] requires a benevolent and compassionate attention on the part of all our partners, even those who have encountered unfortunate and disastrous consequences, for there was a time when these same persons were enjoying the benefit of the good situation of the State of Zaire." See *AMT v. Zaire*, at ¶7.17.

40. For example, the awards in *LG&E v. Argentina* and *PSEG v. Turkey* display a noticeable desire on the part of the arbitrators to look for means of minimizing the compensation to be paid by the host state. In the former case, the tribunal rejected the application of the DCF method as well as the award of lost future profits, judging them speculative and uncertain in nature. In the second case, the tribunal did not accept claimant's arguments in favor of recovering lost profits under a concession contract for a power project because of the start-up nature of the project and the gaps in the concession contract with respect to the pricing terms. See *LG&E v. Argentina* and *PSEG Global Inc et.al v. Republic of Turkey*, ICSID Case No. ARB/02/5, Award of January 19, 2007. Other tribunals, including some panels of the Iran-U.S. Claims Tribunals, have taken a similar approach. For instance, in *CMI v. Iran* the panel declined to apply certain argued-for rules of the governing law of the purchase orders, which the claimant argued would have served to increase the amount of compensation due. Instead, the panel noted that the assessment of compensation involved a "search [...] for justice and equity, even in cases where arguably relevant national laws might be designed to further other and doubtless quite legitimate goals." Consequently, the tribunal held that profits on resales of equipment should be taken into account to reduce claimant's compensation.

See *CMI International, Inc. v. Ministry of Roads and Transportation and The Islamic Republic of Iran*, Case 245, 4 Iran-U.S. C.T.R. 267–8.

41. See *AMT v. Zaire*, at ¶7.19–7.21. It is interesting to note that Mr. Kéba Mbaye, the arbitrator appointed by ICSID in the absence of Zaire's appointment of its arbitrator, stated in a separate declaration that "[...] I am still convinced that the sum of U.S. Dollars 9,000,000 (nine million) awarded to the Claimant exceeds by far the injuries actually sustained by the Claimants and the profits including the interests it could have reasonably expected. In my opinion, the total amount of compensation, inclusive of the principal, interests and other claims, should not exceed U.S. Dollars 4,000,000 (four million)." No further explanation was provided for departing from the majority's position.

42. See *Sola Tiles Inc. v. Islamic Republic of Iran*, Award 298-317-1 14 US C.T.R 223, (hereinafter, *Sola v. Iran*), at 64.

43. See *Metalclad v. Mexico*, at ¶120.

44. The concept of "liquidation value" corresponds to the "net amount that can be realized in either an orderly sale or a forced sale." It is appropriate if "use of 'going concern' is unrealistic" (Kantor 2008, 251).

45. For example, the International Glossary of Business Valuation Terms defines "going concern" as "an ongoing operating business enterprise" and "going concern value" as "the value of a business enterprise that is expected to continue to operate into the future. The intangible elements of Going Concern Value result from factors such as having a trained work force, an operational plant, and the necessary licenses, systems, and procedures in place." International Glossary of Business Valuation Terms, available at www.bvappraisers.org/glossary/glossary.pdf, in Kantor (2008, 9, 95). This glossary has been jointly adopted by the American Society of Appraisers, the American Institute of Certified Public Accountants, the Canadian Institute of Chartered Business Valuators, the National Association of Certified Valuation Analysis, and the Institute of Business Appraisers.

46. In this regard, the tribunal in *Vivendi v. Argentina* closely followed the reasoning of the *CMS v. Argentina* and *Azurix v. Argentina* awards. See *Vivendi v. Argentina*, at ¶8.2.10. See also "Measure of damages for breach of treatment obligations" section of this chapter.

47. See *Vivendi v. Argentina*, at ¶8.2.11. As noted by the tribunal, the reference to "at least in part" relates to Vivendi's need to fund the investment's ongoing costs after expropriation.

48. *Vivendi v. Argentina*, at ¶8.3.3.

49. *Vivendi v. Argentina*, at ¶¶8.3.12–8.3.13.

50. See Kantor (2008, 35). *AAPL v. Sri Lanka*, the first investment case based on a BIT, offers another interesting example of the disparity in the application of standards, measures, and methods of valuation by

tribunals in investment awards. In this case, the parties and the tribunal agreed that compensation should reflect "the full value of the investment lost as a result of said destruction and damages incurred as a result thereof." According to the tribunal, the value of the investment corresponded to the value of the claimant's shareholding in the joint venture entity (Serendib). The tribunal indicated that this value was to be determined by the stock market at which the price of the shares was quoted on the date before the destruction took place. In the absence of such a stock quote, the value of the investment should be calculated by the alternative method of calculating the "reasonable price a willing purchaser would have offered to AAPL to acquire its shareholding in Serendib." This reasonable price was to be determined by establishing a "comprehensive balance sheets which reflects the results of assessing the global assets of Serendib in comparison with all the outstanding indebtedness thereof at the relevant time."

The tribunal noted, in addition, that it would consider the question of whether Serendib was a going concern only for the purposes of establishing the reasonable market value of the shares but that as a "general rule all elements related to subsequent developments should not be taken as such into consideration, and *lucrum cessans* in the proper sense could not be allocated in the present case [...]." The relevant issue for the tribunal was to determine whether the company had developed a "goodwill" and a "standard of profitability" that would influence the prospective purchaser to pay a "premium over the value of tangible assets for the benefit of the Company's 'intangible' assets." Because the evidence did not show the existence of these elements the tribunal concluded that Serendib was not a going concern and granted compensation only on the basis of the value of the tangible assets. Apart from the unusual characterization of a going concern, it should be noted that, although the tribunal stated its intention to establish the market value of the investment, it took recourse to the method of net book value, a method that does not reflect market value. See *Asian Agricultural Products LTD v. Republic of Sri Lanka*, ICSID Case No. ARB/87/3, Award of June 27, 1990, at ¶¶88, 96, 98, 102.

51. For a detailed description of the methods and their use, see Kantor (2008).

52. The invested capital or sunk investment costs approach provides recovery of the reliance interest by seeking to put the investor back into the position it was in before making the investment. As noted by Wells (2003), sunk investment costs may be the appropriate measure "when the investment is very recent or still in the process of being made." This approach is consistent with business valuation practices. For instance, the International Private Equity Valuation Guidelines (Kantor 2008, 42–3, 50, 83) point out that "where the

Investment being valued was itself made recently, its costs will generally provide a good indication of Fair Value." It should be noted, however, that this approach will not take into account changes in value (up or down) after the investment is made and that it has no relation at all to market value. The guidelines recommend employing sunk investment costs only for "recent" investments: "[t]his length of period will depend on the specific circumstances of the case, but should not generally exceed a period of one year" (Kantor 2008, 83).

53. DCF is one of the most widely used methods for business valuations. It measures the present value of the future cash flows available to equity, which corresponds to the "[n]et income after taxes, plus depreciation and other non-cash charges, less increases in working capital, less capital expenditures, less decreases in invested debt capital principal, plus increases in invested capital debt principal" (International Valuation Standards Council [2007] in Kantor [2008, 131–207]).

54. See, for example, the cases of *Sola v. Iran* and *Metalclad v. Mexico* discussed in the Valuation Practices section of this chapter.

References

Ahee, L. A., and R. E. Walck. 2009. "Investment Arbitration Update as of December 31, 2008." Transnational Dispute Management. http://www.gfa-llc.com/images/Investment_Arbitration_Update_2008_-_TDM.pdf.

Dunn, R. L. 2005. *Recovery of Damages for Lost Profits*, sixth ed. Alameda, CA: Lawpress Corporation.

Franck, S. D. 2007. "Empirically Evaluating Claims about Investment Treaty Arbitration." *North Carolina Law Review* 86: 1.

International Valuation Standards Council. 2007. "Guidance Note GN6 on Business Valuation." In *International Valuation Standards*, 8th ed. London: IVSC.

Kantor, M. 2008. *Valuation for Arbitration: Compensation Standards, Valuation Methods and Expert Evidence*. Amsterdam: Wolters Kluwer.

Legum, B. 2004. "Lessons Learned from the NAFTA: The New Generation of U.S. Investment Treaty Arbitration Provisions." *ICSID Review: Foreign Investment Law Journal* 19: 344–47. In Franck, S. D. 2007. "Empirically Evaluating Claims about Investment Treaty Arbitration." *North Carolina Law Review* 86.

Marboe, I. 2006. "Compensation and Damages in International Law. The Limits of 'Fair Market Value.'" *The Journal of World Investment and Trade* 7 (5).

Wells, L. 2003. "Double Dipping in Arbitration Awards? An Economist Questions Damages Awarded to Karaha Bodas Company in Indonesia." *Arbitration International* 19 (4): 471.

ANNEX 12A CALCULATING DAMAGES: ARBITRATORS, COUNSEL,
AND EXPERTS CAN DO BETTER THAN THEY HAVE IN THE PAST

I. LAW OF DAMAGE CLAIMS

A. Standards and measures of compensation

Points of Discussion	*Valuable Tools*
1.The standard introduced by Chorzów	**Clarifying the difference between "expectancy" and "reliance" interests in the invocation of the** *Chorzów* **standard**

Standard introduced by Chorzów: "The essential principle contained in the actual notion of an illegal act—a principle which seems to be established by international practice and in particular by decisions of arbitral tribunals—is that reparation must, so far as possible wipe out all the consequences of the illegal act and re-establish the situation that would, in all probability, have existed if that act had not been committed."

Adopted by the ILC's Draft Articles on State Responsibility (Arts. 31, 36) as well.

Counsel and arbitrators: In practice, the standard is understood to require "full reparation." The full reparation standard has been invoked by investors and states in equal measure to support differing claims for compensation. It has also been accepted by arbitrators as the starting point for the analysis of investment treaty damage claims.

The standard introduced by Chorzów seems capable, in practice, of being interpreted in divergent fashions. For example, in four different cases against Argentina (Vivendi, Enron, LG&E, and BG) the standard was invoked as the starting point for the tribunals' analysis of compensation.

The Chorzów rule calls for compensation of the injured party's "expectancy interest," that is, compensation that seeks to return the investor to a position in which the investment has been made but the injury had not occurred. Therefore, the Chorzów formulation should be invoked only when compensation is intended to protect the injured party's expectancy interest.

The standard set out in Chorzów does not support the award of compensation based solely on the "reliance interest" or compensation that seeks to return the investor to the position it would have been in if the investment had never been made.

Prof. Marboe's "differential method"

To conduct the calculation of the full compensation required by Chorzów, Professor Marboe points to the use of the "differential method," according to which

"What has to be done is a comparison of the actual financial situation of the injured person with the financial situation that would have existed if the illegal act had not been committed.

Points of Discussion	*Valuable Tools*
However, when calculating compensation, Vivendi used a "sunk investment costs" approach, Enron relied upon a "DCF" valuation, LG&E applied a "business interruption" model, and BG relied on a "comparable transactions" valuation method.	The adjudicating body must therefore make an assumption regarding the situation that 'would, in all probability, have existed' if the illegal act had not occurred and compare it to the actual situation after the breach. The difference is the damage that was caused by the illegal act."

Varying applications of the "differential method"

Tribunals differ widely in the methods they employ to calculate the value of the injured enterprise before and after the illegal act. The tribunals in both Enron and LG&E expressly stated that their intent was to put the investor in the situation as if the illegal act had never occurred, by comparing the company's situation before and after the measures adopted by Argentina. To do so, though, the Enron tribunal used a DCF methodology to value the claimant's equity interest. LG&E, in contrast, rejected this approach and opted to calculate the difference between the amount of dividends actually received and the dividends that would have been received but for the adoption of the Argentine measures. This difference in the measure of compensation is explained by a different understanding of the application of the notion of FMV.

2. Measure of damages for expropriation	**FMV as *de minimus* compensation for unlawful expropriation**
Counsel and arbitrators. There seems to be considerable agreement that the measure of damages for expropriation is the FMV of the investment. This approach has largely been incorporated into investment	FMV is particularly useful when the purpose of compensation is to compensate for the total loss or destruction of an asset or the permanent diminution in value of that asset. In such a case, it would serve as the

Points of Discussion	Valuable Tools

treaties, and tribunals in numerous awards have referred to FMV as the proper measure of compensation for expropriation.

FMV has been defined by tribunals along the lines of the definition used by accountants, regulators, and valuation professionals as

"[...] the price expressed in terms of cash equivalents, at which the property would change hands between a hypothetical willing and able buyer and a hypothetical willing and able seller, acting at arms length in an open and unrestricted market, when neither is under compulsion to buy or sell and when both have reasonable knowledge of the relevant facts."

Investment treaties, however, are largely silent regarding the proper compensation standard for so-called unlawful expropriations, for example, expropriations not effected for a public purpose, conducted in a discriminatory manner, or made pursuant to a process denying the injured investor due process or compensation.

Should a difference be made between lawful and unlawful expropriation?

Counsel. It comes as no surprise that counsel for investors use the distinction between lawful and unlawful expropriations to argue for larger compensation amounts in the latter case.

Arbitrators. Arbitrators have invoked this distinction to introduce equitable considerations. Examples included moving the valuation date from the

basis for calculating damages and as a minimum value for compensation. As noted, the majority of BITs expressly require the use of FMV to calculate compensation for a lawful expropriation. Given the use of FMV as the standard for compensation with respect to lawful expropriations, it is essentially impossible to argue persuasively that the amount of compensation for an unlawful expropriation should be less than FMV.

Alternative measures of compensation

Alternatives to FMV may be considered depending on the factual circumstances surrounding the dispute. When the investment is very recent or is in the process of being made, "sunk investment costs" appears to be a useful measure of compensation. As noted, this is a measure of the "reliance interest" and seeks to provide for the recovery of invested sums plus a reasonable rate of return on those sums up until the date of recovery. If, however, there are significant intervening events between the date of investment and the date of the injury, the amount of invested capital will not reflect the FMV (up or down) of the investment on the injury date.

When the loss or destruction of the asset is not permanent, but rather is temporary, "business interruption" appears to be a useful measure of compensation. This method seeks to compensate the injured party for the diminution in value of the business for the period of time necessary for the business to restore itself. The business interruption computation

Points of Discussion	*Valuable Tools*
injury date to the award date to prevent unjust enrichment, protecting the amount awarded from foreign exchange fluctuations after the injury date, and granting restitution of property unlawfully seized. For example, the tribunal in *ADC v. Hungary* considered that, because Hungary's expropriation of the airport concession was unlawful, the claimants were entitled to the benefits of the significant increase in value of the concession that followed the expropriation. To reflect this conclusion, the tribunal departed from the injury date rule and used the date of the award as the valuation date.	calculates the amount of the temporary loss resulting from interruption of or interference with the injured business; in effect, the normal outcome is compared with the actual outcome. The UN Compensation Commission regularly used business interruption analyses to compensate injured businesses for the consequences of the Iraqi invasion of Kuwait. **Use of general legal principles** General legal principles may also find application in the process of determining compensation and assessing the use of FMV. These include causation, foreseeability, a requirement in many legal systems that lost profits be proven with reasonable certainty and not be speculative, mitigation, and equitable considerations, including unjust enrichment.

3. Measure of damages for breach of treatment obligations

Counsel. Investors' counsel are inclined to consider that the FMV of the asset provides the full compensation required by the Chorzów standard for breach of all treatment obligations. State's counsel consider that FMV is, perhaps, the proper measure for expropriations, but not for unlawful conduct such as breach of "fair and equitable treatment" or discriminatory treatment contrary to MFN or "national treatment" commitments.

Arbitrators. Arbitrators have not been consistent in their approach, as illustrated by the following awards.

Points of Discussion	*Valuable Tools*

■ CMS referred to the FMV measure,
based on the proximity of the circumstances of the case to expropriation. The tribunal was "persuaded that the cumulative nature
of the breaches discussed here is
best dealt with by resorting to the
standard of fair market value."
The tribunal also indicated that
"[...] it is not excluded that it
[FMV] might also be appropriate
for breaches different from expropriation if their effect results in
important long-term losses." The
tribunal proceeded to define FMV
and to calculate the amount of
compensation by comparing the
estimated market values in the
"*pesification* scenario" (the actual
situation under the measures
adopted by Argentina) and the
"*nonpesification* scenario" (in the
absence of such measures). The
difference between the two scenarios was, for the CMS tribunal,
the amount of damage caused by
the adoption of the regulatory
measures that resulted in violation
of the treaty. To avoid the problem
of leaving CMS with continuing
ownership of the shares when it
was possible that those shares
might in the future recover their
value or drop further in value, the
tribunal also granted Argentina an
option for one year to purchase
CMS's shares for US$2.1 million
(their postinjury reduced value).
In that way, if Argentina later
chose to rescind its unlawful acts
and, as a result, the share value
rose, Argentina would have made
a choice by exercising (or not exercising) the share option as to
whether CMS or Argentina would
capture that future change in

Points of Discussion	*Valuable Tools*

value. That share option is an
often overlooked, but crucial,
component of the CMS compensation decision.

■ In departing from the approach in
CMS, the tribunal in *LG&E v.
Argentina* concluded that the
expropriation standard applied in
the treaty to lawful expropriations
was not suitable for determining
the consequences of unlawful acts
such as breach of the treaty's fair
and equitable treatment commitment. The LG&E tribunal also
argued that FMV is not the appropriate measure for compensation
when the investor retains title to
its investment and when the
state's unlawful interference with
property rights does not result in a
loss equivalent to the total loss of
the investment. The tribunal
decided that the proper measure in
this "case [...] is that of the identification of the 'actual loss' suffered
by the investor 'as a result' of
Argentina's conduct. The question
is one of 'causation': what did the
investor lose by reason of the
unlawful acts?" The tribunal determined that "the actual damage
inflicted by the measures is the
amount of dividends that could
have been received but for the
adoption of the measures" and
proceeded to calculate the amount
of dividends that the claimant
would have received but for the
measures and subtracted from that
amount the amount of dividends
actually received to obtain the
value of compensation. By limiting
compensation solely to forgone
dividends, the LG&E tribunal
effectively declined to compensate
the investor for any capital gains

Points of Discussion	*Valuable Tools*

on the investment. Said another way, if a portion of the company's earnings is reinvested in the company to grow the enterprise, rather than being paid to the shareholders as dividends, that value is ignored in a "dividends forgone" calculation. The dividends forgone calculation would also result in zero compensation if the company was in a negative cash flow situation because it was in the midst of development or construction, even if the company was nevertheless acknowledged to be very valuable.

■ The subsequent *BG v. Argentina* and *National Grid v. Argentina* decisions, in contrast, refer to the FMV measure of compensation as "being made available by reference to customary international law." Those tribunals cite the ILC's Draft Articles as support for that conclusion. In particular, the tribunal in BG noted that "[...] principles of treaty hermeneutics militate for the conclusion that one should not read into Article 2.2 of the BIT [containing the standard of FET] a standard that Argentina and the U.K. expressly confined to Article 5 of the BIT [provision on expropriation]. For other reasons, however, 'fair market value' can be relied upon as a standard to measure damages for breach of the obligation to accord investors treatment in accordance with Article 2.2 of the BIT. While the Tribunal is disinclined to automatically import such standard from Article 5 of the BIT, this standard of compensation is nonetheless available by reference to customary international law." In their calculations of

Points of Discussion	Valuable Tools
the FMV of the affected investment, the tribunals in the BG and National Grid cases were guided by the values used in actual transactions relating to the companies affected by the measures adopted by Argentina—a "comparable transactions" method of measuring FMV. ■ The tribunal in *Sempra v Argentina* followed closely the CMS approach and stated, "In [...] cases [where] it might be very difficult to distinguish the breach of fair and equitable treatment from indirect expropriation or other forms of taking [...] it is [...] reasonable that the standard of reparation might be the same." ■ In the context of NAFTA, tribunals have interpreted the silence of the treaty in respect to the standard of compensation for breaches of protections other than expropriation as limiting application of FMV as the measure of compensation for breaches of treatment obligations.	

B. Locus of the burden of evidence

Where does the burden of evidence lie?	Allocating the burden of proof
Counsel. State parties point out the uncertainty of forward-looking compensation. Accordingly, states regularly argue in investment treaty cases that such compensation should be awarded only upon proof satisfying a high threshold of evidence (that is, proof with "reasonable certainty"— not "speculative" amounts). Investors retort that the reason the evidence of future revenues is subject to uncertainty is the conduct of the host state,	When considering matters of evidence, it should be noted that the ordinary burden of proof for factual matters is "preponderance of the evidence." By requiring proof of forward-looking damages (such as lost profits) to a reasonable certainty, arbitrators impose a higher evidentiary standard on the claimant investor. The purpose behind the higher evidentiary standard is, of course, to avoid compensation for a future that is inherently uncertain.

Points of Discussion	*Valuable Tools*
which prevented that future from crystallizing. Therefore, the claimant-investor should not be held to an unusually high standard of evidence.	The uncertainty about that future has been created, however, by the state's conduct preventing that future from crystallizing, an obvious equitable consideration. Investment treaty awards often impose the reasonable certainty test on both the fact of forward-looking damages and the amount of those damages. Some national courts (for example, U.S. and UK courts) take account of the equitable considerations involved by requiring the higher reasonable certainty evidentiary burden for the fact of forward-looking damages, but a lower evidentiary burden for the proof of the amount of those damages. No investment treaty award has yet followed this approach.
Arbitrators. In recent practice, arbitrators have tended to impose a high evidentiary burden on the claimant (high threshold for reasonable certainty) and to grant the benefit of the doubt to states. Unlike the situation in many national courts, no difference is drawn between the standard of evidence (reasonable certainty) required to prove the existence in those awards of forward-looking damages (the "expectancy interest") and the standard of evidence required to prove the amount of those damages (again, reasonable certainty).	
The concern over the certainty of damages lies at the core of the decision of the tribunal in *LG&E v. Argentina*. Despite having evidence of prior dividends from 1993 through 2005 at hand, the tribunal rejected the investor's claim for future dividends because "future loss to the Claimants is uncertain and any attempt to calculate it is speculative." The tribunal also noted that "[t]he uncertainty concerning lost future profits in the form of lost dividends results from the fact, noted above, that Claimants have retained title to their investments and are therefore entitled to any profit that the investment generates and could generate in the future. Any attempt to calculate the amount of the lost dividends in both the actual and 'but for' scenarios is a highly speculative exercise. If the Tribunal were to compensate LG&E for lost	

Points of Discussion	Valuable Tools
future dividends while it continues to receive dividends distributed by the Licensees at a hypothetical low amount, a situation of double recovery would arise, unduly enriching the Claimants." Finally, the tribunal in LG&E considered that respect for due process obliged it to consider only the evidence that both parties were able to contest. Therefore, the panel set February 2005—the date indicated at the hearing as the final date for submitting evidence—as the date for calculating accrued losses. The panel rejected the investor's efforts to submit further valuation evidence after that date. Notably, the LG&E tribunal did not discuss the share option tool employed in CMS to address the potential for double recovery. Moreover, the tribunal did not discuss the impact on the investor of continuing injuries after the award period despite Argentina's stated intention to continue the conduct the tribunal had already ruled was unlawful. The *Vivendi v. Argentina* case also illustrates how some investment treaty arbitral tribunals have set the reasonable certainty threshold very high.	

C. Treatment of a state party

Should a state respondent be treated differently from private respondents when calculating compensation in investment arbitration? *Counsel.* States claim differential treatment based solely on their being states and having to respond to political demands; investors reject this claim.	**Providing reasons** Arbitrators should fully explain their reasons for deciding to treat states the same as, or different from, private respondents for compensation purposes.

Points of Discussion	*Valuable Tools*
Arbitrators. By applying a stricter test of reasonable certainty (setting the threshold higher and requiring reasonable certainty for both the fact of lost profits and the amount of those lost profits), using "equitable considerations" to limit compensation and giving the benefit of the doubt to states (the party causing the injury) rather than claimants (the injured party), some investor-state tribunals grant states protective treatment. In the majority of awards, this position is neither fully explained nor is any justification set out.	**Counsel advocacy points** Counsel for investor claimants will wish to argue that a state respondent has the burden of persuading the tribunal that states should be treated more favorably than private respondents in calculating compensation.
In the case of *AMT v. Zaire*, the tribunal expressly stated that it based its decision on "equitable principles." The tribunal asserted that in the calculation of damages it would consider the particular circumstances and risks taken when investing in a country like Zaire. It then criticized AMT's proposed valuation method for encompassing "interests practicable in the normal circumstances prevailing in an ideal country where the climate of investments is very stable [...]." Accordingly, the *AMT v. Zaire* tribunal rejected in large part AMT's claim for *lucrum cessans* (lost profits). In spite of this approach, the tribunal exercised its "discretionary and sovereign power to determine the quantum of compensation" and awarded the claimant an "all-inclusive" total sum that doubled the value of destroyed goods and property as calculated by the expert appointed by the tribunal. Presumably, the excess over the value of the tangible assets reflected the tribunal's attempt to value the investment's goodwill as a going concern. However, the tribunal provided no explanation for how this sum was calculated.	Conversely, counsel for state respondents will wish to argue that international investment law derives from different sources of law than commercial law. States are only bound by international customary rules and general principles of law evidenced by longstanding state conduct and by treaties specifically agreed to by the state. Therefore, the concept of state consent lies at the heart of international investment law. Thus, according to state respondents, differential treatment of states is justified.

Points of Discussion	Valuable Tools
Also, the awards in *LG&E v. Argentina* and *PSEG v. Turkey* display a noticeable desire on the part of the arbitrators to look for means of minimizing the compensation to be paid by the host state.	

II. VALUATION OF DAMAGE CLAIMS

A. Valuation Practice

Existing arbitral practice displays insufficiencies, including (i) a tendency to depart from accepted business concepts and (ii) a degree of inconsistency when matching the standard of compensation to the measure and method to calculate such compensation.

Departure from accepted business concepts

There is a tendency for arbitrators to depart from widely accepted business concepts and valuation principles (such as the common meaning of the phrase "going concern"). The following cases are illustrative of this situation. In the Sola Tiles award, the Iran-U.S. Tribunal concluded that, although the enterprise (SIMAT) had been operating for almost three years before the expropriation date, it was not a "going concern" because, among other factors, "Simat has the briefest past record of profitability having shown a loss in 1976, its first year of trading, and a small profit the next year." Since the enterprise was not a going concern the tribunal rejected claimant's request for goodwill and lost profits.

Citing with approval the *Sola v. Iran* award, the NAFTA tribunal in *Metalclad* asserted that a minimum period of two or three years of continuing market presence was required before an enterprise would be treated as a going concern. The tribunal noted, "However, where the enterprise has not operated for a sufficiently long time to establish a performance record or where it has failed to make a profit, future profits cannot be used to determine going concern or fair market value."

Accountants, valuation professionals, regulators, and the business community use the expression "going concern" to refer to operating business enterprises, in contrast with "liquidation value." Thus, outside the hermetically sealed world of public international law, there is no requirement that a business entity have a continuous record of profitability to be treated as a going concern.

Inconsistency when matching the standard of compensation to the measure and method to calculate such compensation

Many existing awards exhibit a degree of inconsistency when trying to reconcile the standard of compensation with the measure and method to calculate such compensation, in particular when it comes to the calculation of market value.

The *Vivendi v. Argentina* award illustrates this point. In this case, the tribunal first ruled that the standard of FMV was applicable to treaty breaches other than expropriation. In particular, the tribunal observed that "it is appropriate to assess compensation, at least in part, based on the fair market value of the concession." The tribunal then proceeded to calculate such value and noted that "[a]t international law, depending on the circumstances arising in a particular case, there are a number of ways of approximating fair market value."

The tribunal rejected a DCF "lost profits" valuation for lack of certainty. Then, after considering the application of alternative approaches to calculating FMV, the tribunal concluded that "investment value," understood as "the amount actually invested prior to the injurious acts," offered the "[...] closest proxy, if only partial, for compensation sufficient to eliminate the consequences of the Province's actions." Historical investment costs, however, are not a measure of the current market value of an asset. Consequently, the tribunal applied a non-market measure of compensation despite its initial ruling that FMV was the appropriate standard of compensation.

The award in the first investment case based on a BIT, *AAPL v. Sri Lanka* offers another interesting example of the disparity in the application of standards, measures, and methods of valuation by tribunals in investment awards.

It is, therefore, necessary to define the purposes of the different methods of valuation and whether they are suitable for the determination of market value.

B. Methods to Calculate Compensation

Providing a consistent analysis

Methods of valuation should correspond to the decision taken by arbitrators as to whether the investor should be compensated on the basis of the expectancy interest or the reliance interest. A careful consideration of the available methods is fundamental.

Becoming familiar with available methods

Methods that do not establish market value

Net book value. This is a calculation of the difference between the enterprise's assets and its liabilities as recorded in its financial statements in accordance with Generally Accepted Accounting Principles (GAAP) or International Accounting Principles (IAP). An NBV calculation uses the value of assets recorded on a company's financial statements at historical costs, rather than using the fair value (for example, changes in tangible assets that appreciate in value, such as the value of seedlings planted by a forest products company). Nor does this method take account of assets expensed (for example, internally developed intellectual property such as "Windows" or drugs rights) or changes in goodwill.

Sunk investment costs (invested capital). This method calculates the amount of capital invested in a project, plus a rate of return (usually an interest rate) from the date of investment to the award date. In certain cases, the amount is reduced for dividends received and returns on capital. Unless the capital was invested at a recent date in an arm's-length transaction, this method does not take account of the impact of intervening events on market value.
Methods that establish market value

Income-based approach. Methods employing an income-based approach convert forward-looking anticipated economic benefits into a single present value amount; they can accommodate uncertainties by "risk-adjusting" the discount rate used to calculate the present value of the future stream of projected earnings or by "risk-adjusting" growth rates or revenue and expense assumptions using the following methods.

- *Discounted cash flow* (DCF). This method measures the present value of the future net cash flows available to the company.
- *Adjusted present value* (APV). This method is a variant of DCF that measures the company's enterprise value as the value of the company without debt (the "unlevered enterprise") plus the present value of tax savings from the company's debt, then adjusts the resulting sum to introduce both the debt (the "leveraged enterprise") and the incremental bankruptcy risk created by adding that debt. Each of these components may be discounted at different rates representing different risks.
- *Capitalized cash flow* (CCF). Another popular income-based calculation, CCF relies on a company's historical income levels. The reliability of the CCF method depends on the reliability of these historical figures. The CCF method is often preferred by valuation professionals for companies with significant intangible assets and few fixed assets.

Market-based approach. This method relies on a market value estimated by comparing the business under review with similar businesses or business ownership interests and securities that have been sold in the market, or with transactions involving similar companies. A comparability analysis seeks to attribute to the company being valued the characteristics of a comparable company. Often, however, the extent of comparability is subject to question. Once the identity of the comparable companies is agreed on, the comparison can be made by using the comparable's CCF value as a proxy for the subject company's value.

Asset-based approach. This method estimates value by using methods based on the current market value of assets net of liabilities. The adjusted book value (ABV) is a calculation of the difference between a business's total assets (net of depreciation, depletion, and amortization) and its total liabilities (including material assets and liabilities not found in accounting balance sheets, such as depreciated assets, internally developed intellectual property, and goodwill). Unlike an NBV calculation that relies on GAAP or IAP financial statements, however, all of the assets and liabilities in an ABV calculation are adjusted to their fair market values, not the historical book amounts found on balance sheets prepared in accordance with accounting principles.

C. Additional Remarks

Working with experts and communication with arbitrators

First, counsel and experts should focus on the need to simplify and communicate their positions to the tribunal. Too often, arbitrators are left confused by highly complicated damages presentations. Counsel should also work with the experts and the other party to determine points of agreement. Experts could be asked to exchange their reports in draft form with the opposing party and then confer regarding differences. Following that process, which might create pressure for experts to retreat from exaggerated positions, the experts may revise their reports and submit final reports to the tribunal. Those reports may be accompanied by a schedule of material disagreements, thereby enabling the tribunal to focus its attention on the material issues in dispute.

Facing damages and managing expert reports

Second, arbitrators need to come to grips with compensation calculations and provide sufficient and clear reasoning for their findings. To focus the issues, arbitrators may, as recommended above, request that experts submit a list of agreed-upon matters and of material differences. Arbitrators could then decide if supplemental reports seeking the use of more comparable methodologies and assumptions are required. In appropriate cases, arbitrators may also employ their own expert. In this event, arbitrators must pay attention to the expert's background and to giving the parties full and fair opportunity to be heard. Arbitrators should be mindful of the risk that the tribunal-appointed expert may improperly become the "fourth arbitrator." To avoid this risk, all interactions between the tribunal and their tribunal-appointed expert should be transparent to the parties and subject to examination and comment by the parties. Arbitrators should be especially mindful of the costs involved in asking for additional reports and in appointing their own expert. Those steps may be appropriate only in disputes sufficiently large to justify the significant additional expense.

Understanding business concepts

A more thorough grasp of business concepts by all parties involved seems warranted. A clear example of the divergence between a common understanding of valuation concepts among state regulatory and tax authorities, accountants, valuation experts, and the business community, on the one hand, and the investment arbitration community, on the other hand, is the use of the expression "going concern" in international investment law cases. As noted above, some investment treaty tribunals have employed the expression to require a business to have enjoyed several previous years of profitability. These tribunals appear, in fact, to be concerned about the uncertainty of future earnings estimations, not whether the business is a going concern. By treating the concept of going concern as a rule of international law, rather than a question of whether the evidence in the case is sufficiently persuasive to support forward-looking damages, some arbitrators treat a question of the weight of evidence as, instead, a matter of legal principle. This contravenes accepted usage and creates confusion for participants in the compensation process.

Appreciating the relevance of facts

Third, looking first at the facts surrounding a compensation dispute may enable arbitrators and counsel to narrow the range of possible compensation theories available for application in the dispute. For example, if the date the capital was invested in a business was some time ago, and a number of intervening events have occurred, an arbitrator is unlikely to rely on the amount of invested capital to determine FMV. The impact of those subsequent events will have caused FMV to diverge from the amount of capital originally invested.

An Approach to Financial Valuation for Arbitration Awards

Faisal A. Quraishi

There is only one certainty in determining the amount of an arbitration award to compensate for an injury to a business interest: that the amount will seldom capture the intrinsic value of the loss. The basis for payment will be shaped by the legal and financial considerations relating to the arbitration, which in many cases shift the argument from discovering the true value to positioning for a more favorable outcome by the parties involved. The methods for quantifying award outcomes vary widely, as Mark Kantor (2008) points out in numerous examples. And the difficulties in arriving at a common solution to dealing with claims—specifically for expropriation, as discussed by Srilal M. Perera in "Expropriation and the Share Pledge Dilemma: An Assessment of Individual Rights and Compensation Claims" (chapter 9 in this volume)—further highlight legal issues faced by stakeholders. Adding financial valuation to an already complicated framework makes it a challenge to perform any exercise to arrive at an intrinsic value of loss agreeable to the parties involved in an arbitration case.

Faisal A. Quaraishi is a Financial Officer at MIGA.

This chapter supports the idea that the valuation exercise should be impartial; that it should use all broadly accepted methods of enterprise valuation, such as discounted cash flow (DCF; income based), market-based multiples (market based), and book value (net book value); and that it should incorporate scenario analysis by varying economic assumptions in the valuation methods. Once the parties agree to all three proposed tenets, a valuation close to the intrinsic value may result. An agreement between parties, such as a contract termination agreement, may exist at the outset to describe the methodology by which to value the company at hand. If well crafted, it may obviate the need to perform a separate valuation. To illustrate the use of valuation methodologies in combination with scenario analysis, an example is presented for a hypothetical hydropower company expropriated by a host government. A calculation of enterprise value when a termination payment clause exists is presented, followed by a discussion of a past arbitration decision. Finally, the results are studied and conclusions are drawn regarding the benefits of the proposed three tenets.

Structured Approach to Valuation

The broadly accepted valuation methods allow a degree of flexibility to accommodate for the specifics of a case. In some instances a valuation method may not work because of an absence of data, and therefore should be discarded. In the following example, DCF and market-based price multiples methodologies are presented for enterprise valuation, in conjunction with sensitivity analysis on key assumptions. A recent proliferation of spreadsheet tools has allowed complex financial analysis to be performed in an easier and more efficient manner, further encouraging the use of practitioner-preferred DCF and price-multiples methodologies among various methods for enterprise valuation. Developing a plausible range of valuations may result in better negotiated outcomes between parties. Table 13.1 provides sensitivity analysis for the value of a hydropower company.[1] Under the DCF framework, assumptions for a 2008 operating margin and weighted average cost of capital (r_{WACC}) were varied and a resulting range of enterprise values determined.

At the baseline scenario, the investment company's value is $1,263 million (2008 operating margin = 86 percent and r_{WACC} = 11.5 percent). At one extreme, the lowest operating margin at 80 percent and

TABLE 13.1 PROJECT COMPANY SENSITIVITY ANALYSIS
TOTAL FIRM VALUE (US$ MILLIONS) FOR COMBINATIONS OF r_{WACC} AND
2008 OPERATING MARGIN

		13.5	12.5	11.5	10.5	9.5
2008 Operating	92	1,158	1,247	1,351	1,474	1,623
Margin (%)	89	1,121	1,207	1,307	1,426	1,571
	86	1,084	1,166	1,263	1,379	1,518
	83	1,046	1,126	1,220	1,331	1,466
	80	1,009	1,086	1,176	1,283	1,413

Source: Author's illustration.
Note: r_{WACC} = weighted average cost of capital (percent).

the highest r_{WACC} at 13.5 percent give the lowest valuation of $1,009 million. This can be compared with the highest valuation estimate of $1,623 million. The lower and upper limits provide a range of valuations under this methodology. The sensitivity analysis shows a number of cases where the firm value is lower or higher than the baseline. Because the true underlying assumptions are not known with certainty, valuation experts, in consultation with their legal counterparts, should assess which set of assumptions best reflects the economics of the enterprise being valued. This process may lead to a scenario more suitable than the baseline. Furthermore, all of the assumptions in the DCF model can be scrutinized, leading to a better understanding of the total firm value and its drivers. The results of the DCF analysis can then be compared with those of market-based approaches, where available. An example of market-based price multiples is shown in table 13.2.

TABLE 13.2 MARKET-BASED PRICE MULTIPLES

	Price/earnings	Price/book	Price/sales
Average of comparable firms at Dec. 31, 2007	8.5	1.0	4.5
Implied firm value[a] at Dec 31, 2007 ($ million)	992.0	976.6	1,440.0
Average of DCF and multiples ($ million)	1,168.0		

Source: Author's illustration.
Note: a. Year-end 2007 data from annex 13A Project Company Sample Financial Earnings = 116.7; Book = 976.6; and Sales = 320.0.

Commonly used enterprise valuation market-based price multiples include price-to-earnings (P/E), price-to-book (P/B), and price-to-sales (P/S).[2] The application of these methodologies depends on the availability of data for comparable firms, which may be a challenge in emerging economies. Once the ratios of the comparable firms are determined, they are simply multiplied by values of the enterprise to arrive at firm value. Using the P/E multiple of 8.5 at December 2007 and multiplying it by the firm's 2007 earnings of $116.7 million results in an enterprise value of $992.0 million. This process is carried out for the other ratios.

Termination Payment

A termination payment is calculated using the termination payment clause from a project agreement. The termination agreement also covers other causes of termination, including project company default. Table 13.3 shows the amount of compensation due from the

TABLE 13.3 PROJECT COMPANY SAMPLE TERMINATION

Project description	200 MW Hydropower Project
Host government	Country ABC
Subsovereign agency	EMC2 Transmission
Investor	H2O-NRG Global Capital
Capital structure	$300 million equity, $700 million debt

Assuming expropriation of the project company occurs on Jan. 1, 2008, the value of firm at Dec. 31, 2007, is as follows:

Item	Descripton	Value[a] ($ millions)
DSR	Debt service reserve	5.8
YP	Equity yield[b]	401.4
INS	Insurance proceeds (*force majeure*)	-
OTD	Outstanding tariff debt	607.8
OTE	Outstanding tariff equity	100.0
PCP	Past-due capacity payments	64.0
Government ABC Default Purchase Price (DPP) DPP = YP + OTD + OTE + PCP - INS - DSR		1,167.4

Source: Author's illustration.
Notes: a. Annex 13A Project Company Sample Financial Statements; b. Present value of dividends, including terminal dividend in 2012.

government of country ABC. The amount is clearly specified by a formula, the main components of which are outstanding debt amounts due to the lenders and the outstanding equity plus return on equity due to the investors. A well-specified termination agreement avoids the ambiguity often associated with determining payments due to the affected parties and will help lenders, investors, and political risk insurers alike negotiate the amount of compensation owed by the host government.

In the absence of a termination clause, the claimants should seek recovery using one or more agreed-upon enterprise valuation approaches to determine the amount of compensation.[3]

Past Arbitration Decision

The decisions of arbitral tribunals on international expropriations show a varied and often ad hoc approach to valuing expropriated property and ownership rights. In the *Phillips Petroleum Co. Iran v. Iran* case[4] on expropriation, the tribunal considered a number of methodologies, including the claimants' DCF approach,[5] to establish the amount of compensation due. Given the disparities in the production forecasts prepared by the claimants' experts and the respondents' experts, the tribunal challenged each assumption and indicated why it had found the claimants' assumptions in many cases to produce a higher than warranted valuation. The tribunal accepted DCF as a central (but not exclusive) method of valuation, based on the reasoning that a prospective buyer would likely undertake such an analysis as well (Becker 1997). However, it also recognized a need to adjust the DCF result in light of other considerations. In concluding its analysis, the tribunal examined the validity of a net book value approach and noted that this approach failed to capture the full economic value because it was only an accounting measure.[6] Ultimately, the tribunal based the award on an adjusted net book value plus future profits calculated based on a market value price-to-earnings multiple.

In this case, the valuation process, which began with DCF, changed course based on the failure of the parties to agree on the parameters underlying the DCF valuation. The tribunal judge correctly ascertained the unreasonable nature of both the claimants' and defendants' assumptions in the DCF methodology and proposed an alternate hybrid result. While satisfactory in many respects, the processes and methodology failed to correctly capture the underlying economics, thus failing to capture the intrinsic value of the company.

Final Analysis

A summary illustrates the variability in outcomes from the various enterprise valuation approaches. Table 13.4 presents the DCF and market-based multiples as well as the termination payment valuation. The table shows the range of results that can be derived based on an underlying economic, market-based, and financial framework. Several iterations may be needed to refine the results, eventually arriving at a range that can be the starting point for negotiating the settlement amount.

Execution of a pre-agreement, whether as specific as a termination clause or just generally specifying the valuation methodologies to be used, is strongly recommended. A pre-agreement helps to ensure that parties, when placed in a position to claim or defend in an arbitration, will benefit from the process already identified.

In summary, parties involved in the settlement should agree on the methods (DCF, market based) to be used as well as on the ranges for key economic assumptions in the valuation (for example, discount rate, sales growth rate). By specifying these important business and economic drivers, the analysis can be performed and arguments for one position over the other can be presented with the hope that the values produced by each side are reasonable. Following this process without partiality will increase the likelihood of arriving at a settlement close to the intrinsic loss, rather than an alternative based on an ad hoc approach to determining the final firm value.

TABLE 13.4 SUMMARY OF VALUATION RESULTS
TOTAL FIRM VALUE ($ MILLIONS)

	Low	Mid	High
Termination agreement	n.a.	1,167	n.a.
DCF	1,009	1,263	1,623
Price multiples	977	992	1,440

Source: Author's illustration.
Note: n.a. = Not applicable.

ANNEX 13A PROJECT COMPANY SAMPLE FINANCIAL

Project description:	200 MW Hydropower Project	Cost of Capital (percent)	
Host government:	Country ABC	Equity:	15.0
Subsovereign agency:	EMC2 Transmission	Debt:	10.0
Investor company:	H2O-NRG Global Capital	WACC:	11.5
Capital structure:	$300 million equity, $700 million debt		

Required Rate of Return
After Tax

Income Statement ($ millions)
Years ending December 31

	Actual 2004	Actual 2005	Actual 2006	Actual 2007	Fcst 2008	Fcst 2009	Fcst 2010	Fcst 2011	Fcst 2012
Revenues	0	0	300.0	320.0	280.0	280.0	260.0	240.0	240.0
Selling and General Administrative Expense									
Administrative Expenses	0	0	(6.0)	(7.0)	(7.8)	(10.6)	(9.9)	(11.5)	(11.5)
Insurance	0	0	(12.0)	(14.1)	(15.7)	(21.3)	(19.8)	(23.0)	(23.0)
Labor	0	0	(7.5)	(8.8)	(9.8)	(13.3)	(12.4)	(14.4)	(14.4)
Maintenance Expenses	0	0	(3.0)	(3.5)	(3.9)	(5.3)	(4.9)	(5.8)	(5.8)
Management Fee	0	0	(1.5)	(1.8)	(2.0)	(2.7)	(2.5)	(2.9)	(2.9)
S&GA Total	0	0	(30.0)	(35.2)	(39.2)	(53.2)	(49.4)	(57.6)	(57.6)
Operating Income (EBITDA)	0	0	270.0	284.8	240.8	226.8	210.6	182.4	182.4
Depreciation Expense	0	0	(45.0)	(45.0)	(45.0)	(45.0)	(45.0)	(45.0)	(45.0)
Interest Expense	0	0	(70.0)	(65.6)	(60.8)	(55.5)	(49.6)	(43.2)	(36.1)
Income before Taxes	0	0	155.0	174.2	135.0	126.3	116.0	94.2	101.3
Taxes at 30%	0	0	(51.2)	(57.5)	(44.6)	(41.7)	(38.3)	(31.1)	(33.4)
Net Income after Tax	0	0	103.9	116.7	90.5	84.6	77.7	63.1	67.9
Common Dividends	0	0	100.0	100.0	75.0	75.0	75.0	50.0	50.0

Balance Sheet ($ millions)
Years ending December 31

	2004	2005	Actual 2006	Actual 2007	Fcst 2008	Fcst 2009	Fcst 2010	Fcst 2011	Fcst 2012
Current Assets									
Cash/Debt Service Reserve	50.0	0	6.8	5.8	25.6	27.1	20.1	17.8	9.9
Accounts Receivable	0	0	45.0	64.0	56.0	56.0	52.0	48.0	48.0
Total	50.0	0	51.9	69.8	81.6	83.1	72.1	65.8	57.9
Fixed Assets									
Capitalized Project Costs	450.0	900.0	900.0	900.0	900.0	900.0	900.0	900.0	900.0
Less: Accum. Depreciation	0	0	(45.0)	(90.0)	(135.0)	(180.0)	(225.0)	(270.0)	(315.0)
Net Cap. Project Costs	450.0	900.0	855.0	810.0	765.0	720.0	675.0	630.0	585.0
Land	100.00	100.00	100.00	100.00	100.00	100.00	100.00	100.00	100.00
Total Assets	600.0	1,000.0	1,006.9	979.8	946.6	903.1	847.1	795.8	742.9
Accounts Payable	0	0	3.0	3.2	2.8	2.8	2.6	2.4	2.4
Current Portion of Long-Term Debt	0	0	43.9	48.3	53.1	58.5	64.3	70.7	77.8
Long-Term Debt	300.0	700.0	656.1	607.8	554.6	496.2	431.9	361.1	283.3
Common Stock	300.0	300.0	300.0	300.0	300.0	300.0	300.0	300.0	300.0
Retained Earnings	0	0	3.8	20.6	36.0	45.7	48.4	61.5	79.4
Total Liabilities and Equity	600.0	1,000.0	1,006.9	979.8	946.6	903.1	847.1	795.8	742.9

ANNEX 13A CONTINUED

Cash Flow Statement ($ millions)
Years ending December 31

	2004	2005	Actual 2006	Actual 2007	Fcst 2008	Fcst 2009	Fcst 2010	Fcst 2011	Fcst 2012
Net Income	0	0	103.9	116.7	90.5	84.6	77.7	63.1	67.9
Depreciation & Amortization	0	0	45.0	45.0	45.0	45.0	45.0	45.0	45.0
Changes in Working Capital									
Accounts Receivable	0	0	(45.0)	(19.0)	8.0	0	4.0	4.0	0
Accounts Payable	0	0	3.0	0.2	(0.4)	0	(0.2)	(0.2)	0
Cash from Operations	0	0	106.9	142.9	143.1	129.6	126.5	111.9	112.9
Purch Fixed Assets (Cap. Ex.)	(555.0)	(450.0)	0	0	0	0	0	0	0
Proceeds Sale Fixed Assets	0	0	0	0	0	0	0	0	0
Cash from Investing	(555.0)	(450.0)	0	0	0	0	0	0	0
Common Stock	300.0	0	0	0	0	0	0	0	0
Common Dividends	0	0	(100.0)	(100.0)	(75.0)	(75.0)	(75.0)	(50.0)	(50.0)
Increases/(Decreases) in Debt	300.0	400.0	0	(43.9)	(48.3)	(53.1)	(58.5)	(64.3)	(70.7)
Cash from Financing	600.0	400.0	(100.0)	(143.9)	(123.3)	(128.1)	(133.5)	(114.3)	(120.7)
Total Cash Flow	50.0	(50.0)	6.8	(1.0)	19.8	1.5	(7.0)	(2.4)	(7.9)

Income Statement Assumption % of Revenues

	Actual 2004	Actual 2005	Actual 2006	Actual 2007	Fcst 2008	Fcst 2009	Fcst 2010	Fcst 2011	Fcst 2012
Revenue Forecasts			Based on Tariff Schedules						
Operating Income (EBITDA) Margin			90	89	86	81	81	76	76
Tax Rate			33	33	33	33	33	33	33
Incremental Fixed Capital Investment			0	0	0	0	0	0	0
Incremental Working Capital Investment			14	6	0	0	0	0	0

Debt Schedule ($ millions)
Years ending December 31

	Actual 2004	Actual 2005	Actual 2006	Actual 2007	Fcst 2008	Fcst 2009	Fcst 2010	Fcst 2011	Fcst 2012
Beginning Balance		300.0	700.0	656.1	607.8	554.6	496.2	431.9	361.1
Interest		27.0	70.0	65.6	60.8	55.5	49.6	43.2	36.1
Principal Repayment		0	43.9	48.3	53.1	58.5	64.3	70.7	77.8
Drawdown	300.0	373.0	0	0	0	0	0	0	0
Ending Balance	300.0	700.0	656.1	607.8	554.6	496.2	431.9	361.1	283.3

Source: Author's illustration.

Annex 13B.
Description and Commentary on Discounted Cash Flow and Market-Based Price-Multiples Valuation Methods

Detail on the discounted cash flow and market-based multiples valuation methods are provided in this annex, which is based on Stowe and others (2002).

Discounted Cash Flows

DCF is a general approach with enough flexibility to value companies in most any industry. Judgment and sound knowledge are required to develop the numerous assumptions, such as future revenue growth rates, operating margins, and discount rates, by reviewing historical trends as well as looking at prospective economic and business conditions, and the specific project company context. With these assumptions, forward-looking financial statements can be generated, from which future free cash flows can be developed.

Free cash flows to the firm (FCFF) are those amounts available (distributable) to all providers of capital after all operating expenses (including taxes) have been paid and necessary investments in working capital (for example, inventory) and fixed capital (for example, equipment) have been made. Free cash flows are the cash flows from operations minus capital expenditures. For DCF valuation, these cash flows are projected for the life of the project and then discounted using a weighted average cost of capital (r_{WACC}), which reflects the overall riskiness of the project and considers the proportion of debt and equity used to finance the project.[7] The assumptions in the DCF calculations should reflect the situation immediately before the occurrence of the expropriation event. A key advantage of using DCF to value a company is that the calculated total firm value can be simply and fairly allocated between equity and debt holders. This is especially important for parties involved in a joint recovery effort. The method is outlined below.

$$Firm\ Value = \sum_{t=1}^{N} \left(\frac{FCFF_t}{(1 + r_{WACC})^t} \right)$$

Free Cash Flow to the Firm at time t = $FCFF_t$
= Net income available to shareholders at time t
+ Net noncash charges[8] at time t
+ Interest expense at time t $\times$ (1 $-$ tax rate)
$-$ Investment in fixed capital at time t
$-$ Investment in working capital at time t.

N is the number of years.

Firm value represents the total value of the company; the value of equity is simply firm value minus the market value of its debt:

Equity value = Firm value - Market value of debt.

The market value of debt equals the present value of cash flows due to the debt holders at a discount rate equal to the current market rate for loans or bonds of similar risk and terms:

$$Value\ of\ Debt = \sum_{t=1}^{N} \left(\frac{DebtCF_t}{(1 + r_{Debt})^t} \right)$$

The DCF approach also has limitations because the valuation of the project company relies on the availability of transparent financial statements, data on the sector and economic environment in which the company operates, and the competitive advantages it enjoys. A lack of information in any of these areas will make the valuation exercise more challenging. The DCF approach also tends to be sensitive to underlying assumptions; thus, sensitivity analysis around key variables such as discount rate and growth rate is recommended to produce a range of valuations.

Market-Based Multiples

In comparison with DCF, a market-based price-multiples method is easier to implement. This approach suggests that competitor companies with similar operating characteristics should have similar valuations. Ratios such as price-to-earnings (P/E), price-to-sales (P/S), or price-to-book (P/B) of comparable companies are determined and then used to calculate the value of the project company. For example, say the average P/E is the best representation of the value of comparable companies. This multiple is then multiplied by the earnings of the project company to arrive at the value of the project company. Examples of DCF and market-value based price multiples approaches are illustrated in table 13B.1.

In the context of calculating firm values, the market-based price multiples approach has shortcomings. Most important, relevant comparables for determining multiples can be hard to find, especially in the absence of pure-play companies with operations very similar to those of the project being analyzed. If a similar entity is found, it may be subsumed as part of a larger entity and thus not have an identifiable stand-alone market value. This approach also suffers from lack of detail and does not capture unique aspects of a particular project, such as the risk situation and specific geographic conditions.

Notes

1. The results are based on changing the assumptions in annex 13A, Project Company Sample Financial Statements.

2. See annex 13B, Description and Commentary on Discounted Cash Flow and Market-Based Price-Multiples Valuation Methods.

3. In classic expropriation cases, the value is determined as of the day before the date of the expropriation because the underlying assumption is that the project company could be sold in the market in an arm's-length transaction, but would have no value if the date of the expropriation were used. The date of calculation could also be determined by contract, for example, in the termination payment clauses in a concession agreement.

4. *Phillips Petroleum Company Iran, Claimant v. The Islamic Republic of Iran, The National Iranian Oil Company,* Respondents Award No. 425-39-2, ¶¶111–165.

5. See annex 13B, Description and Commentary on Discounted Cash Flow and Market-Based Price-Multiples Valuation Methods.

6. A number of past awards in expropriation cases have been determined on a net book value basis. The net book value for company valuation purposes is defined as total assets minus total liabilities, less any equity attributable to preferred stock. While this approach is straightforward in application, it employs the historical purchase cost of assets less accumulated depreciation, which may cause the book value to differ substantially from its actual value. An alternate use of net book value in valuation is to multiply it by a price-to-book multiple of comparable companies to arrive at a representative market value. See annex 13B for this approach.

Project Description:	200 MW Hydropower Project
Host Agency:	Country ABC
Subsovereign:	EMC2 Transmission
Investor:	H2O-NRG Global Capitol
Capital Structure:	$300 million equity, $700 million

Cost of Capital (percent)		Required Rate of Return
Equity	15.0	After Tax
Debt	10.0	
WACC	11.5	

Discounted Cash ($ millions)
Years ending December 31

	Actual 2004	Actual 2005	Actual 2006	Actual 2007	Fcst 2008	Fcst 2009	Fcst 2010	Fcst 2011	Fcst 2012
Net Income	0	0	103.9	116.7	90.5	84.6	77.7	63.1	67.9
Plus: Dep. & Amort.	0	0	45.0	45.0	45.0	45.0	45.0	45.0	45.0
Plus: Int. Exp. x (1 - Tax Rate)	0	0	49.0	45.9	42.5	38.8	34.7	30.2	25.3
Less: Inv. in Fixed Capital	(550.0)	(450.0)	0	0	0	0	0	0	0
Less: Inv. in Woring Capital	0	0	42.0	18.8	(7.6)	0	(3.8)	(3.8)	0
Total free cash flow	(550.0)	(450.0)	239.9	226.4	170.4	168.5	153.6	134.6	138.1

Present Value of Free Cash Flows to Firm at 11.5% (WACC) over 2008–12	566.4
Present Value of Terminal Value[a] FCFF @ 2012 No Growth–Perpetual	697.0
Total firm value	1,263.4
Value to Debt Holders[b]	607.8
Value to Equity Holders[c]	655.7

a. Terminal Value = $(FCFF_{2012} (1+g))/(r_{WACC}-g)/(1+r_{WACC})^5$, where ($FCFF_{2012}$ = 138.1, g = 0%; and r_{WACC} = 11.5%, where g = growth rate r_{WACC} = weighted average cost of capital.

b. Assume book value of debt equals market value (that is, discount future debt payments at 10%).

c. Value of Equity = Value of Firm – Value of Debt.

7.
$$r_{WACC} = \frac{MVEquity}{MVDebt + MVEquity} r_{EQUITY} + \frac{MVDebt}{MVDebt + MVEquity} r_{DEBT}(1 - TaxRate)$$

8. Such as depreciation and amortization.

References

Becker, Judy. 1997. "Valuing the Depletion of Natural Resources under International Law." *Review of European Community and International Environmental Law* 6 (2): 181–90.

Kantor, M. 2008. *Valuation for Arbitration, Compensation Standards, Valuation Methods and Expert Evidence.* New York: Kluwer Law International.

Stowe, J. D., T. R. Robinson, J. E. Pinto, and D. W. McLeavy. 2002. *Analysis of Equity Investments: Valuation.* Charlottesville, VA: Association for Investment Management and Research.

Concluding Comments

Gero Verheyen and Srilal M. Perera

Potential investors pay considerable attention to the role that political risk insurance (PRI) can play in their investment decisions. From the investor's perspective, considerations include the cost of PRI, coverage available from the insurer, and the likelihood that a claim will be paid if a loss event takes place. The various crises over the past 20 years have proven that considerable doubts prevail even after decisions to procure PRI have been made—not only because an insurer may have decided that a loss was not considered eligible under a certain cover, but also because the investor may not have had the proper coverage to begin with.

To determine if providing PRI makes business sense, insurers must consider the viability of the investment, the country risk (both economic and political), and the costs associated with covering against such risks. Unlike short-term credit insurance, which is issued on an annual basis, thereby allowing the flexibility to adjust terms and conditions from one policy period to the next, PRI is typically structured with fixed terms and conditions over a medium- to long-term tenor (in some cases as long as 20 years). Consequently, insurers must incorporate into their risk assessment and pricing assumptions the likelihood that a loss event might take place in the future.

Over the past decade, the number of crises that have led to arbitration or another form of dispute resolution points to both the effectiveness of PRI as well as its shortcomings. Claims have been paid for the nationalization of financial-sector and resource-related investments; at the same time, however, claims have been denied in some cases because insurers deemed the loss to have been commercial in nature, to have come within the scope of an excluded category, or to have not been eligible under the coverage elected by the investor. A few cases before the International Center for the Settlement of Investment Disputes (ICSID) and other arbitral bodies have rendered awards but, in the critical areas for insurers, such as expropriation, have not been instructive. Most of the cases are still pending final rulings, and investors and insurers alike are awaiting the outcomes of the awards decisions with concerned anticipation. An award in favor of the investor not only validates that a loss has occurred, but that the event itself has taken place. An award in favor of the government not only raises considerable concerns for the investor, but calls into question the scope and definition of the coverage under which the event took place. In the Argentine cases, much of the debate has revolved around whether the asymmetric *pesification* that took place in 2001 constituted expropriatory events, or whether it was well within Argentina's police powers to take emergency actions in its efforts to stabilize the economy.

The discussion of how to define expropriation coverage is ongoing, and new events continue to redefine and realign the boundaries of this critical risk. Recent rulings by arbitral panels that cases brought against Argentina had to be considered under the fair and equitable treatment standard provided in the applicable bilateral investment treaties (BITs) only serve to intensify the discussion. While some countries have reexamined the value of continuing ICSID membership, other countries are making an effort to strengthen the language of their BITs to afford investors better protection. At the previous MIGA-Georgetown symposium in 2004, one of the papers discussed the coverage of breaches of BIT obligations under PRI policies. At the time, consensus indicated that such breaches were not included under PRI policies for the simple reason that investors generally did not request such coverage. To cover breaches of BITs without qualification would present the insurer with a range of liabilities traditionally not covered by PRI because BITs cover a wider range of subjects than the risks traditionally covered under PRI. Recent discussions have suggested that breaches of BITs could be covered narrowly so long as the event would also fall within the definition of expropriation as provided by the insurance policy. The current economic crisis has raised fears of new waves of nationalizations as governments take control of failing companies and financial institutions in their efforts to stabilize their economies. However, given the importance of the support provided by foreign parent companies to their subsidiaries and the extent to which this support has contributed to maintaining stability in the economies, host governments are less likely to intervene in these subsidiaries than they are in domestic companies and banks. Moreover, governments are more likely to intervene in a stronger bank whose failure would have a much more catastrophic impact on the financial system than they are to intervene in behalf of failing smaller banks. Even if a government steps in and, through a capital injection, assumes a majority stake in a financial institution, this may not necessarily constitute an expropriatory event if the institution is able to continue functioning. An example of this would be the U.S. government's intervention to prevent the collapse of AIG. Despite the government assuming 82 percent ownership of AIG, the company has continued functioning, although it has been selling off assets to repay the government and remain afloat. Yet, questions will be asked about whether such interventions by governments can be covered under PRI and even if covered, whether causality would direct to commercial rather than political reasons for the losses faced by investors. Some would argue that a government's infusion of capital is itself, in effect, a form of compensation.

In addition to defining and redefining the scope of the cover they provide, PRI providers are also continually working to fine-tune the mechanisms they use to price risks. As models evolve, providers factor in new variables that reflect the different risk components that must be measured; in turn, each variable must be properly weighted so that the final calculation reflects a reasonable rate to both the insurer and the investor. Insurers must cover costs, factoring in their claims history, the likelihood that a claim may arise for a given investment, and the chances for recovery. Some models, such as the economic capital model being used by MIGA, also factor in the consumption of economic capital for each project. Unlike short-term credit insurance, which allows insurers to respond to economic crises by reducing or cancelling cover during the contract period and adjusting the rates at the annual renewal, PRI providers generally issue medium- to long-term contracts with rates fixed for the duration of the contract.

In the event of a crisis, PRI providers must either work to resolve the dispute or prepare to pay the claim. These risks must be factored into the premium rates. Whether a PRI provider is private or public will also play a role in pricing. A private insurer's PRI portfolio is typically a small percentage of its overall insurance portfolio, which comprises property and casualty insurance, credit insurance, and other lines. Public insurers such as export credit agencies offer both trade credit insurance and PRI, and in most cases, their non-PRI portfolios are substantially larger than their PRI portfolios. The advantage to them is that they can offer more competitive rates for their PRI because of the support provided by premium income from non-PRI products. However, when these insurers, particularly the private insurers, face a high volume of claims from their credit insurance exposures, as we have witnessed during the past two years, their natural tendency is to become more conservative in their overall underwriting approach. This conservative slant is reflected in both the premium rates offered and the capacity available for a given project.

MIGA's role as a development agency is first and foremost to promote foreign direct investment into developing countries, and to do so, it must charge a premium for its PRI that is attractive to investors but sufficient to cover MIGA's operating costs. As the only multilateral institution offering PRI, MIGA brings an added dimension in its ability to interact directly with host country authorities to avert claims situations. The agency's leverage as a World Bank Group institution provides a level of comfort and security for the investments it covers. These considerations add value to an investor obtaining PRI cover from MIGA.

As the economic crisis unfolds and economies begin the long road to recovery, PRI providers and investors alike will reflect on the impact that the crisis has had upon them, and this will help to shape their strategies going forward. Sovereign wealth funds, which traditionally invested heavily in what seemed to be solid, fail-proof investments, will reconsider their future investment strategies, and perhaps seek PRI cover more actively. If they refocus their investments toward more developmentally oriented projects, PRI could play an important role in protecting and promoting these investments, and the potential for the insurers would be significant, with regard to both new exposure and further advancing the science and innovation of PRI products.

Islamic-financed projects have recently appeared on the radar screens of political risk insurers. The most significant Islamic-financed project for which PRI was offered is the Doraleh Port Project in Djibouti. Although some Islamic-financed projects have been underwritten by traditional PRI providers, the concept of *Shariah*-compliant coverage still represents uncharted territory for a number of them. This market offers significant potential because the number of traditional Islamic providers of PRI is limited—very few providers of Islamic finance have investment insurance portfolios or the underwriting expertise and capacity to provide PRI. The challenge will be for insurers to bridge the cultural differences that may arise as they seek to cover *Shariah*-compliant projects. Coverage requires significant modification to policy terms and conditions, an understanding of the myriad agreements that define the relationships among the various parties, as well as review and approval by the applicable *Shariah* board responsible for sanctioning the project. This can be a lengthy and complex process, with frequent revisions and amendments. Ultimately, the insurer benefits from having underwritten a PRI policy with a deeper understanding of Islamic financing practices, and the investor is able to move forward knowing that the project is protected from political risk events. As more PRI providers begin to underwrite Islamic financing structures, an increasing number of non-Islamic banks will look to insure their financing under Islamic structures because they know that PRI is available, and available from providers with whom they are already familiar.

As PRI continues to evolve, providers will combine the lessons from the current financial crisis with their experience from previous years to further refine the manner in which they structure their insurance coverage and pricing; thus, the product can keep pace with the continuously changing needs of the investor community. By default, private insurers will react more quickly because they have greater flexibility to modify their insurance coverage. Public and multilateral insurers may need more time to respond—they must subject any changes to a more extensive review process, and modify relevant agreements and policies to accommodate such demand-based changes that depart from the norm. Nevertheless, PRI will continue to evolve and provide an important risk mitigant to investors, and continue to contribute to the flow of investments into developing countries.

Previous Volumes in This Series

Previous volumes in this series can be ordered from the World Bank

P.O. Box 960
Herndon, VA 20172-0960, U.S.A.
Tel. 703-661-1580, 800-645-7247
Fax 703-661-1501

or accessed online at http://publications.worldbank.org/Previous volumes in this series can be ordered from the World Bank:

P.O. Box 960
Herndon, VA 20172-0960, USA
Tel. 703-661-1580, 800-645-7247
Fax 703-661-1501

or accessed online at http://publications.worldbank.org/

International Political Risk Management: Needs of the Present, Challenges for the Future

Published by the World Bank from the Fifth MIGA-Georgetown Symposium, 2006

Introduction
  Yukiko Omura, **Multilateral Investment Guarantee Agency**

PART ONE
New Perspectives on Political Risk Insurance Products

Overview
  Theodore H. Moran and Gerald T. West, Editors

A BIT of Insurance
Kenneth W. Hansen, Chadbourne & Parke LLP

The Convergence of the Terrorism Insurance and Political Risk Insurance Markets for Emerging Market Risk: Why It is Necessary and How It will come About
Charles Berry, BPL Global

Commentary
David Neckar, Willis

Commentary
Edie Quintrell, OPIC

Discussion of New Perspectives on Political Risk Insurance Products
Symposium Panelists and Partipants

PART TWO
Private Power Projects in Emerging Markets: New Models for Financing and Risk Management

Overview
Theodore H. Moran and Gerald T. West, Editors

Managing International Political Risk: Lessons from the Power Sector
Erik J. Woodhouse, Program on Energy and Sustainable Development Stanford University

AES's Experience in Developing Countries
Jeffery A. Safford, AES

Commentary
Barry Metzger, Baker & McKenzie LLP

Discussion of Private Power Projects in Emerging Markets: New Models for Financing and Risk Management
Symposium Panelists and Participants

The New Scramble for Commodities: Medium-Term Trends in Political Risk Insurance
Greg Ansermino, Standard Bank of South Africa

Einstein and Cinderella
Julie Martin, Marsh

Discussion of the International Political Risk Insurance Industry in 2010
Symposium Panelists and Participants

Appendixes

International Political Risk Management: Looking to the Future

Published by the World Bank from the Fourth MIGA-Georgetown Symposium, 2004

Discussion of New Products and new Perspectives in Political Insurance
   Symposium Panelists and Participants

Appendixes
   I   Biographies of Authors
   II   Whither the Political Risk Insurance Industry?
         Gerald T. West and Kristofer Hamel, MIGA
   III   Previous Volumes in the Series
   IV   More About MIGA

International Political Risk Management: The Brave New World

Published by the World Bank from the Third MIGA-Georgetown Symposium, 2002

Introduction
 Motomichi Ikawa, Multilateral Investment Guarantee Agency

PART ONE

Political Risk Insurance Providers: In the Aftermath of the September 11 Attacks and Argentine Crisis

Overview
 Theodore H. Moran, Editor

Political Risk Insurance after September 11 and the Argentine Crisis: A Public Provider's Perspective
 Vivian Brown, Berne Union

Political Risk Insurance after September 11 and the Argentine Crisis: An Underwriter's View from London
 David James, Ascot Underwriting

The Impact of September 11 on Trade Credit and Political Risk Insurance: A Private Insurer's Perspective from New York
 John J. Salinger, AIG Global Trade & Political Risk Insurance Co.

In the Aftermath of September 11 and the Argentine Crisis: A Private Reinsurer's Perspective
 Brian Duperreault, ACE Limited

Commentary on Political Insurance Providers in the Aftermath of September 11 and the Argentine Crisis
 Julie, A. Martin, MMC Enterprise Risk

Political Risk Management: A Strategic Perspective
Witold J. Henisz, Wharton School, and *Bennet A. Zelner*, McDonough School of Business

Commentary on Finding Common Ground or Uncommon Solutions: A Private Provider's View
David J. Bailey, Sovereign Risk Insurance, Ltd.

Commentary on Finding Common Ground or Uncommon Solutions: A Public Provider's View
Edith Quintrell, Overseas Private Investment Corporation

Appendixes

International Political Risk Management: Exploring New Frontiers

Theodore H. Moran, Editor

Published by the World Bank from the Second MIGA-Georgetown Symposium, 2000

Introduction
  Motomichi Ikawa, Multilateral Investment Guarantee Agency

PART ONE
The Multiple Pledge-of-Shares Problem

Overview
  Theodore H. Moran, Editor

The Multiple Pledge-of-Shares Problem:
Report of a Little Progress
  Kenneth Hansen, Chadbourne & Parke LLP

Comments
  Julie A. Martin, Overseas Private Investment Corporation, and
  Anne Predieri, Banc of America Securities

PART TWO
Preferred Creditor Status

Overview
  Theodore H. Moran, Editor

Preferred Creditor Status: Husbanding a Valuable Asset
  Felton (Mac) Johnston, FMJ International Risk Services, LLC

Comments
  Suellen Lazarus, International Finance Corporation, and
  Anne Predieri, Banc of America Securities

PART THREE
Breach of Contract Coverage

Overview
Theodore H. Moran, Editor

Breach of Contract Coverage in Infrastructure Projects: Can Investors Afford to Wait for Arbitration
Frederick E. Jenney, Morrison & Foerster

OPIC Modified Expropriation Coverage Case Study: MidAmerican's Projects in Indonesia-Dieng and Patuha
Julie A. Martin, Overseas Private Investment Corporation

Comments
Anne Predieri, Banc of America Securities

PART FOUR
Securitizing Political Risk Insurance

Overview
Theodore H. Moran, Editor

Securitizing Political Risk Insurance: Lessons from Past Securitizations
John D. Finnerty, PricewaterhouseCoopers LLP

Comments
Kevin B. Callahan, Aon Capital Markets;
Neil Doherty, Wharton Risk Management Center;
Gerald T. West, Multilateral Investment Guarantee Agency;
Anthony Faulkner, Export Credits Guarantee Department of the United Kingdom; *and*
David Bailey, Export Development Corporation of Canada

APPENDIX II

More About MIGA

1. MIGA Member Countries
2. MIGA Contact Information
3. MIGA Publications
4. MIGA's Websites

1. MIGA Member Countries (as of July 10, 2009)

Industrialized Countries (25)

Australia, Austria, Belgium, Canada, Czech Republic, Denmark, Finland, France, Germany, Greece, Iceland, Ireland, Italy, Japan, Luxembourg, Netherlands, New Zealand, Norway, Portugal, Slovenia, Spain, Sweden, Switzerland, United Kingdom, United States

Developing Countries (150)

Africa
Angola, Benin, Botswana, Burkina Faso, Burundi, Cameroon, Cape Verde, Central African Republic, Chad, Congo (Democratic Republic of), Congo (Republic of), Côte d'Ivoire, Djibouti, Equatorial Guinea, Eritrea, Ethiopia, Gabon, Gambia, Ghana, Guinea, Guinea-Bissau, Kenya, Lesotho, Liberia, Madagascar, Malawi, Mali, Mauritania, Mauritius, Mozambique, Namibia, Nigeria, Rwanda, Senegal, Sierra Leone, Seychelles, South Africa, Sudan, Swaziland, Tanzania, Togo, Uganda, Zambia, Zimbabwe

Asia and the Pacific
Afghanistan, Bangladesh, Cambodia, China, East Timor, Fiji, India, Indonesia, Korea, Republic of, Lao People's Democratic Rep., Malaysia, Maldives, Micronesia, Mongolia, Nepal, Pakistan, Palau, Papua New Guinea, Philippines, Samoa, Singapore, Solomon Islands, Sri Lanka, Thailand, Vanuatu, Vietnam

Middle East / North Africa
Algeria, Bahrain, Egypt, Iran (Islamic Republic of), Israel, Jordan, Kuwait, Lebanon, Libya, Morocco, Oman, Qatar, Saudi Arabia, Syrian Arab Republic, Tunisia, United Arab Emirates, Yemen

Europe/Central Asia
Albania, Armenia, Azerbaijan, Belarus, Bulgaria, Bosnia-Herzegovina, Croatia (Republic of), Cyprus, Czech Republic, Estonia, Georgia, Hungary, Kazakhstan, Kosovo, Kyrgyz Republic, Latvia, Lithuania, Macedonia, Malta, Moldova, Montenegro, Poland, Romania, Russian Federation, Serbia, Slovak Republic, Tajikistan, Turkey, Turkmenistan, Ukraine, Uzbekistan

Latin America / Caribbean
Antigua and Barbuda, Argentina, Bahamas, Barbados, Belize, Bolivia, Brazil, Chile, Colombia, Costa Rica, Dominica, Dominican Republic, Ecuador, El Salvador, Grenada, Guatemala, Guyana, Haiti, Honduras, Jamaica, Mexico, Nicaragua, Paraguay, Panama, Peru, St. Kitts & Nevis, St. Lucia, St. Vincent, Suriname, Trinidad & Tobago, Uruguay, Venezuela

Countries in the Process of Fulfilling Membership Requirements (2)

Africa: Niger

2. MIGA Contact Information

Multilateral Investment Guarantee Agency
World Bank Group
1818 H Street, NW
Washington, DC 20433 USA
tel: +1-202-458-4798
fax: +1-202-522-0316
e: migainquiry@worldbank.org

3. MIGA Publications

All publications can be accessed or ordered through MIGA's website, www.miga.org.
- MIGA Annual Report 2009
- Investment Guarantee Guide
- Small Investment Program
- Corporate Brochure
- *Sector/theme:* MIGA in Conflict-Affected Countries; Mitigating Risks in Oil, Gas and Mining
- *Case Studies:* Hydropower in Asia: The Nam Theun 2 Project; MIGA: Improving Project Profiles to Get Investments Going- The Case of the Dominican Toll Road; Power Case Study: Maritza East 1, Bulgaria
- *Trust Funds:* Afghanistan Investment Guarantee Facility; European Union Investment Guarantee Trust Fund for Bosnia and Herzegovina; MIGA: Environmental and Social Fund for Africa; West Bank and Gaza Investment Guarantee Trust Fund
- *Factsheets* (by regions): MIGA in Africa; MIGA in the Middle East and North Africa
- *Factsheets* (by sectors):Agribusiness; Telecommunications; Oil and Gas; Mining; Financials; Infrastructure; Manufacturing; Services and Tourism

- *Brokers/Insurance:*
  Insurance Broker's Program
  Syndications: Facultative Reinsurance and Cooperation Underwriting Program
- *Advisory Services:*
  EIOP The Western Balkans-Europe's Next High-Value Location for Manufacturer's; European Investor Outreach Program (EIOP): Grow your Business in the Western Balkans

4. MIGA Websites

www.miga.org — MIGA's general external website

www.fdi.net — offers prospective foreign investors information on investment opportunities in 26 sectors across 175 countries, including specific investment opportunities, key industry news, and many other documents on investment laws, BITs, etc.

www.pri-center.com — a one-stop portal that provides in-depth information, including ratings, research, tools, interactive directories, etc., on political risk analysis and management issues affecting 160 countries.

www.fdipromotion.com — an online knowledge-sharing and learning portal for investment promotion professionals in developing countries, providing access to knowledge and learning resources that help them attract and retain foreign direct investment.

Index

ECO-AUDIT
Environmental Benefits Statement